TRADING WITH THE ENEMY:

An Exposé of The
Nazi-American Money Plot
1933-1949

Books by Charles Higham

Theater and Film

HOLLYWOOD IN THE FORTIES
(with Joel Greenberg)

THE CELLULOID MUSE:
Hollywood Directors Speak
(with Joel Greenberg)

THE FILMS OF ORSON WELLES

HOLLYWOOD AT SUNSET

HOLLYWOOD CAMERAMEN

ZIEGFELD

CECIL B. DEMILLE:
A Biography

THE ART OF THE AMERICAN FILM

AVA

KATE:
The Life of Katharine Hepburn

CHARLES LAUGHTON:
An Intimate Biography

MARLENE:
The Life of Marlene Dietrich

CELEBRITY CIRCUS

ERROL FLYNN:
The Untold Story

BETTE:
The Life of Bette Davis

TRADING WITH THE ENEMY:

An Exposé of The Nazi-American Money Plot 1933-1949

CHARLES HIGHAM

DELACORTE PRESS/NEW YORK

Published by
Delacorte Press
1 Dag Hammarskjold Plaza
New York, N.Y. 10017

Manufactured in the United States of America

Second Printing

Library of Congress Cataloging in Publication Data

Higham, Charles, 1931–
Trading with the enemy.

Bibliography: p.
Includes index.
1. United States—Commerce—Germany—History.
2. Germany—Commerce—United States—History.
3. Trading with the enemy—History—20th century.
4. World War, 1939–1945—Finance—United States.
5. World War, 1939–1945—Finance—Germany. I. Title.
HF3099.H5   1983   382'.0943'073   82-14959
ISBN 0-440-09064-4

For
George Seldes

Contents

Acknowledgments

I am indebted to I. F. Stone, John Toland, George Seldes, and the staffs of various institutions of learning and record that made the difficult task of declassification possible. Among these are the administrators of the manuscripts rooms of the Library of Congress, Georgetown University in Washington, D.C., and the Franklin D. Roosevelt Memorial Library at Hyde Park, New York. I am grateful to John Taylor, George Wagner, Kathie Nicastro, William Lewis, Fred Pernell, Michael Miller, and James Paulauskas of the National Archives and Records Service in Washington, D.C., and Suitland, Maryland; to James Hall of the FBI; to Ralph V. Korp and Michael O'Connor of the Department of the Treasury; to Jeanne Giamporcaro of the State Department; to the staff of Army Intelligence, Fort Meade, Maryland; to Bradford Snell, whose forthcoming book on General Motors will exhaustively explore its international dealings; and to John Costello, Norman Littell, Josiah E. DuBois, Dr. Beatrice Berle, Henry Morgenthau III, Professor Irwin Gellman, and my indispensable research assistants Howard Davis, Frances Rowsell, and David Anderson; to the inspired guidance and advice of Pierre Sauvage; to the late Drew Pearson, who got wind of the story long ago but only knew part of the facts; to Jeanne Bernkopf, my editor and friend, who helped me weave the mass of complicated data into a coherent whole; to Professor Robert Dallek, who read and commented brilliantly on the manuscript; and to the late Joseph Borkin, who gave good advice and supplied the last line of the book.

Preface

It would be comforting to believe that the financial Establishment of the United States and the leaders of American industry were united in a common purpose following the Day of Infamy, the Japanese attack on Pearl Harbor on December 7, 1941. Certainly, the American public was assured that Big Business along with all of the officials of government ceased from the moment the war began to have any dealings whatsoever with the enemy. That assurance sustained the morale of millions of Americans who bore arms in World War II and their kinfolk who stayed at home and suffered the anguish of separation.

But the heartbreaking truth is that a number of financial and industrial figures of World War II and several members of the government served the cause of money before the cause of patriotism. While aiding the United States' war effort, they also aided Nazi Germany's.

I first came across this fact in 1978 when I was declassifying documents in the course of writing a biography that dealt with motion picture star Errol Flynn's Nazi associations. In the National Archives Diplomatic Records Room I found numerous cross-references to prominent figures who, I had always assumed, were entirely committed to the American cause, yet who had been marked down for suspected subversive activities.

I had heard over the years about a general agreement of certain major figures of American, British, and German commerce to continue their relations and associations after Pearl Harbor. I had also heard that certain figures of the warring governments had arranged to assist in this. But I had never seen any documentary evidence of it. Now, pieces of information began to surface. I started to locate documents and have them declassified under the Freedom of Information Act—a painfully slow and exhausting process that lasted two and a half years. What I found out was very disturbing.

I had been born to a patriotic British family. My father had raised the first battalions of volunteers against Germany in World War I, and had built the Star and Garter Hospital at Richmond, Surrey, for ex-servicemen. He had been knighted by King George V for his services to the Crown and had been a member of Parliament and a Cabinet member. I feel a strong sense of loyalty to Britain, as well as to my adopted country, the United States of America. Moreover, I am part Jewish. Auschwitz is a word stamped on my heart forever.

It thus came as a severe shock to learn that several of the greatest American corporate leaders were in league with Nazi corporations before and after Pearl Harbor, including I.G. Farben, the colossal Nazi industrial trust that created Auschwitz. Those leaders interlocked through an association I have dubbed The Fraternity. Each of these business leaders was entangled with the others through interlocking directorates or financial sources. All were represented internationally by the National City Bank or by the Chase National Bank and by the Nazi attorneys Gerhardt Westrick and Dr. Heinrich Albert. All had connections to that crucial Nazi economist, Emil Puhl, of Hitler's Reichsbank and the Bank for International Settlements.

The tycoons were linked by an ideology: the ideology of Business as Usual. Bound by identical reactionary ideas, the members sought a common future in fascist domination, regardless of which world leader might further that ambition.

Several members not only sought a continuing alliance of interests for the duration of World War II but supported the idea of a negotiated peace with Germany that would bar any reorganization of Europe along liberal lines. It would leave as its residue a police state that would place The Fraternity in postwar possession of financial, industrial, and political autonomy. When it was clear that Germany was losing the war the businessmen became notably more "loyal."

Then, when war was over, the survivors pushed into Germany, protected their assets, restored Nazi friends to high office, helped provoke the Cold War, and insured the permanent future of The Fraternity.

From the outset I realized that in researching the subject I would have to carve through an ice cream mountain of public relations. I searched in vain through books about the corporations and their histories to find any reference to questionable activities in World War II. It was clear that the authors of those volumes, granted the cooperation of the businesses concerned, predictably backed off from disclosing anything that would be revealing. To this day the bulk of Americans do not suspect The Fraternity. The government smothered everything, during and even (inexcusably) after the war. What would have happened if millions of American and British people, struggling with coupons and lines at the gas stations, had learned that in 1942 Standard Oil of New Jersey managers shipped the enemy's fuel through neutral Switzerland and that the enemy was shipping Allied fuel? Suppose the public had discovered that the Chase Bank in Nazi-occupied Paris after Pearl Harbor was doing millions of dollars' worth of business with the enemy with the full knowledge of the head office in Manhattan? Or that Ford trucks were being built for the German occupation troops in France with authorization from Dearborn, Michigan? Or that Colonel Sosthenes Behn, the head of the international American telephone conglomerate ITT, flew from New York to Madrid to Berne during the war to help improve Hitler's communications systems and improve the robot bombs that devastated London? Or that ITT built the Focke-Wulfs that dropped bombs on British and American troops? Or that crucial ball bearings were shipped to Nazi-associated customers in Latin America with the collusion of the vice-chairman of the U.S. War Production Board in partnership with Göring's cousin in Philadelphia when American forces were desperately short of them? Or that such arrangements were known about in Washington and either sanctioned or deliberately ignored?

For the government did sanction such dubious transactions—both before and after Pearl Harbor. A presidential edict, issued six days after December 7, 1941, actually set up the legislation whereby licensing arrangements for trading with the enemy could officially be granted. Often during the years after Pearl Harbor the government permitted such trading. For example, ITT was allowed to continue its relations with the Axis and Japan until 1945, even though that conglomerate was regarded as an official instrument of United States Intelligence. No attempt was made to prevent Ford from retaining its interests for the Germans in Occupied France, nor were the Chase Bank or the Morgan Bank expressly forbidden to keep open their branches in Occupied Paris. It is indicated that the Reichsbank and Nazi Ministry of Economics made promises to certain U.S. corporate leaders that their properties would not be injured after the Führer was victorious. Thus, the bosses of the multinationals as we know them today had a six-spot on every side of the dice cube. Whichever side won the war, the powers that really ran nations would not be adversely affected.

And it is important to consider the size of American investments in Nazi Germany at the time of Pearl Harbor. These amounted to an estimated total of $475 million. Standard Oil of New Jersey had $120 million invested there; General Motors had $35 million; ITT had $30 million; and Ford had $17.5 million. Though it would have been more patriotic to have allowed Nazi Germany to confiscate these companies for the duration—to nationalize them or to absorb them into Hermann Göring's industrial empire—it was clearly more practical to insure them protection from seizure by allowing them to remain in special holding companies, the money accumulating until war's end. It is interesting that whereas there is no evidence of any serious attempt by Roosevelt to impeach the guilty in the United States, there is evidence that Hitler strove to punish certain German Fraternity associates on the grounds of treason to the Nazi state. Indeed, in the case of ITT, perhaps the most flagrant of the corporations in its outright dealings with the enemy, Hitler and his postmaster general, the venerable Wilhelm Ohnesorge, strove to impound the German end of the business. But even they were powerless in such a situation: the Gestapo leader of counterintelligence, Walter Schellenberg, was a prominent director and shareholder of ITT by arrangement with New York—and even Hitler dared not cross the Gestapo.

As for Roosevelt, the Sphinx still keeps his secrets. That supreme politician held all of the forces of collusion and betrayal in balance, publicly praising those executives whom he knew to be questionable. Before Pearl Harbor, he allowed such egregious executives as James

D. Mooney of General Motors and William Rhodes Davis of the Davis Oil Company to enjoy pleasant tête-à-têtes with Hitler and Göring, while maintaining a careful record of what they were doing. During the war, J. Edgar Hoover, Adolf A. Berle, Henry Morgenthau, and Harold Ickes kept the President fully advised of all internal and external transgressions. With great skill, he never let the executives concerned know that he was on to them. By using the corporate leaders for his own war purposes as dollar-a-year men, keeping an eye on them and allowing them to indulge, under license or not, in their international tradings, he at once made winning the war a certainty and kept the public from knowing what it should not know.

Because of the secrecy with which the matter has been blanketed, researching it presented me with a nightmare that preceded the greater nightmare of discovery. I embarked upon a voyage that resembled nothing so much as a descent into poisoned waters in a diving bell.

Why did even the loyal figures of the American government allow these transactions to continue after Pearl Harbor? A logical deduction would be that not to have done so would have involved public disclosure: the procedure of legally disconnecting these alliances under the antitrust laws would have resulted in a public scandal that would have drastically affected public morale, caused widespread strikes, and perhaps provoked mutinies in the armed services. Moreover, as some corporate executives were never tired of reminding the government, their trial and imprisonment would have made it impossible for the corporate boards to help the American war effort. Therefore, the government was powerless to intervene. After 1945, the Cold War, which the executives had done so much to provoke, made it even more necessary that the truth of The Fraternity agreements should not be revealed.

I began with the conveniently multinational Bank for International Settlements in Basle, Switzerland. The activities of this anomalous institution in wartime are contained in Treasury Secretary Henry Morgenthau's official diaries at the Roosevelt Memorial Library at Hyde Park, New York. Other details are contained in reports by the estimable Lauchlin Currie, of Roosevelt's White House Economics Staff, whom I interviewed at length by telephone at his home in Bogotá, Colombia, to which city he had been banished, his citizenship stripped from him in 1956 for exposing American-Nazi connections.

Another source lay in reports by the late Orvis Schmidt of Treasury Foreign Funds Control. German records were a useful source: Emil Puhl, vice-president and real power of the Reichsbank, a most crucial figure in The Fraternity's dealings, had sent reports to his nominal superior, Dr. Walther Funk, from Switzerland to Berlin late in the war.

I turned to the matter of the Rockefeller-controlled Chase National Bank, which had conducted its business for the Nazi High Command in Paris until the war's end. Evidently realizing that future historians might want to examine the highly secret Chase Bank files, Morgenthau had left subtle cross-references at Hyde Park that could lead future investigators to Treasury itself. I asked Ralph V. Korp of Treasury for access to the sealed Chase boxes, which had been under lock and key since 1945. Under the Freedom of Information Act, Mr. Korp obtained permission from his superiors to unseal the boxes and to declassify the large number of documents contained therein.

From the Chase Bank it was a natural progression to Standard Oil of New Jersey, the chief jewel in the crown of the Rockefeller empire. Records of Standard's dealings with the Axis were contained in the Records Rooms of the Diplomatic Branch of the National Archives and were specially declassified. There, too, I found records of Sterling Products, General Aniline and Film, and William Rhodes Davis, whose FBI files were also most revealing. Documents on ITT and RCA were classified. After waiting out the better part of the year, I was able to obtain them from the National Archives. Classified SKF Industries files are held in the Suitland, Maryland, annex of the Archives. General Motors matters are covered in the James D. Mooney public access collection of Georgetown University, Washington, D.C. The unpublished post–Pearl Harbor diaries of Harold Ickes were invaluable; they are to be found in the manuscript room of the Library of Congress.

The most elusive files were those on Ford in Occupied France. I could find no reference to them in the Treasury documentary listings. I knew that a Treasury team had investigated the company. I wondered if any member of the team could be alive.

Something jolted my memory. I remembered that a book entitled *The Devil's Chemists* had appeared after World War II, written by Josiah DuBois, an attorney who had been part of the Treasury team at Nuremberg. The book was a harrowing account of the trial of the executives of I.G. Farben, the Nazi industrial trust, that showed Farben's links to Wall Street.

I reread the book's pages, looking for a clue. In it DuBois mentioned that he came from Camden, New Jersey. I decided to call information in the Camden area because I had a theory that, embittered by his experience in Germany and Washington, DuBois might have returned to live there after the war. It was only a hunch, but it paid off. In fact, it turned out that DuBois had gone back to his family law firm in Camden. I wrote to him, asking if he had records of the Ford matter. I figured that these might have been so important that he would have been given personal custody of them; that Secretary Morgenthau might not even have risked leaving them at Treasury.

DuBois replied that he believed he still had the documents, including the letters of Edsel Ford to his managers in Nazi-occupied France after Pearl Harbor, authorizing improvements in automobile and truck supplies to the Germans. After several weeks, DuBois wrote to say that he had searched his attic to no avail. The documents were missing. However, he would keep looking.

He was admitted to a hospital where he underwent major surgery. Although enfeebled, he returned to the attic and began searching again. Compelled by a desire to disclose the truth, he pursued his task whenever he could find the strength. At last, when he was about to give up hope, he uncovered the documents.

However, he explained that the main file was so incendiary that he would not send it by mail or even by messenger—I was at liberty to examine it in his office. I was faced with a new dilemma. Since I was expecting delivery of an important set of documents, I couldn't risk an absence from my house for a prolonged journey to the East. I said I would call him back.

I knew that Rutgers University was close to DuBois's offices. I called the Law department and asked for a student researcher. Within an hour I received a call from a young man who needed work. I contacted DuBois's secretary and arranged for the student to copy the documents on the premises. He did so; I sent an air courier to his home to pick them up. As I read the documents, the last details of the puzzle fell into place.

I have tried to write this book as dispassionately as possible, without attempting a moral commentary, and without, of course, intending implication of present corporations and their executive boards. It will be claimed that the people in this book, since they are dead, cannot answer and therefore should not be criticized. To that I would reply: Millions died in World War II. They, too, cannot answer.

GENERAL LICENSE UNDER SECTION 3(a)
OF THE TRADING WITH THE ENEMY ACT

By virtue of and pursuant to the authority vested in me by sections 3 and 5 of The Trading with the Enemy Act as amended, and by virtue of all other authority vested in me, I, Franklin D. Roosevelt, President of the United States of America, do prescribe the following:

A general license is hereby granted, licensing any transaction or act proscribed by section 3(a) of The Trading with the Enemy Act, as amended, provided, however, that such transaction or act is authorized by the Secretary of the Treasury by means of regulations, rulings, instructions, licenses or otherwise, pursuant to the Executive Order No. 8389, as amended.

FRANKLIN D. ROOSEVELT

THE WHITE HOUSE,

December 13, 1941

H. MORGENTHAU, JR.
Secretary of the Treasury
FRANCIS BIDDLE
Attorney General of the United States

TRADING
WITH
THE ENEMY:

An Exposé of The
Nazi-American Money Plot
1933-1949

1

A Bank for All Reasons

On a bright May morning in 1944, while young Americans were dying on the Italian beachheads, Thomas Harrington McKittrick, American president of the Nazi-controlled Bank for International Settlements in Basle, Switzerland, arrived at his office to preside over a fourth annual meeting in time of war. This polished American gentleman sat down with his German, Japanese, Italian, British, and American executive staff to discuss such important matters as the $378 million in gold that had been sent to the Bank by the Nazi government after Pearl Harbor for use by its leaders after the war. Gold that had been looted from the national banks of Austria, Holland, Belgium, and Czechoslovakia, or melted down from the Reichsbank holdings of the teeth fillings, spectacle frames, cigarette cases and lighters, and wedding rings of the murdered Jews.

The Bank for International Settlements was a joint creation in 1930 of the world's central banks, including the Federal Reserve Bank of New York. Its existence was inspired by Hjalmar Horace Greeley Schacht, Nazi Minister of Economics and president of the Reichsbank, part of whose early upbringing was in Brooklyn, and who had powerful Wall Street connections. He was seconded by the all-important banker Emil Puhl, who continued under the regime of Schacht's successor, Dr. Walther Funk.

Sensing Adolf Hitler's lust for war and conquest, Schacht, even before Hitler rose to power in the Reichstag, pushed for an institution that would retain channels of communication and collusion between the world's financial leaders even in the event of an international conflict. It was written into the Bank's charter, concurred in by the respective governments, that the BIS should be immune from seizure, closure, or censure, whether or not its owners were at war. These owners included the Morgan-affiliated First National Bank of New York (among whose directors were Harold S. Vanderbilt and Wendell Willkie), the Bank of England, the Reichsbank, the Bank of Italy, the Bank of France, and other central banks. Established under the Morgan banker Owen D. Young's so-called Young Plan, the BIS's ostensible purpose was to provide the Allies with reparations to be paid by Germany for World War I. The Bank soon turned out to be the instrument of an opposite function. It was to be a money funnel for American and British funds to flow into Hitler's coffers and to help Hitler build up his war machine.

The BIS was completely under Hitler's control by the outbreak of World War II. Among the directors under Thomas H. McKittrick were Hermann Schmitz, head of the colossal Nazi industrial trust I.G. Farben, Baron Kurt von Schröder, head of the J. H. Stein Bank of Cologne and a leading officer and financier of the Gestapo; Dr. Walther Funk of the Reichsbank, and, of course, Emil Puhl. These last two figures were Hitler's personal appointees to the board.

The BIS's first president was the smooth old Rockefeller banker, Gates W. McGarrah, formerly of the Chase National Bank and the Federal Reserve Bank, who retired in 1933. His successor was the forty-three-year-old Leon Fraser, a colorful former newspaper reporter on the muckraking New York *World,* a street-corner soapbox orator, straw-hat company director, and performer in drag in stage comedies. Fraser had little or no background in finance or economics, but he had numerous contacts in high business circles and a passionate dedication to the world of money that acknowledged no loyalties or frontiers. In the first two years of Hitler's assumption of power, Fraser was influential in financing the Nazis through the BIS. When he took over the position of president of the First National Bank at its Manhattan headquarters in 1935, he continued to exercise a subtle influence over the BIS's activities that continued until the 1940s.

Other directors of the Bank added to the powerful financial group.

Vincenzo Azzolini was the accomplished governor of the Bank of Italy. Yves Bréart de Boisanger was the ruthlessly ambitious governor of the Bank of France; Alexandre Galopin of the Belgian banking fraternity was to be murdered in 1944 by the Underground as a Nazi collaborator.

The BIS became a bête noire of U.S. Secretary of the Treasury Henry Morgenthau, a deliberate, thorough, slow-speaking Jewish farmer who, despite his origins of wealth, mistrusted big money and power. A model of integrity obsessed with work, Morgenthau considered it his duty to expose corruption wherever he found it. Tall and a trifle ungainly, with a balding high-domed head, a high-pitched, intense voice, small, probing eyes, pince-nez, and a nervous, hesitant smile, Morgenthau was the son of Woodrow Wilson's ambassador to Turkey in World War I. He learned early in life that the land was his answer to the quest for a decent life in a corrupt society. He became obsessed with farming and, at the age of twenty-two, in 1913, borrowed money from his father to buy a thousand acres at East Fishkill, Dutchess County, New York, in the Hudson Valley, where he became Franklin D. Roosevelt's neighbor. During World War I he and Roosevelt formed an intimate friendship. Elinor Morgenthau became very close to her near namesake, Eleanor Roosevelt. While Roosevelt soared in the political stratosphere, Morgenthau remained rooted in his property. In the early 1920s he published a newspaper called *The American Agriculturist* that pushed for government credits for farmers. When Roosevelt became governor of New York in 1928, he appointed Morgenthau chairman of the Agricultural Advisory Commission. Morgenthau showed great flair and a passionate commitment to the cause of the sharecropper.

Legend has it that on a freezing winter day in 1933, FDR and Morgenthau met and talked on the borderline of their two farms. Morgenthau is supposed to have said to Roosevelt, "Life is getting slow around here." And FDR replied, "Henry, how would you like to be Secretary of the Treasury?"

What he lacked in knowledge of economics, Morgenthau rapidly made up in his Jeffersonian principles and role as keeper of the public conscience. Close to a thousand volumes of his official diaries in the Roosevelt Memorial Library at Hyde Park give a vivid portrait of his inspired conducting of his high office. He was aided by an able staff, which he ran with benign but military precision. His most trusted aide was his Assistant Secretary, Harry Dexter White. Unlike Morgenthau, White came from humble origins. Jewish also, he was the child of penniless Russian immigrant parents who were consumed with a hatred of the czarist regime. White's early life was a struggle: this short, energetic, keen-faced man fought to help his father's hardware business succeed, finally forging a career as an economist with the aid of a Harvard scholarship and a professorship at Lawrence College, Wisconsin. He was opinionated and self-confident to a degree. Although he was frequently accused of being a communist sympathizer, he was in fact simply an old-fashioned liberal driven by his ancestral memories of Russian imperialism.

It is unfortunate that Morgenthau did not appoint White as his representative at BIS meetings, but White was too valuable in Washington. Instead, Morgenthau sent the more questionable Merle Cochran to investigate the BIS. Cochran was on loan to Treasury from the State Department; he represented the State Department's sophisticated neutralism before (and during) the war. Cochran became Secretary of the American Embassy in Paris, working directly under Roosevelt's friend the duplicitous, Talleyrand-like Ambassador William Bullitt. Cochran spent most of his time in Basle conveying to both Morgenthau and Cordell Hull details of what the BIS was up to. Very much opposed to White—indeed, violently so—Cochran was sympathetic with the BIS and to the Nazis, as his various memoranda made clear. Morgenthau took Cochran's political judgments with a degree of skepticism, but continued to use him over White's objections because he knew the Germans would trust Cochran and confide much in him. Day after day, Cochran lunched with Schmitz, Schröder, Funk, Emil Puhl, and the other Germans on the BIS board, obtaining a clear picture of the BIS's plans for the future.

In March 1938, when the Nazis marched into Vienna, much of the gold of Austria was looted and packed into vaults controlled by the Bank for International Settlements. The Nazi board members forbade any discussion of the transaction at the BIS summit meetings in Basle. Cochran, in his memoranda to Morgenthau, failed to score this outrageous act of theft. The gold flowed into the Reichsbank under Funk, in the special charge of Reichsbank vice-president and BIS director, Emil Puhl. On March 14, 1939, Cochran wrote to Morgenthau, "I have known Puhl for several years, and he is a veteran and efficient officer." He also praised Walther Funk.

His timing was not good. One day later, Hitler followed his forces into Prague. The storm troops arrested the directors of the Czech National Bank and held them at gunpoint, demanding that they yield up the $48 million gold reserve that represented the national treasure of that beleaguered country. The Czech directors nervously announced that they had already shifted the gold to the BIS with instructions that it be forwarded to the Bank of England. This was an act of great naiveté. Montagu Norman, the eccentric, Vandyke-bearded governor of the Bank of England, who liked to travel the world disguised as Professor Skinner in a black opera cloak, was a rabid supporter of Hitler.

On orders from their German captors, the Czech directors asked the Dutch BIS president, J. W. Beyen, to return the gold to Basle. Beyen held an anxious discussion with BIS general manager Roger Auboin of the Bank of France. The result was that Beyen called London and instructed Norman to return the gold. Norman instantly obliged. The gold flowed into Berlin for use in buying essential strategic materials toward a future war.

There the matter might have been buried had it not been for a young, very bright, and idealistic London journalist and economist named Paul Einzig, who had been tipped off to the transaction by a contact at the Bank of England. He published the story in the *Financial News*. The story caused a sensation in London. Einzig held a hasty meeting with maverick Labour Member of Parliament George Strauss. Strauss through Einzig began investigating the matter.

Henry Morgenthau telephoned Sir John Simon, British Chancellor of the Exchequer, on a Sunday night in an effort to determine what was going on. Merle Cochran had telegraphed him with a characteristic whitewash of the BIS and an outright dismissal of Einzig's charges that the BIS was a Nazi outfit. Sir John said icily on the transatlantic wire, "I'm in the country, Mr. Secretary. We are enjoying our dinner. It is not our custom to do business by telephone."

"Well, Sir John," Morgenthau replied, "we've been doing business by telephone over here for almost forty years!"

Sir John Simon continued to dodge Morgenthau's questions. On May 15, George Strauss asked Prime Minister Neville Chamberlain,

"Is it true, sir, that the national treasure of Czechoslovakia is being given to Germany?" "It is not," the Prime Minister replied. Chamberlain was a major shareholder in Imperial Chemical Industries, partner of I.G. Farben whose Hermann Schmitz was on the board of the BIS. Chamberlain's reply threw the Commons into an uproar. Einzig refused to let go. He was convinced that Norman had transferred the money illegally in collusion with Sir John Simon. Simon, in answer to a question from Strauss, denied any knowledge of the matter.

Next day, Einzig tackled Sir Henry Strakosch, a prominent political figure. Strakosch refused to disclose the details of the conversation he had had with Simon. But Strakosch finally cracked and admitted that Simon had discussed the transfer of the Czech gold.

Einzig was jubilant. He called Strauss with the news. Strauss put a further question to Sir John Simon in a debate on May 26. Once again, Simon hedged. Winston Churchill was the leader of a violent onslaught on the unfortunate Chancellor of the Exchequer.

Morgenthau demanded to know more. Cochran's letter from Basle dated May 9 and received May 17 brushed over the issue once more. Cochran wrote,

> There is an entirely cordial atmosphere at Basle; most of the central bankers have known each other for many years, and these reunions are enjoyable as well as profitable to them. I have had talks with all of them. The wish was expressed by some of them that their respective statesmen might quit hurling invectives at each other, get together on a fishing trip with President Roosevelt or to the World's Fair, overcome their various prides and complexes, and enter into a mood that would make comparatively simple the solution of many of the present political problems.

This picture of good cheer scarcely convinced Morgenthau. On May 31, Associated Press reported from Switzerland that transactions were completed between the BIS and the Bank of England and the Czech gold was now firmly in Berlin.

During World War II, Einzig, who had never forgotten the Czech gold affair, ran into J. W. Beyen in London and asked him if he would now admit what had taken place. Beyen said smoothly, "It is all technical. The gold never left London.'' Einzig was amazed. He wrote an apology to Beyen in his book of memoirs, *In the Center of Things*.

The truth was that the gold had not had to leave London in order to be available in Berlin. The arrangement between the BIS and its member banks was that transactions were not normally made by shipping money—dangerous and difficult when the shipments would show up in customs manifests—but simply by adjusting the gold deposit accounts. Thus, all Montagu Norman had to do was to authorize Beyen to deduct $40 million from the Bank of England's holdings in Basle and replace the same amount from the Czech National Bank holdings in London.

By 1939, the BIS had invested millions in Germany, while Kurt von Schröder and Emil Puhl deposited large sums in looted gold in the Bank. The BIS was an instrument of Hitler, but its continuing existence was approved by Great Britain even after that country went to war with Germany, and the British director Sir Otto Niemeyer, and chairman Montagu Norman, remained in office throughout the war.

In the middle of the Czech gold controversy, Thomas Harrington McKittrick was appointed president of the Bank, with Emil Meyer of the Swiss National Bank as chairman. White-haired, pink-cheeked, smooth and soft-spoken, McKittrick was a perfect front man for The Fraternity, an associate of the Morgans and an able member of the Wall Street establishment. Born in St. Louis, he went to Harvard, where he edited the *Crimson,* graduating as bachelor of arts in 1911. He worked his way up to become chairman of the British-American Chamber of Commerce, which numbered among its members several Nazi sympathizers. He was a director of Lee, Higginson and Co., and made substantial loans to Germany. He was fluent in German, French, and Italian. Though he spent all of his career inland, he wrote learned papers on the life and habits of seabirds. His wife, Marjorie, and his four pretty daughters, one of whom was at Vassar and a liberal enemy of the BIS, were popular on both sides of the Atlantic.

Early in 1940, McKittrick traveled to Berlin and held a meeting at the Reichsbank with Kurt von Schröder of the BIS and the Gestapo. They discussed doing business with each other's countries if war between them should come.

Morgenthau grew more aggravated by McKittrick and the BIS as the war in Europe continued, but did not insist he be withdrawn. He was forced to rely upon Treasury Secret Service reports rather than upon Cochran for information on the BIS's doings. He learned that in June 1940, Belgian BIS director Alexandre Galopin had intercepted $228 million in gold sent by the Belgian government to the Bank of France and had shifted it to Dakar in North Africa and thence the Reichsbank and Emil Puhl.

The Bank of Belgium's exiled representatives in New York sued the Bank of France, represented by New York State Senator Frederic Coudert, to recover their gold. Ironically, they were represented by John Foster Dulles, whose law firm, Sullivan and Cromwell, had represented I.G. Farben. The Supreme Court ruled in favor of the Bank of Belgium, ordering the Bank of France to pay out from its holdings in the Federal Reserve Bank.

But when Hitler occupied all of France in November 1942, State Senator Coudert stepped in with the excuse that since Germany had absorbed the Bank of France, that bank no longer had any power of appeal against the verdict. He pretended that contact with France was no longer possible, while fully aware of the fact that he himself was still retained by the Bank of France. He claimed that only a Bank of France representative could allow the release of funds from the Federal Reserve Bank. As a result, the gold remained in Nazi hands.

On May 27, 1941, Secretary of State Cordell Hull, at Morgenthau's suggestion, telegraphed U.S. Ambassador John G. Winant in London, asking for a report on the continuing relationship between the BIS and the British government. It infuriated Morgenthau that Britain remained a member of a Nazi-controlled financial institution: Montagu Norman and Sir Otto Niemeyer of the Bank of England were still firmly on the board. Winant had lunch with Niemeyer. He gave an approving report of the meeting on June 1.

Niemeyer had said that the BIS, "guaranteed immunity from constraint in time of war," was still "legal and intact." He admitted that Britain retained an interest in the Bank through McKittrick twenty-one months after war had broken out. He said that he was in touch with the Bank through the British Treasury and that British Censorship examined all of the mail by his own wish. Asked about the issue of the Czechoslovakian gold, Niemeyer admitted, "Yes, it had a bad public press. However, that was due to the mishandling of the question in Parliament." He further admitted that the government of Great Britain was still a client of the Bank and had accepted a dividend from it. The dividend, it scarcely needs adding, came largely from Nazi sources. Niemeyer said that he believed the British should continue the association for the duration as well as lend the Bank their tacit approval, "If only for the reason that a useful role in post-war settlements might later have an effect."

Niemeyer went on, "It would be of no use at this time to raise difficult legal questions with respect to the relationship of the various countries overrun by the Germans. . . . McKittrick should stay in Switzerland because he is . . . guardian of the Bank against any danger that might occur . . . McKittrick might want to get in touch with the American Minister in Switzerland and explain his problem to him."

On July 13, 1941, Ivar Rooth, governor of the Bank of Sweden, wrote to his friend Merle Cochran—who had returned to Washington—about the latest general meeting of the Bank and the luncheon at the Basle restaurant Les Trois Rois afterward. He said that it was agreed at lunch that McKittrick should soon travel to the United States to explain BIS's position to "your American friends . . . [in the] very correct and neutral way." Rooth continued, "I hope that our friends abroad will understand the political necessity of committing the Germans to send a division to Finland by railway through Sweden."

On February 5, 1942, almost two months after Pearl Harbor, the Reichsbank and the German and Italian governments approved the orders that permitted Thomas H. McKittrick to remain in charge of the BIS until the end of the war. One document of authorization included the significant statement, "McKittrick's opinions are safely known to us." McKittrick gratefully arranged a loan of several million Swiss gold francs to the Nazi government of Poland and the collaborative government of Hungary. Most of the board's members traveled freely across frontiers throughout the war for meetings in Paris, Berlin, Rome, or (though this was denied) Basle. Hjalmar Schacht spent much of the war in Geneva and Basle pulling strings behind the scenes. However, Hitler correctly suspected him of intriguing for the overthrow of the present regime in favor of The Fraternity and imprisoned him late in the war. From Pearl Harbor on, the BIS remained listed in Rand McNally's directory as Correspondent Bank for the Federal Reserve Bank in Washington.

In London, Labour Member of Parliament George Strauss kept hammering away at the BIS. In May 1942 he challenged Sir John Simon's successor, Chancellor of the Exchequer Sir Kingsley Wood, on the matter. Wood replied, "This country has various rights and interests in the BIS under our international trust agreements between the various governments. It would not be in our best interest to sever connections with the Bank."

George Strauss and other Labour members of Parliament insisted upon knowing why the Bank's dividend was still being divided equally in wartime among the British, German, Japanese, and American banks. It was not until 1944 that they discovered Germany was receiving most of the dividends.

On September 7, 1942, Thomas H. McKittrick issued the Bank's first annual report after Pearl Harbor. He went through the bizarre procedure of addressing an empty room with the report to be able to say to Washington that none of the Axis directors was present. In fact, all of the Axis directors received the report soon afterward and the mixed executive staff of warring nations discussed it through the rest of the day. The report was purely Nazi in content. It assumed an immediate peace in Germany's favor and a distribution of American gold to stabilize the currencies of the United States and Europe. This was a line peddled by every German leader starting with Schacht. When Strauss told the House of Commons on October 12 that the report had delighted Hitler and Göring, Sir Kingsley asserted that he had not seen it. Strauss went on, "It is clear some form of collaboration between the Nazis and the Allies exists and that appeasement still lives in time of war."

In the summer of 1942, Pierre Pucheu, French Cabinet member and director of the privately owned Worms Bank in Nazi-occupied Paris, had a meeting at the BIS with Yves Bréart de Boisanger. Pucheu told Boisanger that plans were afoot for General Dwight D. Eisenhower to invade North Africa. He had obtained this information through a friend of Robert Murphy, U.S. State Department representative in Vichy. Boisanger contacted Kurt von Schröder. Immediately, Schröder and other German bankers, along with their French correspondents, transferred 9 billion gold francs via the BIS to Algiers. Anticipating German defeat, they were seeking a killing in dollar exchange. The collaborationists boosted their holdings from $350 to $525 million almost overnight. The deal was made with the collusion of Thomas H. McKittrick, Hermann Schmitz, Emil Puhl, and the Japanese directors of the BIS. Another collaborator in the scheme was one of the Vatican's espionage group who leaked the secret to others in the Hitler High Command—according to a statement made under oath by Otto Abetz to American officials on June 21, 1946.

In the spring of 1943, McKittrick, ignoring the normal restrictions of war, undertook a remarkable journey. Despite the fact he was neither Italian nor diplomat and that Italy was at war with the United States, he was issued an Italian diplomatic visa to travel by train and auto to Rome. At the border he was met by Himmler's special police, who gave him safe conduct. McKittrick proceeded to Lisbon, whence he traveled with immunity from U-boats by Swedish ship to the United States. In Manhattan in April he had meetings with Leon Fraser, his old friend and BIS predecessor, and with the heads of the Federal Reserve Bank. Then McKittrick traveled to Berlin on a U.S. passport to provide Emil Puhl of the Reichsbank with secret intelligence on financial problems and high-level attitudes in the United States.

On March 26, 1943, liberal Congressman Jerry Voorhis of California entered a resolution in the House of Representatives calling for an investigation of the BIS, including "the reasons why an American retains the position as president of this Bank being used to further the designs and purposes of Axis powers." Randolph Paul, Treasury counsel, sent up the resolution to Henry Morgenthau on April 1, 1943, saying, "I think you will be interested in reading the attached copy of [it]." Morgenthau was interested, but he made one of his few mistakes and did nothing. The matter was not even considered by Congress.

Washington State Congressman John M. Coffee objected and introduced a similar resolution in January 1944. He shouted, angrily, "The Nazi government has 85 million Swiss gold francs on deposit in the BIS. The majority of the board is made up of Nazi officials. Yet American money is being deposited in the Bank."

Coffee pointed out that the American and British shareholders were receiving dividends from Nazi Germany and Japan and that the Germans and Japanese were receiving dividends from America. The resolution was tabled.

There the matter might have lain had it not been for an energetic Norwegian economist of part-German origin named Wilhelm Keilhau. He was infuriated by Washington's continuing refusal to break with the Bank and its acceptance of a flagrant financial alliance with its country's enemies.

Keilhau introduced a resolution at the International Monetary Conference at Bretton Woods, New Hampshire, on July 10, 1944. He called for the BIS to be dissolved "at the earliest possible moment." However, pressure was brought to bear on him to withdraw a second resolution, and he was forced to yield. The second resolution called for an investigation into the books and records of the Bank during the war. Had such an investigation taken place, the Nazi-American connection would undoubtedly have been exposed.

Bankers Winthrop Aldrich and Edward E. (Ned) Brown of the American delegation and the Chase and First National banks tried feebly to veto Keilhau's resolution. They were supported by the Dutch delegation and by J. W. Beyen of Holland, the former president of BIS and negotiator of the Czech gold transference, despite the fact that Holland's looted gold had gone to the BIS. Leon Fraser of the First National Bank of New York stood with them. So, alas, did the British delegation, strongly supported by Anthony Eden and the Foreign Office. After initial support, the distinguished economist Lord Keynes was swayed into confirming the British official opposition calling for a postponement of the Bank's dissolution until postwar—when the establishment of an international monetary fund would be completed. Keynes's wife, the former Lydia Lopokova, the great star of the Diaghilev Ballet who had made her debut opposite Nijinsky, was a member of a wealthy czarist family who influenced her husband toward delaying the BIS's dissolution and a tabling of all discussion of looted gold—according to Harry Dexter White.

Dean Acheson, representing the State Department in the American delegation, was firmly in Winthrop Aldrich's camp as a former Standard Oil lawyer, smoothly using delaying tactics as the master of compromise he was. The minutes of the meetings between Morgenthau, Edward E. Brown, Acheson, and other members of the delegation on July 18–19, 1944, at the Mount Washington Hotel at Bretton

Woods show Acheson arguing for retention of the BIS until after the war. He used the spurious argument that if McKittrick resigned and the Bank was declared illegal by the United States government, all of the gold holdings in it owned by American shareholders would go direct to Berlin, via a Nazi president. Acheson must surely have known that the gold was already deposited for the Axis via the BIS partner, the Swiss National Bank, which shared the same chairman. Acheson also argued that the Bank would help restore Germany post-war. That at least was true.

Senator Charles W. Tobey of New Hampshire emerges with great credit from the minutes of the meetings at the Mount Washington. At the July 18 meeting he said, savagely, to the company in general, "What you're doing by your silence and inaction is aiding and abetting the enemy." Morgenthau agreed. Acheson, rattled, said that the BIS must go on as "a matter of foreign policy." At least there was a degree of honesty in that. Morgenthau felt that the BIS "should be disbanded because to disband it would be good propaganda for the United States."

There were jocular moments during the discussion on July 19. Dr. Mabel Newcomer of Vassar said that she "would not dissolve the Bank." Morgenthau asked her cheerfully whether McKittrick's daughter was one of her students. She replied in the affirmative. Morgenthau said, "She has informed my daughter that she is against the Bank." Dr. Newcomer replied, "She didn't inform me, except that she wanted her father to come home—so she might favor the dissolution!"

Everyone laughed. Morgenthau said, "She is very cute. She has read this article in *PM* about it, and she said [referring to an attack on the BIS in that liberal publication] 'I think *PM* is right and father is wrong.' " Morgenthau threw back his head and laughed again. "That is what Vassar does to those girls!"

Under pressures from Senator Tobey and from Harry Dexter White, Morgenthau stated that Leon Fraser, McKittrick, and Beyen all had sympathies "that run there." In other words, in the direction of Germany. He said,

> I think in the eyes of the Germans, they would consider this as the kind of thing which can go on, and it holds out to them a hope, particularly

to people like Dr. Schacht and Dr. Funk, that the same [associations] will continue [between America and Germany] after the war. It strengthens the position of people like Mr. Leon Fraser and some very important people like Mr. Winthrop Aldrich, who have openly opposed this dissolution.

Dean Acheson, fighting hard with Edward E. Brown at his side, said he "would have to take the matter up with Cordell Hull." He was sure Hull would want the BIS retained since Hull had approved its existence up till now. Morgenthau promised to call Hull, who had become acutely embarrassed by press criticism. After four years of tacitly approving the BIS, Hull told Morgenthau he called for its dissolution. Morgenthau telephoned him and said, "What about McKittrick?" Hull replied icily, "Let him read about it in the papers!" Later, he repeated angrily to Acheson, "Let him read about it in the papers!"

Acheson went to see the British delegation on July 20. Closely connected to high-level politicians in England, he was well regarded in Whitehall. Lord Keynes felt that the BIS might be too quickly abolished if Acheson were beaten by the Morgenthau faction. Although Keynes was advanced in years and had a heart condition, he and his wife abruptly left a British summit meeting and, finding the elevator jammed with conferencers, ran up three flights of stairs and knocked on the Morgenthaus' door. Elinor Morgenthau was astonished to see the normally imperturbable British economist trembling, red-faced, and sweating with rage.

Keynes repeated, as calmly as he could, that what he was upset about was that he felt that the BIS should be kept going until a new world bank and an international monetary fund were set up. Lady Keynes also urged Morgenthau to let the Bank go on. Finally, Keynes, seeing that Morgenthau was under pressure to dissolve the BIS, shifted his ground and took the position that Britain was in the forefront of those who wanted the BIS to go—but only in good time. Morgenthau insisted the BIS must go "as soon as possible." At midnight an exhausted Keynes said he would go along with the decision.

Keynes returned to his rooms and contacted his fellow delegates from the Foreign Office. The result of this late-night meeting was that he largely compromised his original agreement and at 2 A.M. sent a letter by hand to the Morgenthaus' suite again calling for the BIS to go on for the duration.

Next day, over the objections of Edward E. Brown and the great irritation of Dean Acheson, Morgenthau's delegation approved the disposal of the BIS.

Immediately after the liquidation of the BIS was voted, McKittrick did everything possible to combat it. He sent letters to Morgenthau and the Chancellor of the Exchequer, Sir John Anderson, in London. He stated that when the war ended, huge sums would have to be paid to Germany by the Allies and the BIS would have to siphon these through. There was no mention of the millions owed by Germany to the Allies and the conquered nations. Harry Dexter White sent a memorandum to Morgenthau dated March 22, 1945, saying, "McKittrick's letters are part of an obvious effort to stake out a claim for the BIS in the postwar world. As such, they are, in effect, a challenge to Bretton Woods. . . . The other signatories to the Bretton Woods Act should be advised of the BIS action, should be reminded of Bretton Woods' resolution Number Five, and should be advised that we are not answering the letters."

The same day, Treasury's indispensable Orvis A. Schmidt held a meeting with McKittrick in Basle. His comment on McKittrick's remarks was sharp: "I was surprised that a voluntary recital intended as a defense of the BIS could be such an indictment of that institution." When Schmidt asked McKittrick why the Germans had been willing to allow the BIS to be run as it had and had continued to make payments to the BIS, McKittrick replied, "In order to understand, one must first understand the strength of the confidence and trust that the central bankers had had in each other and the strength of their determination to play the game squarely. Secondly, one must realize that in the complicated German financial setup, certain men who have their central bankers' point of view are in very strategic positions and can influence the conduct of the German Government with respect to these matters."

McKittrick went on to say that there was a little group of financiers who had felt from the beginning that Germany would lose the war; that after defeat they might emerge to shape Germany's destiny. That they would "maintain their contacts and trust with other important banking elements so that they would be in a stronger position in the postwar period to negotiate loans for reconstruction of Germany.''

McKittrick declined to name all save one of the little group, taking particular care to hide the name of Kurt von Schröder. Since he had to name someone, he selected Emil Puhl. Nevertheless, he pretended that Puhl ''does not share the Nazi point of view.'' Orvis Schmidt was not deceived by this. He knew perfectly well that it was Puhl who had authorized the looting of Allied gold and its transferal to Switzerland and who had been talking to McKittrick the day before in Basle about that very subject.

Schmidt closed in. He asked McKittrick whether he knew what had happened to the Belgian gold deposited in the Bank of France. McKittrick replied: ''I know where it is. I will tell you. But it is extremely important that word does not leak out. It is in the vaults of the Reichsbank.'' Evidently he realized he had said too much: that he had let slip his own role in the transaction. He added hastily: ''I'm sure it will be in Berlin when you get there. Puhl is holding it for return to the Belgians after the war.'' This barefaced lie scarcely impressed Schmidt. The gold was already in Switzerland.

McKittrick did not end there. He admitted that the Germans had sent gold to the BIS and said, ''When the war is over you'll find it all carefully segregated and documented. Anything that's been looted can be identified. When gold was offered to us, I thought it would be better to take it and hold it rather than to refuse it and let the Germans keep it for other uses.''

McKittrick continued, ''I'm so sorry I can't ask you to take a look at the books and records of the Bank. When you do see them at the end of the war, you will appreciate and approve of the role that I and the BIS have played during the war.'' They were, of course, never released.

Orvis Schmidt went on to see the executives of the Swiss National Bank, which maintained its partnership in the BIS and shared the same chairman, Ernst Weber. Schmidt raised the question of the looted gold: the $378 million in gold of Belgium, Czechoslovakia, Holland, and other occupied countries, including the treasure of the Jews. He knew that by a technicality the BIS no longer siphoned the gold through directly but sent it to its associated earmarked account at the Swiss National Bank.

The Swiss National Bank officials told Schmidt that in order to be sure they were not obtaining looted gold, they had requested a member of the Reichsbank, whom they "regarded to be trustworthy," to certify that each parcel of gold that they purchased had not been looted. Schmidt asked who that person might be. He was not surprised when the directors of the Swiss National Bank informed him that that personage was none other than Emil Puhl, who had just left ahead of his arrival. At the Nuremberg Trials in May 1946, Walther Funk, still listed as a BIS director, testified that Puhl had American connections and had been offered a major post at Chase in New York shortly before Pearl Harbor. Funk admitted that Puhl was in charge of gold shipments. He admitted receiving the gold reserve of the Czech National Bank and the Belgian gold, and he added, "It was very difficult to pay [in foreign exchange] in gold. . . . Only in Switzerland could we still do business through changing gold into foreign currency." Funk said that Puhl had informed him in 1942 that the Gestapo had deposited gold coins, and other gold, from the concentration camps, in the Reichsbank. Puhl had been in charge of this. Jewels, monocles, spectacle frames, watches, cigarette cases, and gold dentures had flowed into the Reichsbank, supplied by Puhl from Heinrich Himmler's resources. They were melted down into gold bars; he did not add how many bars were marked for shipment to Switzerland. Each gold bar weighed 20 kilograms. An affidavit was read to Funk, signed by Puhl, confirming the facts. Puhl stated that Funk had made arrangements with Himmler to receive the gold.

Funk unsuccessfully sought to disclaim responsibility for the scheme. He dismissed Puhl's charges that the gold was plowed into a revolving fund. Faced with a film showing as many as seventy-seven shipments of gold teeth, wedding rings, and other loot at one time, he stuck to his story. At one stage he said that the loot was brought to the Reichsbank by mistake! His lies became so absurd that they were laughable. When prosecutor Thomas E. Dodd said to him, "There was blood on this gold, was there not, and you knew this since 1942?" Funk replied weakly, "I did not understand."

On May 15, 1946, Puhl took the witness stand. Puhl claimed that he had objected to the shipments as "inconvenient" and "uncomfortable"—a curious description. He admitted that his "objections" were "subordinated to the broader consideration of assisting the SS, all the more—and this must be emphasized—because these things were for the account of the Reich."

The prosecuting counsel read items from a report that included the statement, "One of the first hints of the sources of [the gold] occurred when it was noticed that a packet of bills was stamped with a rubber stamp, 'Lublin.' This occurred some time early in 1943. Another hint came when some items bore the stamp, 'Auschwitz.' We all knew that these places were the sites of concentration camps. It was in the tenth delivery, in November 1942, that dental gold appeared. The quantity of the dental gold became unusually great."

In October 1945 the Senate Committee on Military Affairs produced further evidence of Puhl's activities. His letters to Funk from Switzerland in March 1945 were read out. They showed his desperate and successful efforts to overcome the effects of the mission that month headed by Lauchlin Currie and Orvis Schmidt. Puhl had constantly hammered away at McKittrick and the Swiss National Bank in order to secure the flow of the looted gold of Europe. McKittrick, brutally exposed by the Bretton Woods Conference's Norwegian delegation, had—the letters showed—panicked, seeking to avoid direct receipt of the gold. Instead, the Swiss National Bank, as BIS shareholder, would take it into its vaults. But in order to camouflage the receipt of it, since the Swiss National Bank had promised the Americans they would not receive it, the Swiss National Bank had disguised it as payments to the American Red Cross and the German legations in Switzerland. There was a starkly ironical humor in this. General Robert C. Davis, head of the New York chapter of the American Red Cross, was also chairman of the part-Nazi network Transradio. As late as 1943, the German Legation in Berne was buying Standard Oil for its heating and automobiles, which were supplied and repaired by U.S. subsidiaries. Tons of gold, thus laundered, poured into the Swiss National Bank in those last months of the war.

In 1948, under great pressure from Treasury, the Bank for International Settlements was compelled to hand over a mere $4 million in looted gold to the Allies.

Despite the fact that the evidence of the Puhl-McKittrick conspiracy was overwhelming, McKittrick was given an important post by the Rockefellers and Winthrop Aldrich: vice-president of the Chase

National Bank, a position he occupied successfully for several years after the war. In 1950 he invited Emil Puhl to the United States as his honored guest. And the Bank for International Settlements, despite the Bretton Woods Resolution, was not dissolved.

2

The Chase Nazi Account

It was only appropriate that Thomas Harrington McKittrick should have been so amply rewarded by Winthrop Aldrich, John D. Rockefeller's brother-in-law, because Joseph J. Larkin, one of Aldrich's most trusted vice-presidents, in charge of European affairs, figured prominently in The Fraternity.

The Rockefellers' Chase National Bank (later the Chase Manhattan) was the richest and most powerful financial institution in the United States at the time of Pearl Harbor. The Rockefellers owned Standard Oil of New Jersey, the German accounts of which were siphoned through their own bank, the Chase, as well as through the independent National City Bank of New York, which also handled Standard, Sterling Products, General Aniline and Film, SKF, and ITT, whose chief, Sosthenes Behn, was a director of the N.C.B. Two executives of Standard Oil's German subsidiary were Karl Lindemann and Emil Helfferich, prominent figures in Himmler's Circle of Friends of the Gestapo—its chief financiers—and close friends and colleagues of the BIS's Baron von Schröder.

Larkin kept the Chase Bank open not only in the neutral countries of Europe and South America but in Nazi-occupied Paris throughout World War II. After Pearl Harbor, Chase's Paris branch provided financial arrangements for the German embassy and German businesses in Paris, under the "guidance" of Emil Puhl's right-hand man at the Reichsbank, Hans-Joachim Caesar, and with the full acceptance of New York.

In common with most members of The Fraternity, Winthrop Aldrich was politically schizophrenic, capable of playing both ends against the middle in the interests of Big Money. On the one hand he was a most generous supporter of Great Britain in her beleaguered state, raising millions for British war relief in a campaign that in 1942 earned him audiences at 10 Downing Street and Buckingham Palace. Yet with great duplicity he turned a blind eye to Larkin's continuances of the Chase interests and banking headquarters in Occupied Paris.

Joseph J. Larkin resembled Aldrich in his immaculate tailoring, perfect manners, austere deportment, and in his dedication to The Fraternity. A distinguished member of a Roman Catholic family, he had received the Order of the Grand Cross of the Knights of Malta from Pope Pius XI in 1928. He was an ardent supporter of General Franco and, by natural extension, Hitler. Morgenthau first suspected him as a fascist sympathizer in October 1936, when Fernando de los Ríos, the ambassador of Loyalist Spain, dedicated to Franco's defeat, went to see Larkin to open an account of $4 million. The account was to be used to raise local assistance for the Spanish government, including the Lincoln Brigade. Larkin said firmly that the $4 million account would not be allowed.

Larkin went a step further in the service of fascism. When the Loyalist government deposited a similar amount in the Chase Bank in Paris, Larkin was furious with the subordinate who accepted the account. He immediately contacted the Loyalist emissary in Paris and had him withdraw the deposit. Simultaneously, with the encouragement of Schacht, Larkin took on the Franco account and the Reichsbank account, though the Reichsbank was under the personal control of Hitler. In 1942, introducing a book entitled *Patents for Hitler* by Gunther Reimann, the lawyer Creekmore Fath wrote:

> Since the middle thirties, whenever a German business group wanted to make an agreement with any business concern beyond the borders of Germany, it was required first to submit a full text of the proposed agreement to the Reichsbank. The Reichsbank rejected or rewrote until the agreement met its approval. The Reichsbank approved no agree-

ment which did not fit into the plans of the Nazi State and carry that
state another step toward its goal of world domination. In other words,
any American firm which reached an agreement or dealt with a German
firm . . . was dealing . . . with Hitler himself.*

As war approached, the links between the Rockefellers and the
Nazi government became more and more firm. In 1936 the J. Henry
Schröder Bank of New York had entered into a partnership with the
Rockefellers. Schröder, Rockefeller and Company, Investment Bank-
ers, was formed as part of an overall company that *Time* magazine
disclosed as being "the economic booster of the Rome-Berlin Axis."
The partners in Schröder, Rockefeller and Company included Avery
Rockefeller, nephew of John D., Baron Bruno von Schröder in
London, and Kurt von Schröder of the BIS and the Gestapo in Co-
logne. Avery Rockefeller owned 42 percent of Schröder, Rockefeller,
and Baron Bruno and his Nazi cousin 47 percent. Their lawyers were
John Foster Dulles and Allen Dulles of Sullivan and Cromwell. Allen
Dulles (later of the Office of Strategic Services) was on the board of
Schröder. Further connections linked the Paris branch of Chase to
Schröder as well as the pro-Nazi Worms Bank and Standard Oil of
New Jersey in France. Standard Oil's Paris representatives were di-
rectors of the Banque de Paris et des Pays-Bas, which had intricate
connections to the Nazis and to Chase.

Six months before the war broke out in Europe, Joseph J. Larkin
brought off his most audacious scheme in the Nazi interest, acting in
collusion with the Schröder Bank. Aldrich and the Schröders secured no less than $25 million American for the use of Germany's
expanding war economy and accompanied it with a detailed record
(supplied direct to the Chase Bank in Berlin for forwarding to the
Nazi government) of the assets and background of ten thousand Nazi
sympathizers in the United States. The negotiations were engineered
with the help of Dr. Walther Funk and Emil Puhl.

In essence, the Nazi government through the Chase National Bank
offered Nazis in America the opportunity to buy marks with dollars
at a discount. The arrangement was open only to those who wished
to return to Germany and would use the marks in the interest of the
Nazis. Before any transaction could be made, such persons had to

---

*Through, of course, the indispensable Emil Puhl.

convince the Nazi embassy in Washington that they were bona fide supporters of German policy. They were told in pamphlets sent out by the Chase National Bank in Manhattan that Germany could offer glorious opportunities to them and that marks would provide a hedge against inflation and would have much increased value after victory in the expected war.

As a result, there was a rush on marks. On February 15, 1939, there was a summit meeting at the Chase in New York of representatives of both Chase and Schröder banks on what was known as the Rückwanderer (Reimmigrant) scheme. Alfred W. Barth was the personal representative of Winthrop Aldrich and Joseph J. Larkin, while E. II. Meili of J. Henry Schröder represented that side of the association. At the meeting the members discussed a proposal that the Reichsbank should send a special representative to the Nazi consulate in New York, which served as the headquarters of the Gestapo and had its accounts at the Chase. The American group decided that they should not take such a risk because their importing such a person might reveal to the American public that they were supporting Nazis. The minutes show that it was decided to "let well enough alone" and to conduct future business on behalf of Berlin through

> the employment of numerous agents and sub-agents who operate through the country. These agents and sub-agents in cooperation with their respective principals, ourselves, can go a long way towards educating Germans in exile and those sympathetic to the Nazi cause through extensive newspaper advertising campaigns, radio broadcasts, as well as through literature, etc. . . .
>
> It is unanimously felt that it would be to the greatest advantage of everyone concerned if . . . Berlin would instruct the various consulates in the United States that all inquiries about . . . transactions should be referred to ourselves, whose name should be supplied not only to the various consular offices in the U.S. but also to those who inquire at the consulates in respect to the procedure.

The bankers agreed that special attention should be focused on shopkeepers, factory workers, and others with little money but great potential for Germany. They should be able-bodied young men and women of pure Aryan stock. Above all, the present meeting must never come to the attention of the American government. The minutes of the meeting state:

The ensuing publicity and the agitation that has been furthered in certain quarters of this country [against similar schemes] might possibly compel our Department of State to enforce a clearing system between Germany and America, under which monies due to American citizens such as inheritances, etc., would have to be cleared. The results are too obvious: firstly, no benefits are likely to accrue to Germany; secondly, the final outcome might prove disadvantageous from Germany's standpoint.

Thus, the Chase directors and the barons von Schröder were afraid that if Morgenthau discovered the true facts, the U.S. government might take measures detrimental to the German government. It was an act of total collaboration with the Nazis.

In May 1940 a prominent diamond merchant in New York City, Leonard Smit, began smuggling commercial and industrial diamonds to Nazi Germany through Panama. Smit's company was theoretically Dutch, which placed it under the provenance of the Nazis, but its stock was in fact owned by the International Trading Company, which was located in Guernsey in the Channel Islands. President Roosevelt had issued a freezing order precluding the shipment of monies to Europe, especially if these might seem to be to the advantage of the Axis. A few days after the Smit account was frozen, Chase officials unblocked the funds at Smit's request. The funds flowed out to Panama, allowing diamonds to be sent through the Canal Zone to Berlin.

On June 17, 1940, when France was collapsing, Morgenthau via Roosevelt again blocked the French account to prevent money going to the enemy. Within hours of the blocking, somebody at Chase authorized the South American branches of the Banque Française et Italienne pour l'Amérique du Sud to transfer more than $1 million from New York to special accounts in the Argentine and Uruguay. The Banque was 50 percent owned by the Banque de Paris et des Pays-Bas (a Chase and Standard affiliate), and 50 percent owned by the Mussolini-controlled Banca Commerciale Italiana. In South America, these banks were working partly for the Axis. Larkin continued to permit free withdrawals from the special accounts even though he knew perfectly well that such accounts were cloaks for Banque Française et Italienne funds.

On June 23, 1941, J. Edgar Hoover wrote to Morgenthau: "During the monitoring of foreign funds at the Chase Bank, FBI discovered various payments to oil companies in the United States. There are indications that the Standard Oil Company of New Jersey has been receiving money from German oil sales by order of the Reichsbank.''

Throughout 1941, *The German-American Commerce Association Bulletin*, a pro-Nazi publication, repeatedly disclosed connections between the Chase Bank and Emil Puhl at the Reichsbank; it revealed that the Reichsbank maintained its account at the Chase. It also maintained an account at the National City Bank when the Reichsbank was personally under the directorship of Hitler. Any transactions between Winthrop Aldrich and Dr. Walther Funk had to be approved by Hitler in person.

Meanwhile, the Germans were permitted to retain accounts at Chase banks throughout neutral Europe. Reports on these accounts were siphoned through Madrid and Lisbon by special couriers. The U.S. ambassador to Spain held up many of the transshipments of accounts, reporting to the Department of State on trading with Germany.

With the advent of Pearl Harbor, most American firms in Paris closed down for the not surprising reason that their nation was now at war with Nazi Germany. Unfortunately, Joseph J. Larkin and Emil Puhl's right-hand man, Hans-Joachim Caesar, both authorized the retention of the Chase Bank in the Nazi-occupied city for the duration.

Otto Abetz, the smooth ambassador to Paris and comptroller of German interests in that city, specifically requested that the Chase manager in Paris, Carlos Niedermann, not close his doors to German business. Such a request was pointless since Emil Puhl and the Chase had already entered into an arrangement that the bank would not close.

The Chase Bank in Paris was the focus of substantial financing of the Nazi embassy's activities throughout World War II with the full knowledge of New York. In order to assure the Germans of its loyalty to the Nazi cause, Carlos Niedermann in Paris and Albert Bertrand and his colleagues in the Vichy branch of Chase at Chateauneuf-sur-Cher were strenuous in enforcing restrictions against Jewish property, even going so far as to refuse to release funds belonging to Jews because they anticipated a Nazi decree with retroactive provisions prohibiting such release. When this matter was drawn to the attention of the New York office by an angry Harry Dexter White in May

1942, Larkin refused to act, since to do so "might react against our interests as we are dealing, not with a theory, but with a situation."

The German administrator Hans-Joachim Caesar reinstated the Chase officials who were suspended as a result of complaints in the Nazi hierarchy. On June 5, 1942, Albert Bertrand wrote Larkin that Niedermann was collaborating still further with the Nazis; on June 16, Bertrand revealed that Niedermann was making arrangements to centralize in the Paris office all deposits, securities, and general records of the branches in France. In September 1942 more deposits were placed. By May 1943, they had virtually doubled. German-controlled funds of some 15 million francs flowed in so that Chase could meet its operating expenses. Chase acted as an intermediary for banks in Brazil and Chile in transmitting to Berlin instructions, transfers, orders, statements, and account details at a time when Brazil was at war with Germany. Brazilian censorship prohibited such communications, and the branches were on Allied blacklists.

Simultaneously, Bertrand transferred securities and large sums of money from Vichy to Germany and German-occupied countries abroad via Emil Puhl with Larkin's approval throughout 1942.

The Chase also handled transactions for the Nazi Banco Aleman Transatlantico, which was, according to a Uruguayan Embassy report dated August 18, 1943, "No mere financial institution. It was in actuality treasurer or comptroller of the Nazi Party in South America. It received local party contributions, supervised and occasionally directed party expenditures, received party funds from Germany under various guises and juggled the deposits . . . all under the guidance of the German Legations." It was in fact a branch of the Deutsche Überseeische Bank of Berlin.

Most Nazi businesses in South America handled their affairs through the Banco Aleman. Thus, the German legations throughout Latin America possessed channels for distribution and receipt of Nazi funds. The Paris Chase received large amounts of money from Nazi sources through the medium of the Bank.

Most important of all, the Chase, with the full knowledge of Larkin, handled the accounts of Otto Abetz, German ambassador to Paris, and the embassy itself.

It is interesting to consider what, among other things, Abetz and the German Embassy dealt with during the war. They poured millions of francs into various French companies that were collaborating with the Nazis. On August 13, 1942, 5.5 million francs were passed through in one day to help finance the military government and the Gestapo High Command. This money helped to pay for radio propaganda and a campaign of terror against the French people, including beatings, torture, and brutal murder. Abetz paid 250,000 francs a month to fascist editors and publishers in order to run their vicious anti-Semitic newspapers. He financed the terrorist army known as the Mouvement Synarchique Revolutionnaire, which flushed out anti-Nazi cells in Paris and saw to it they were liquidated. In addition, Abetz used embassy funds to trade in Jewish art treasures, including tapestries, paintings, and ornaments, for the benefit of Göring, who wanted to get his hands on every French artifact possible.

The Chase board in New York could not claim that it was unfamiliar with these activities on the ground that communication with Occupied France was impossible. The purpose of retaining diplomatic relations with Vichy was that the U.S. government could determine what was going on in Occupied France. A constant flow of letters, telegrams, and phone calls between Paris and the Vichy branch of Chase in Châteauneuf-sur-Cher kept Albert Bertrand informed, and in return he kept New York informed; Washington was advised by Larkin. Despite some criticism by Nazi comptroller Hans-Joachim Caesar, Vichy had under French law the power to close the Paris branch at any minute if New York so instructed. No such instructions were ever received.

When the local branch of the New York Guaranty Trust Bank refused to deal with the Nazis, Niedermann unsuccessfully urged its managers to agree to the demands. In a report marked 1942 (no month or date), Albert Bertrand wrote to Larkin from Vichy, ''The present basis of our relationship with the authorities of Germany is as satisfactory as the modus vivendi worked out with German authorities by Morgan's.* We anxiously sought and actually obtained substantial deposits of German funds . . . which funds were invested by Chase in French treasury banks to produce additional income.'' Reports to New York during the war gave repeated statements by Nazi bank comptroller H-J Caesar of the high esteem in which the German

---

* The Morgan Bank also stayed open in Paris throughout the war, with New York's knowledge.

authorities held Chase and even had minutes of meetings between the Chase people and Caesar. In one response from New York, date and signator not given in the secret Treasury report recently declassified, an American officer of the bank in Manhattan described Chase as "Caesar's beloved child." All of this was known to the U.S. Embassy in Vichy, and to Washington. But nothing was done.

A Treasury report in Morgenthau's files dated December 20, 1944, reveals that Carlos Niedermann was an outright collaborator with the Nazi government; that Larkin knew this but took no steps to remove him; that Larkin viewed Niedermann's good relations with the Germans as an excellent means of preserving, unimpaired, the position of the bank in France; that the Nazis took exceptional measures to provide sources of revenue for the bank; that they desired to be friends with the American banks "because they expected that these banks would be useful after the war as an instrument of German policy in the United States"; and that the Chase zealously maintained, with authorization from New York, the account of the German Embassy under Otto Abetz in Paris, "as every little thing helps to maintain excellent relations between Chase and the German authorities."

Meanwhile, on December 24, 1943, Winthrop Aldrich, the Chase, Leonard J. Smit, and his company were indicted for violations of the freezing order on shipments to foreign nationals in the matter of the diamond accounts and Smit and his company paid fines of over $100,000; Smit went to prison for five years. In the midst of the indictments, Aldrich was often closeted with the President, discussing his activities on behalf of Allied war relief.

Attorney General Francis Biddle was miserably slow in dealing with the indictment and bringing the Chase to trial. It was only through Morgenthau and his team of Treasury agents that the matter was brought up at all.

In a note from Harry Dexter White to Morgenthau dated January 24, 1945, White warned that if the Department of Justice "continued in its delaying tactics," the case "would have no meaning." He blamed Biddle for being swayed by "pressures from Chase." Simultaneously, now that Paris had fallen to the Allies, Morgenthau sent a team into Paris to investigate the Chase records. The team discovered a new and shocking fact. It found that at the time of the fall of Paris in June 1940, S. P. Bailey, U.S. citizen and manager of the Paris

office, had announced to Larkin that he would "immediately liqui-
date the branch in the interests of patriotism." Larkin had thereupon
revoked Bailey's powers and conferred authority on the known Nazi
collaborators who continued in office.

It also turned out that Larkin's staff were sending instructions to
the bank direct until six months after Pearl Harbor and that they refused to exercise their right to veto on any transactions from that
moment and remained in possession of monthly reports. They even
took a step further by having American accounts at Chase in Paris
blocked while the Nazi accounts remained open. There are records of
Carlos Niedermann and his colleagues being in direct touch with Emil
Puhl's office at the Reichsbank, offering to be "at your disposal to
continue to undertake the execution of banking affairs in France for
your friends as well as for yourselves."

In 1945, as soon as he got wind of Treasury's full-scale inquiry,
Aldrich rushed Joseph J. Larkin there to fire Niedermann immediately and clean the nest. He issued statements to the U.S. government
that there was "no connection" between Paris and Chase after the
United States entered the war. Larkin's so-called job "to get to the
bottom of the situation and make the necessary adjustments in personnel" was clearly just a way of covering the fact.

In a telegram marked "Secret" and dated January 12, 1945, the
U.S. Embassy in Paris advised Cordell Hull and Henry Morgenthau
of a meeting with Larkin. Larkin had done his best to save Aldrich.
Greatly agitated, he had told the ambassador,

> Aldrich and the board are very much concerned about the situation.
> The investigation. . . . I must emphasize that the managing personnel
> left in Paris were not officers of the Chase Bank. . . .
>
> Chase New York wants the Chase Bank here open for the use of the
> Army. My mission is semi-official. I have been temporarily billeted by
> the Army. I promise my full cooperation with you. The Bank's inter-
> ests and the government's are identical. Both desire to maintain Amer-
> ican prestige in France.

And then he added a revealing piece of information: "The British
government had a good attitude toward British banks abroad. British
banks in Paris did big business during the Occupation."

The fact that Britain had also collaborated with Nazi Germany on an official level was scarcely encouraging to the embattled Secretary of the Treasury. However, there is no evidence that he did anything whatsoever about Larkin.

A curious event followed. Aldrich dispatched Alfred W. Barth, the prime negotiator in the transactions of Leonard Smit and the Rück-wanderer scheme, to Europe to clean up any further ''misunderstand-ings'' about the role of the Chase in dealing with the enemy. A flurry of memoranda went to and from every department of State and Treasury in 1945 as to whether Barth should be allowed to travel to neutral countries. Apparently one of his purposes was to ''uncover secreted German assets''! Morgenthau and White tried without success to stop the mission. Barth proceeded to Spain.

On April 17, 1945, the Chase National Bank of New York—Aldrich being excused (and Larkin not named)—was placed on trial in federal court on charges of having violated the Trading with the Enemy Act in connection with its handling of the Smit diamond accounts. In his opening statement, U.S. Attorney John F. X. McGohey charged the bank with having failed to freeze the accounts. Defense Attorney John T. Cahill placed before the jurors a substantial volume crammed with documents purporting to deal with the alleged violations of the regulations. Cahill said, ''Operations under freezing orders are complicated. Much more so even than operations under your family rationing books. They are, unfortunately, as involved as operations under the Federal Income Tax Law, and it would be as impracticable for all members of the bank staff to become expert in them as it would for such a group to master all the intricacies of income tax legislation.''

In other words, he was saying that the unfreezing of the accounts was due to natural incompetence.

Be that as it may, Cahill overlooked the fact that Smit had already pleaded guilty to trading with the enemy and had paid $110,000 in fines and was serving a jail sentence. Also, that such commitments at the time could scarcely have been unknown to certain officials in the bank.

The trial was complicated and technical. James E. Healey, Jr., vice-president of the Chase National in charge of its Panama branches, testified he had believed that the freeze order was not applicable to the transfer of funds from abroad to the Chase Bank branch in Panama. Fred C. Witty, another vice-president, testified that nothing official had come to his attention to indicate there was anything wrong with the unblocking of the account. Other officers testified that they had never received orders from the Federal Reserve Bank to block any accounts.

Meanwhile, as the trial went on, Winthrop Aldrich, who was not actually prosecuted in the trial, protested wherever he could be heard that the trial was "absurd" and "based on a technicality." On May 5, 1945, at 3:55 P.M., the jury, after twelve hours of deliberation on three weeks of complicated testimony, acquitted the bank. Aldrich expressed his extreme satisfaction in an interview with *The New York Times*. The matter of the proven dealings of Chase that conclusively established wartime connections with the enemy, including the continuing activities of the Chase Bank in Paris, were neither made public nor were even made the subjects of Senate or Congressional investigation. Once more, the ranks of government closed around The Fraternity. And in 1946, Joseph J. Larkin appointed Albert Bertrand, collaborationist head of the Chase in Vichy, to the board of the Chase in Paris.

3

The Secrets of Standard Oil

In 1941, Standard Oil of New Jersey was the largest petroleum corporation in the world. Its bank was Chase, its owners the Rockefellers. Its chairman, Walter C. Teagle, and its president, William S. Farish, matched Joseph J. Larkin's extensive connections with the Nazi government.

Six foot three inches tall, and weighing over two hundred and fifty pounds, Walter C. Teagle was so large a man that it was said that when he stood up from his seat on the subway, it was to make room for two women. He smoked Havana cigars through a famous amber holder. He spoke with measured deliberation, fixing his fellow conversationalists with a frightening, unblinking, and powerful stare.

Teagle came from a prominent Cleveland family just below the millionaire class. He early showed a dominant will, expressed in a thunderous voice, a humorless intensity, and a rugged disrespect for those who questioned his judgment. He was known as a dominant presence at Cornell. Kept out of football by an injury, he worked off his colossal energy in school debates, which he invariably won hands down. Entering the Standard Oil empire under the wing of John D. Rockefeller I, he rose rapidly through his Horatio Alger concern for work and his strong international sense: he drew many foreign countries and their leaders into the Standard Oil web. He weathered scandal after scandal in which Standard stood charged with monopolistic and other illegal practices.

From the 1920s on Teagle showed a marked admiration for Germany's enterprise in overcoming the destructive terms of the Versailles Treaty. His lumbering stride, booming tones, and clouds of cigar smoke became widely and affectionately known in the circles that helped support the rising Nazi party. He early established a friendship with the dour and stubby Hermann Schmitz of I.G. Farben, entertaining him frequently for lunch at the Cloud Room in the Chrysler Building, Teagle's favorite Manhattan haunt of the late 1920s and the 1930s. Teagle also was friendly with the pro-Nazi Sir Henri Deterding of Royal Dutch–Shell, who agreed with his views about capitalist domination of Europe and the ultimate need to destroy Russia.

Teagle, Schmitz, and Deterding shared a passion for grouse shooting and game hunting; they vied with each other as wing shots. Teagle's love of hunting deer and wild birds was to earn him the admiration of Reichsmarschall Hermann Göring.

Teagle was close to Henry Ford. He first met him in the early 1900s when he wanted to make a deal for oil with a new Detroit auto assembly shop. He walked into the shop, saw how miserably rundown it was, and decided that he would have difficulty in collecting for the gasoline contract. But he took a chance on the thin, gaunt proprietor and went ahead. Many years later the two men met again and formed a friendship. Ford looked at him sharply and said, "We've met before." Teagle remembered at once. "Sure," Teagle said, "I sold you your first gasoline contract. You were stripping down a Winton chassis." Ford replied, "I was. And I was so hard up, I didn't even own the goddam thing!"

Because of his commercial and personal association with Hermann Schmitz, and his awareness that he must protect Standard's interest in Nazi Germany, Teagle made many visits to Berlin and the Standard tanks and tank cars in Germany throughout the 1930s. He became director of American I.G. Chemical Corp., the giant chemicals firm that was a subsidiary of I.G. Farben. He invested heavily in American I.G. and American I.G. invested heavily in Standard. He sat on the I.G. board with Fraternity brothers Edsel Ford and William E. Weiss, chairman of Sterling Products.

Following the rise of Hitler to power, Teagle and Hermann Schmitz jointly gave a special assignment to Ivy Lee, the notorious New York publicity man, who had for some years worked for the Rockefellers. They engaged Lee for the specific purpose of economic espionage. He was to supply I.G. Farben, and through it the Nazi government, with intelligence on the American reaction to such matters as the German armament program, Germany's treatment of the Church, and the organization of the Gestapo. He was also to keep the American public bamboozled by papering over the more evil aspects of Hitler's regime. For this, Lee was paid first $3,000 then $4,000 annually, the money paid to him through the Bank for International Settlements in the name of I.G. Chemie. The contract was for obvious reasons kept oral and the money was transferred in cash. No entries were made in the books of the employing companies or in those of Ivy Lee himself. After a short period Lee's salary was increased to $25,000 per year and he began distributing inflammatory Nazi propaganda in the United States on behalf of I.G. Farben, including virulent attacks on the Jews and the Versailles Treaty.

In February 1938 the Securities and Exchange Commission held a meeting to investigate Nazi ownership of American I.G. through a Swiss subsidiary. The commissioners grilled Teagle on the ownership of the Swiss company. He pretended that he did not know the owners were I.G. Farben and the Nazi government. The commissioners tried to make him admit that at least American I.G. was "controlled by 'European' interests." Teagle replied dodgily, "Well, I think that would be a safe assumption." Asked who voted for him as a proxy at Swiss meetings, again he asserted that he didn't know. He also neglected to mention that Schmitz and the Nazi government owned thousands of shares in American I.G.

Teagle was sufficiently embarrassed by the hearing to resign from the American I.G. board, but he retained his connections with the company. He remained in partnership with Farben in the matter of tetraethyl lead, an additive used in aviation gasoline. Göring's air force couldn't fly without it. Only Standard, Du Pont, and General Motors had the rights to it. Teagle helped to organize a sale of the precious substance to Schmitz, who in 1938 traveled to London and "borrowed" 500 tons from Ethyl, the British Standard subsidiary. Next year, Schmitz and his partners returned to London and obtained $15 million worth. The result was that Hitler's air force was rendered capable of bombing London, the city that had provided the supplies.

Also, by supplying Japan with tetraethyl, Teagle helped make it possible for the Japanese to wage World War II.

There was a further irony. The British Royal Air Force had to pay royalties to Nazi Germany through Ethyl-Standard for the gasoline used to fly Göring's bombers that were attacking London. The payments were held in Germany by Farben's private banks for Standard until the end of the war.

Following the embarrassment of the Securities and Exchange Commission hearing, Teagle took more and more of a backseat and handed over his front office to his partner and close friend, William Stamps Farish. Farish was somewhat different in character from Teagle. Tall, bald from youth, bespectacled, given to publishing homilies and pious patriotic articles in the pages of *American Magazine,* he had a reserved, almost scholarly manner that barely concealed a flaring temper and a fierce self-protectiveness that made him seem guilty in controversies over Standard when he was not necessarily so. He was so emotionally locked into the company that he was indivisible from it. He never understood a rule of power: to keep calm and polite when the opposition is angry and threatening. He could not resist striking back at anyone who criticized him, sometimes with a rather feeble attempt at physical violence. He shared with Teagle a mania for salmon fishing, dog training, bird-dogging, quail shooting, and fox hunts. Like Teagle, he devoted as much as eighteen hours a day to office affairs, immense journeys by ship and train, and board meetings that sometimes went on into the small hours of the morning. Both had the capacity of senior executives to exhaust everyone but themselves with their certainties. They allowed little area for discussion and brooked nothing save approval.

Farish, like Teagle, was mesmerized by Germany and spent much time with Hermann Schmitz. With Teagle's approval he staffed the Standard Oil tankers with Nazi crews. When war broke out in Europe, he ran into trouble with British Intelligence, which boarded some of his vessels outside territorial waters on the Atlantic and Pacific seaboards and seized Nazi agents who were passengers. When the British began interrogating Nazi crews on the Hitler-Standard connection, Farish fired the Germans en masse and changed the registration of the entire fleet to Panamanian to avoid British seizure or search. His vessels carried oil to Tenerife in the Canary Islands, where they refueled and siphoned oil to German tankers for shipment to Hamburg. They also fueled U-boats even after the American government declared such shipments morally indefensible and while Roosevelt was fighting an undeclared war in the Atlantic. Standard tankers supplied the self-same submarines which later sank American ships. By a humorous twist of fate, one of the ships the U-boats sank was the S.S. *Walter Teagle*.

It was important for the Nazis to convert the oil in the Canaries to aviation gasoline for the Luftwaffe. Once again, Farish proved helpful. As early as 1936 his associate Harry D. Collier of California Standard had built units for conversion in the Canaries. Simultaneously, Teagle had built a refinery in Hamburg that produced 15,000 tons of aviation gasoline for Göring every week.

With war in Europe, General Aniline and Film, successor to American I.G., stood in danger of being taken over by the U.S. government. Teagle and Farish's friend, the Rockefeller associate Sosthenes Behn of ITT, was narrowly stopped from buying the corporation, thus rendering it "American" and not subject to seizure. Henry Morgenthau prevented the deal. For once, The Fraternity was frustrated. Teagle and Farish could not buy GAF themselves, as it would have too clearly betrayed their association with the Nazis.

By 1939, Americans were dangerously short of rubber. The armed services were hard put to complete wheels for planes, tanks, and armored cars. At this time Standard Oil had made a deal with Hitler whereby he would obtain certain kinds of Standard artificial rubber and America would get nothing. This deal continued until after Pearl Harbor.

When war broke out, Frank A. Howard, one of the more dynamic vice-presidents of Standard (also on the board of Chase), flew to Europe with Farish's authorization. In London he held an urgent meeting with U.S. Ambassador Joseph P. Kennedy, who allegedly wanted to negotiate a separate peace that would bring the European war to an immediate end. Kennedy enthusiastically approved Howard's meeting with Farben's representative Fritz Ringer. The meeting was set up in Holland. Howard flew to The Hague on September 22, 1939, supplied with a special Royal Air Force bomber for the occasion.

At the Hague meeting, held in the Standard Oil offices, Howard and Ringer talked for many hours about their plans for the future. Ringer handed over a thick bundle of German patents that were locked into Standard agreements so that they would not be seized in wartime. The two men drew up an agreement that specified they would remain in business together, "whether or not the United States came into the war." Another clause in the agreement known as the Hague Memorandum guaranteed that the moment war was over, I.G. Farben would get back its patents. Howard returned to London and Kennedy arranged for the patents to be flown by American diplomatic bag to Ambassador William Bullitt in Paris, who forwarded them on by special courier to Farish in New York.

As the war continued in Europe before America's entry, Germany grew more and more desperate for oil. Her domestic supplies were minimal. But for many years Teagle and Farish had exploited the resources of Rumania, setting up extensive oil exploration in the Ploieşti fields and netting millions from Germany in the process. I.G. Farben financed the notorious Rumanian Iron Guard, a fascistic military organization led by General Ion Antonescu. Hermann Schmitz, through Antonescu and in league with Standard, held an exercising control over the oil fields. On March 5, 1941, Göring arranged a special private performance of *Madame Butterfly* by the Austrian State Opera at the Belvedere Palace in Vienna in Antonescu's honor. After the performance, Göring sat down for an urgent discussion with Antonescu on securing the use of the Standard Oil fields if Germany and America should go to war. Antonescu conferred with Schmitz and Standard executives in Bucharest. The result of the meeting was that Göring paid $11 million in bonds for the use of the oil, whether or not America came into the war.

Farish now proceeded to make another deal with Göring. Hungary was second only to Rumania as an oil source for the Nazi war machine. Teagle had started drilling there in 1934.

In July 1941, Farish and Frank Howard filed an application with Treasury for a license to sell its Hungarian subsidiary to I.G. Farben. Farben would, the application said, pay $5.5 million in Swedish, Swiss, and Latin American currencies, $13.5 million in gold to be delivered at Lisbon, Portugal, and later shipped to the United States; and it would supply a promissory note for $5 million by I.G. "to be paid three months after the war ended." This note was to be secured by the blocked assets of General Aniline and Film in America. Treasury refused the application, whereupon Farish asked if the full amount could be paid in gold at Lisbon. That suggestion also was rejected. Farish protested bitterly.

The British blockade ran the length of the Americas upon the Atlantic seaboard, stopping shipments to Nazi Germany wherever possible. Given the problem, how could Farish go on supplying Göring and Hermann Schmitz with oil in time of war? He soon found the solution. He sent large amounts of petroleum to Russia and thence by Trans-Siberian Railroad to Berlin long after Roosevelt's moral embargo. He shipped to Vichy North Africa. In May 1940, British authorities captured a French tanker in U.S. territorial waters that was sailing to Casablanca with 16,000 tons of Standard oil, allegedly for reshipment to Hitler. Cordell Hull demanded the British government yield up the tanker. Restricted by maritime law, the British agreed. The tanker sailed on to Africa, followed by six more.

Farish fueled the Nazi-controlled L.A.T.I. airline from Rome to Rio via Madrid, Lisbon, and Dakar. The airline flew spies, patents, and diamonds for foreign currency. Only Standard could make this shipment possible. Only Standard had the high-octane gasoline that enabled the lumbering clippers to make the 1,680-mile hop across the Atlantic.

A hard-working young man, William La Varre of the Department of Commerce, set about uncovering Standard's deals with this Nazi airline. He knew L.A.T.I. was the means by which the Nazis evaded the British blockade. The airline was not subject to boarding and search. Spies traveled by L.A.T.I. between the United States, Germany, and Italy by way of Brazil.

In addition to spies, the planes flew, in 1941, 2,365 kilos of books containing Nazi propaganda, legal and illegal drugs addressed to Sterling Products, Reichsbank money for the National City Bank in New York, wartime horror pictures prepared by Dr. Joseph Goebbels to frighten Latin Americans out of a world conflict. There were electrical materials and gold and silver jewelry for sale to Brazil. American companies in South America shipped the Nazis thousands of kilos of mica and platinum, which existed in quantity only in Brazil, and which were strategic war materials for Germany. Semiprecious stones were bought cheaply, shipped to Germany, cut in Belgium in slave camps, and shipped back to Brazil for sale.

In order to supply the airline, Farish changed more of his vessels from German to Panamanian registry. Now they were granted immunity under the Panamanian flag by James V. Forrestal, Under Secretary of the Navy, vice-president of General Aniline and Film, and Fraternity member. But U.S. Intelligence constantly checked on the members of the Gestapo, the Abwehr, and the Farben spy network N.W.7. who used the airline. Early in 1941, Adolf Berle of the State Department insisted that Cordell Hull stop these shipments. Hull talked to William Farish. He told him he was going to apply export control to the shipments.

Farish was forced to reach a compromise. He would supply L.A.T.I. and the other Nazi airline, Condor, through Standard's Brazilian subsidiary with permission from the American ambassador in Rio. The ambassador gave permission and the airlines continued to fly. It was not until just before Pearl Harbor that La Varre and Berle realized what Farish was doing: By making the deal through the Brazilian company, he was not subject to blacklisting. Thus, the shipments continued until after Pearl Harbor when the Brazilian government stepped in and closed down the airlines. Farish totally ignored his government's request to be loyal. Germany and money came first.

On March 31, 1941, Sumner Welles of the State Department stepped into the picture with a detailed report on refueling stations in Mexico and Central and South America that were suspected of furnishing oil to Italian or German merchant vessels now in port. Among those suspected of fueling enemy ships were Standard Oil of New Jersey and California. There is no record of any action being taken on this matter.

On May 5, the U.S. Legation at Managua, Nicaragua, reported that Standard Oil subsidiaries were distributing *Época,* a publication filled with pro-Nazi propaganda. John J. Muccio, of the U.S. Consulate, made an investigation and found that Standard was distributing this inflammatory publication all over the world. By a peculiar irony, Nelson Rockefeller was at that moment in his post of Coordinator of Inter-American Affairs, seeking to insure the loyalty to United States interests of all of the governments of Latin America.

On July 17, 1941, Nelson Rockefeller had joined with Dean Acheson, Morgenthau, Francis Biddle, and Secretary of Commerce Jesse Jones to fulfill a presidential order to prepare what was known as the Proclaimed List of enemy-associated corporations with which it was illegal to trade in time of European war. Acheson was appointed chairman of the interdepartmental committee in charge of the group of Cabinet members. Six months later, in a lengthy memorandum to Milo R. Perkins, executive director of the Economic Defense Board, on January 5, 1942, Acheson laid down the conditions of the Proclaimed List. Rockefeller's claim that he was unfamiliar with the details of Standard Oil practices on behalf of the Axis before and after Pearl Harbor is difficult to believe given the fact that he himself sat on the Proclaimed List committee.

In his official capacity, Nelson Rockefeller was in the peculiar position of having to ask the managers of his South American companies how many Germans they employed, despite the fact that his company and official records both contained the information. He was one thing as coordinator and quite something else as Standard Oil executive. In July 1941, Standard, with his knowledge, authorized the continuance of the lease of its headquarters in Caracas, Venezuela, from a Proclaimed List national, Gustav Zingg, because it would be legally very difficult to terminate the lease. The Coordinator of Inter-American Affairs, with billions at his disposal, leased from a Nazi collaborator for the duration because of a technical issue of a leasing arrangement. More surprising still, a doctor who was in constant touch with Nazis in Caracas, and was on a suspect list, was permitted to remain a member of the medical department of Standard Oil of Venezuela.

On July 15, 1941, Major Charles A. Burrows of Military Intelligence reported to the War Department that Standard Oil was shipping oil from Aruba in the Dutch West Indies to Tenerife in the Canary Islands. The report continued:

> [Standard] is . . . diverting about 20 percent of this fuel oil to the present German Government. About six of the ships operating on this route are reputed to be manned mainly by Nazi officers. Seamen have reported to the informant that they have seen submarines in the immediate vicinity of the Canary Islands and have learned that the subma-

rines are refueling there. The informant also stated that the Standard
Oil Company has not lost any ships to date by torpedoing as have other
American companies whose ships operate to other ports.

On July 22, 1941, there was a meeting of several Treasury officials
with Acheson on the subject of oil shipments to Tangier, including
those of Standard Oil. Tangier was an open port that was leaking
supplies to the Nazis. The meeting was inconclusive. Among the subjects discussed was the possible sale by Standard Oil of its Berlin
property. There was no real pressure on the corporation to dispose of
that office.

On October 28, 1941, Cordell Hull sent a peculiar letter to Treasury's Edward H. Foley, Jr., who was acting in Morgenthau's absence
on vacation. Hull asked Foley whether "Standard Oil Company (New
Jersey) may, through its subsidiaries in the other American republics, sell or deliver petroleum or petroleum products, to have other
dealings with" persons whose names appeared on the blacklist of
Nazi collaborators! Incredibly, he even asked whether Standard Oil
might, through its subsidiary, Standard Oil of Brazil, sell petroleum
to Nazi Condor, largely from Aruba. The reply was almost as surprising. Foley said that such transactions fell under Executive Order
8389 and "such transactions, irrespective of whether they are provided for by contract, should not be engaged in *except as specifically
authorized by the Secretary of Treasury under Executive Order
8389.*" * What Foley was pointing out was that it would be quite
possible to trade with Nazi associates with Treasury's specific approval.

This arrangement did not change with Pearl Harbor. Acting in collusion, Treasury and State continued to issue licenses permitting
Standard Oil and other corporations to trade with enemy collaborators
in time of war.

Over three weeks after Pearl Harbor, on December 31, 1941, Warren E. Hoagland of Standard wrote to Green H. Hackworth, legal
advisor to the Department of State, asking which foreign countries
and their residents and corporations should be considered as allies of
the enemy. In reply, Hackworth informed him that the Department

* Author's italics.

had "not issued a list of enemy or allied enemy countries." Hackworth's note, dated January 6, 1942, contains a touch of unconscious humor: "The Congress of the United States has, you doubtless are aware, declared that a state of war exists between the governments of Japan, Germany and Italy and the Government and people of the United States." The letter goes on to refer Hoagland to the presidential license dated December 13, 1941 permitting transactions prohibited by the Trading with the Enemy Act, provided such trading was authorized by the Treasury.

Immediately after Pearl Harbor, Harold Ickes, Secretary of the Interior and Petroleum Administrator and Coordinator for National Defense and War, began to close in on Farish because of his dealings with Nazi Germany. Farish, who already had savage enemies in Morgenthau and Harry Dexter White, had an even more formidable foe in Ickes.

Ickes was popularly known as the Old Curmudgeon: an inspired if irritating gadfly who was almost certainly the most unpopular celebrity of his day in America. A tense, dark, sharp-eyed, impatient man, he deliberately put his worst foot forward on every possible occasion in the hope of provoking widespread fury and the maximum amount of publicity. He began life with a hatred of the privileged: he was the second of seven children of an impoverished Pennsylvania sharecropping family and spent his childhood sweeping and dusting, washing dishes, kneading dough, basting beef, and flipping flapjacks. He was pinch-hit nursemaid, woodchopper, fire builder, and chicken executioner. In 1890, working as a clerk in his uncle's Chicago drugstore, he was so sickened by the rich with their coachmen, footmen, and high-stepping horses that he mixed seidlitz powders so they would explode in the faces of hated wealthy customers. He became a journalist, writing muckraker articles in Chicago that helped run political gangs out of town. He sharply attacked what he called the "turbulent, grasping, selfish men" personified by Farish and Teagle. His greatest moment was when Roosevelt offered him the post of Secretary of the Interior with the words "Mr. Ickes, you and I have been speaking the same language for the past twenty years. I have come to the conclusion that the man I want is you."

Fiercely committed to Roosevelt, Ickes spent much of the war years with his legs knotted together under a battle-scarred desk from his reporting days, banging away at his ancient typewriter and producing reams of rude letters, newspaper column squibs, interoffice memoranda, and diary entries savaging the trusts led by the Rockefellers. He would frequently break off from watering or cross-pollinating his prized dahlia collection to pick up a phone and shower the hated Secretary of Commerce Jesse H. Jones or Walter C. Teagle with a blistering rain of invective. He became known as Roosevelt's conscience. He maddened Roosevelt by his refusal to compromise; his "cumbrous honesty"—as Heywood Broun called it—which led him to disrupt the delicate relationship Roosevelt had established with the Standard Oil leaders to turn them to his own uses.

Ickes constantly complained to Roosevelt that Teagle and Farish were prominent on various government boards including the War Petroleum Board and that American car owners were forming gas lines while the Germans and Japanese had all the gas they needed. Roosevelt was furious.

On June 22, 1941, Roosevelt sent Ickes a rude and peremptory letter on the matter of his restricting oil. He pinned his ears back once and for all by instructing him to release the shipments by arrangement with Cordell Hull. That same day Ickes wrote in his diary (a statement that was censored out of the published version) that for two years now the President had broken promise after promise to him and that he had even begun to lie to him unashamedly. He added that he had often wondered if he could not be of greater assistance to the people on the outside by telling the truth, rather than staying inside, helping to deceive. He was referring to the fact that Roosevelt and Hull were lying to the public about the extent of exports to belligerent powers.

More and more in 1941, Ickes was cut down by pressure from Standard Oil on the State Department. In June, State set up a Caribbean division without even consulting him. This allowed shipments to Axis-influenced neutral countries from Standard and other wells in Venezuela for transshipment via the refineries in Aruba.

Three and a half weeks after Pearl Harbor, Ickes really had his fingers chopped off. Without telling him, Roosevelt set up a committee under the Economic Warfare Council (later the Board of Economic Warfare), which was to handle all duties and responsibilities in the matter of exporting petroleum products. To Ickes's horror,

William S. Farish's right-hand man, Max Thornburg, was appointed Foreign Petroleum Coordinator, with Farish and Harry D. Collier on the board. Thornburg, a smart executive, received $8,000 a year from the State Department for his job—and $13,000 a year from Standard.

Ickes was so maddened by this sign of alleged corruption and collusion that he called Vice-President Henry Wallace at home on January 4, 1942, demanding to know why Wallace, as Economic Warfare Council chairman, could tolerate such an arrangement. Ickes charged Thornburg with being ambitious, not overscrupulous, capable of being disloyal; he insisted to Wallace that Thornburg had schemed for the appointment and even presented Roosevelt with the letter authorizing his appointment, standing over the President while it was signed. He said this indicated the degree of influence Standard had at the White House. Wallace did not reply.

Throughout the early months of 1942, Ickes kept hammering away at Wallace to have Thornburg dismissed. Frustrated in his efforts, he charged Wallace with "trampling on his enemies and betraying his friends." His hatred for Wallace matched his hatred for Thornburg. With his stubborn sense of integrity he simply did not understand that in order to win the war, Roosevelt and Wallace had to get into bed with the oil companies.

As a result of his needling, Ickes was forbidden by Roosevelt and Wallace to attend meetings held by Thornburg and Teagle to which agencies of the government involved in oil were invited. Ickes was under constant threat from Roosevelt not to interfere with anything that happened. He was tempted to resign and indeed drafted his resignation on several occasions but finally decided to dig in and fight the Establishment. Through his spies he unraveled the fact that Secretary of Commerce Jesse Jones and Bill Farish were interlocked in business interests in Texas. And at last he found an ally who had the courage to confront the President and the pro-Standard chief in Washington head on: Thurman Arnold.

Arnold was a man after Ickes's own heart. He was a grass-roots all-American publicity hound who had worked his way up to become head of the Antitrust Division of the Department of Justice. A heavyweight like Walter Teagle and Farish, he could face these men eyeball-to-eyeball. Shock-haired, ruddy-cheeked, with immense shoulders, he would argue or laugh over a dirty joke with equal vehe-

mence, spewing out a stream of witty, filthy words through a heavily chewed cigar. He was described as looking like a small-town
storekeeper and talking like a storm trooper. He was a tough home-
steader, former mayor of Laramie, Wyoming, and a cattle-country
lawyer of the old school. Like Ickes and Morgenthau, he hated the
Big Guys. He was a bitter enemy of corruption. After only a few
months in office he cleaned up the building industry, bringing in 74
indictments against 985 defendants. He was accompanied everywhere
by his beloved dog, Duffy Arnold. He was so boastful that at one
White House banquet, he said to fellow trustbuster Norman Littell,
"You know, I'm the most famous Arnold that ever lived." "How
about Benedict?" Littell's wife quipped.

During the first weeks after Pearl Harbor, Arnold drove his 1930
La Salle automobile with its shaky rear end through the streets of
Washington to a series of meetings with Ickes at Ickes's house. As a
result of these meetings Arnold obtained permission from the nervous
and weak Attorney General Francis Biddle to hold a meeting with
Farish in the matter of the synthetic rubber restrictions that favored
Germany still and drastically inconvenienced American motorists and
the Army, Navy, and Air Force.

On February 27, 1942, Arnold, with documents stuffed under his
arms, followed by his loyal team of secretaries and aides, strode into
the lion's den of Standard at 30 Rockefeller Plaza. Just behind him
were Secretary of the Navy Franklin Knox and Secretary of the Army
Henry L. Stimson. William S. Farish was there to greet them. In the
boardroom Arnold sharply laid down his charges while the others
looked hard at him. He spelled it out that he had the goods on Standard: that by continuing to favor Hitler in rubber deals and patent
arrangements, the Rockefellers, Teagle, and Farish had acted against
the interests of the American government. Chewing his cigar to pulp
as he turned over the documents, Arnold coolly suggested a fine of
$1.5 million and a consent decree whereby Standard would turn over
for the duration all the patents Frank Howard had picked up in Holland.

Farish rejected the proposal on the spot. He pointed out that Standard, which was fueling a high percentage of the Army, Navy, and
Air Force, was making it possible for America to win the war. Where
would America be without it? This was blackmail, and Arnold was

forced into a defensive position. He conferred hastily with Stimson and Knox. The result was that he asked Farish to what Standard would agree. After all, there had to be at least a token punishment. Farish said with icy contempt that he would pay $50,000, to be divided equally among so long a list of executives and corporations that each would wind up paying no more than $600. Arnold, Stimson, and Knox soon realized they had no power to compare with that of Standard. They did manage to reduce the number of defendants to ten. Farish paid $1,000, or a quarter of one week's salary, for having betrayed America.

Standard underwent a process of law in the criminal courts of Newark, New Jersey. This was a technicality in order to satisfy public opinion. The charges of criminal conspiracy with the enemy were dropped in return for Standard releasing its patents and paying the modest fine. Ickes wrote in his diary on April 5 that when the light was thrown on a situation like this, it made it easier to understand why some of the great and powerful in the country were Nazi-minded and were confident of their ability to get along with Hitler. After all, he added, they had been doing business with Hitler right along. They understood each other's language and their aims were common. A complete exposure, he added, would have a very good effect on the United States.

Arnold agreed. Although he had crumbled at the meeting at Rockefeller Plaza, he had another recourse by which he could drag Standard through the mud. He and Ickes had a sturdy ally in Harry S Truman, an enemy of Jesse Jones. The Senator from Missouri was in charge of the Truman defense committee, dedicated to exposing treasonable arrangements. With great enthusiasm Give 'em Hell Harry embarked on a series of hearings in March 1942, in order to disclose the truth about Standard.

On March 26, Arnold appeared before Truman in an exceptionally buoyant mood in order to lay in front of the committee his specific charges against the oil company. He had dug up a great deal of dirt. He produced documents showing that Standard and Farben in Germany had literally carved up the world markets, with oil and chemical monopolies established all over the map. He flourished papers showing that Farish had refused to send vital patent information to

Canada because Germany and Canada were at war. He showed how Farish had flagrantly disregarded Lend-Lease and good neighbor policies in his connivance with Hitler. He zeroed in on the subject of synthetic rubber, pointing out that it had been denied to the U.S. Navy, and that Farish and Howard had deliberately sidetracked a Navy representative from seeing the processes. He charged that cables showed Standard's arrangements with Japan that were to continue throughout any conflict or break in trade. Leaving the Senate chamber on March 28, surrounded by lots of reporters and photographers. Truman was asked, "Is this treason?" He replied in the affirmative.

Farish completely lost his head. Instead of riding out the storm with cool indifference and waiting for his appearance before the committee, he held press conferences, fired off telegrams from Rockefeller Plaza to the President, issued lengthy and complicated statements on the radio, and told *The New York Times* in a statement prepared by Teagle, who sat up all night to write it, that Arnold's charges had "not a shadow of foundation." Appearing before the committee on March 31, he shouted at Truman and Arnold that he repudiated everything said about Standard "with indignation and resentment" and asserted that he had not in any way been disloyal to the United States. He claimed that the deal with I.G. Farben helped the United States since a number of patents were now in America's possession. He neglected to add that the only reason they were in America's possession was that a criminal court judge had ordered them to be.

On April 2 a flushed and irritable Thurman Arnold came to Ickes's office from a further hearing in which Farish had repeated his denials, and told him, "The Standard Oil guys have committed perjury. I know it. I have reported it. Will they be indicted?" He already knew the answer: They would not be indicted. Arnold went on to denounce Secretary Jesse H. Jones to Ickes for complicity with Standard in the whole matter.

Roosevelt was very unhappy with the hearings. Publicly exposing Teagle and Farish was not helping him use them for America's purposes. He had had enough of Arnold as the hearings concluded. He kicked him upstairs to the U.S. Court of Appeals. Ickes wrote in his diary on April 5 that Arnold had been more or less gagged. The War and Navy departments insured that Roosevelt suspended any further antitrust actions against the corporations for the duration. They couldn't (as the Rockefeller Plaza meeting had made clear) run an Army and Navy without Standard.

Teagle was so aggravated and distressed by the attacks of the Truman Committee and Arnold that he sent Roosevelt a letter trying to explain his position and tendering his resignation as chief of the National War Labor Board. On April 2, 1942, Roosevelt wrote to him, "My Dear Mr. Teagle: I have your letter of March 23rd about resigning from the National War Labor Board. I hope you will not do so as your work on the Board has been, and I know will prove to be, of great service to the country. Your connection with the suit against the Standard Oil Company does not in my opinion (and I have discussed this with the Attorney General) afford a reason for your withdrawing from the Board." But in September, Teagle, shattered by the further disclosures of the subsequent Bone Committee, again offered his resignation and Roosevelt this time accepted it with the carefully put together statement, "I do want you to know how much I appreciate the long months of hard work which you have put in . . . and the sincere and very valuable contribution you have made to the war effort."

Farish remained on the War Petroleum Board. On April 3, 1942, Ickes called Roosevelt in the Oval Office. He protested against Farish's being in that position, but Roosevelt instructed him not to ask Farish to resign. That same day Ickes called John D. Rockefeller II at home in Tarrytown. Despite Roosevelt's statement Ickes decided to risk his job and ask Rockefeller to dismiss Farish from the post on the theory that Rockefeller would want to clean his own nest and escape the drastically unfavorable publicity caused by the hearings. He began by telling Rockefeller that he knew of the relationship between Standard and I.G. Farben. Rockefeller was silent. Ickes went on, saying that public opinion would force him to take action; that he was not recommending that Rockefeller get rid of Farish but telling him in advance that an embarrassing situation might develop with further hearings that would force Farish to go.

Rockefeller said that he had the utmost confidence in Farish and Teagle; that he believed in their honesty, their sincerity, and their patriotism. Rockefeller alleged that he took no active part in the affairs of Standard and knew nothing of what was going on, despite

the existence of Schröder, Rockefeller, Inc. He added that he was
going to stand by these two men unless further facts convinced him
they were in the wrong. But he did not expect to discover that they
had been in the wrong. The Rockefellers, he said, always stood by
their friends; perhaps that was the reason why the Rockefellers had
so many friends.

Ickes said he didn't want to make snap judgments, but in a situation like this, where the administration was concerned, one had to
pay some attention to public opinion. He added that he had the people to consider, that the people be persuaded that the government was
not covering up or protecting any individual to the detriment of the
war effort. Unfortunately, as Ickes very well knew, that was exactly
what the government was doing.

The following day Truman came to lunch with Ickes. Truman said
that Ickes ought to fire Farish immediately from the War Petroleum
Board. Ickes didn't have the nerve to tell Truman that the President
had protected Farish. Instead he blamed the newspapers for putting
an effective lid on the stinking pot with the utmost celerity and dex-
terity. He told Truman that he had never seen a better job of under-
playing the news, except for the first stories that came off the presses.
He added that within his experience there had never been a more
complete justification of the charge that big business and advertisers
had tremendous influence with the press. He added, in his diary for
April 11, that there was no use in butting his head against a stone
wall.

Truman told the Secretary of the Interior he was drastically against
the monopolies. He condemned the dollar-a-year men who were
featherbedding their own industries at the government's expense. He
promised to do what he could with further inquiries.

Ickes was not content. He prodded Senator Homer T. Bone into
the Patents Committee, which began hearings in the Senate on May
1. Bone shared the feistiness of Ickes, Arnold, and Truman when it
came to the question of Standard. On May 2, Arnold's keenest friend
in the Antitrust, young Irving Lipkowitz, shoveled up still more dirt:
He could prove that Standard had deliberately retarded production of
the vital war material acetic acid in favor of the Nazis. He charged
Standard with being "I.G. Farben's Charlie McCarthy in the chemicals field." Lipkowitz was followed by Senator Robert M. La Fol-

lette, Jr., who denounced Teagle and Farish for issuing "as despicable a piece of public relations work by a giant corporation as I have ever seen." He went on, "The Standard officials not only did not have guts enough to come before this Committee today where they could be sworn and cross-examined, but they left the officials who made their denials anonymous." He said that Standard and Farish "adopted that age-old rule of debate, 'when you are weak on facts, give 'em hell.' "

On May 6, John R. Jacobs, Jr., of the Attorney General's department, testified that Standard had interfered with the American explosives industry by blocking the use of a method of producing synthetic ammonia. As a result of its deals with Farben, the United States had been unable to get the use of this vital process even after Pearl Harbor. Also, the United States had been restricted in techniques of producing hydrogen from natural gas and from obtaining paraflow, a product used for airplane lubrication at high altitudes. Jacobs produced a document showing that on September 1, 1939, the day Germany invaded Poland, Standard cabled Farben offering $20,000 for its 20 percent interest in a Standard subsidiary handling the patents they shared between them. Jacobs showed a Standard memo that read, "Of course what we have in mind is protecting this minority interest of I.G. in the event of war between ourselves and Germany as it would certainly be very undesirable to have this 20 percent Standard-I.G. pass to an alien property custodian of the U.S. who might sell it to an unfriendly interest."

Jacobs revealed that it had been arranged that Farben in Germany should file applications in France and England for various oil developments in Standard's name during the war. Senator Bone was so shocked by this disclosure that he called it "astounding" and said, "If the war does nothing else, it ought to clean up a system like this." On May 7, Farish hailed the committee with a furious telegram. He denied that he had avoided appearing and said that he had sought to appear to clear the record but had been refused permission. The telegram was several hundred words long and was so complicated as to be virtually unreadable. As usual, Farish was simply trying to confuse and bamboozle the committee, which was in fact perfectly prepared to have him appear. It was quite obvious that he preferred to shelter behind intricate and expensive telegrams rather than face the committee in person.

The hearings resumed on August 7. Texas oil operator C. R. Starnes appeared to testify that Standard had blocked him at every turn in his efforts to produce synthetic rubber after Pearl Harbor. Farish fired off another telegram to Bone, saying he was at a loss to understand why Bone permitted his committee to be used as a sounding board for "reckless, unsupported accusations." He charged Starnes with uttering "glaring falsehoods and misrepresentations," and he flatly denied that he had restricted Starnes in any way. Flying in the face of Starnes's evidence, he said that "like all Americans, who want to get on with this war, we have hesitated to contribute in any way to prolonged public controversy and name-calling. But the abuses of democratic procedures which occurred at yesterday's hearing must be promptly and openly branded for what they are, or we shall be in danger of losing the very things this nation is fighting for." He went on:

> The most slanderous statements of Mr. Starnes were torn from the press release, and these mutilated copies were actually distributed to the press in your committee room by your own committee counsel. Your counsel can hardly plead that he was unaware of the wild and scurrilous nature of the statements the witness was going to make. The circumstances of the witness's appearance are peculiar. Even though you personally stated that he had appeared on his own initiative, it is a singular coincidence that the testimony of this man was presented on the identical mimeograph set-up as had been the testimony of previous witnesses presented under the committee's sponsorship.

These fulminations sat ill with Bone and with Roosevelt's special rubber committee headed by the famous Bernard Baruch, which was holding meetings on park benches in Lafayette Square feeding pigeons while it discussed the rubber crisis. Hatless and in shirtsleeves in the heat, the Baruch committee wrangled desperately in an effort to overcome the rubber shortage.

On August 12, Richard J. Dearborn of the Rubber Reserve Co., a federal agency, angrily denied Starnes's charges. However, since he was affiliated with Standard and with the Texas Company, his denials could scarcely be said to be objective. John R. Jacobs reappeared in an Army private's uniform (he had been inducted the day before) to bring up yet another disagreeable matter: Standard had also in league with Farben restricted production of methanol, a wood alcohol that was sometimes used as motor fuel.

Finally, on August 20, the various complications were ironed out and Farish and Howard turned up before the committee. Howard argued that Standard was aiding the war effort with oils, synthetics, and other products now used in fighting planes, tanks, cannon, and ships. He added that so far as Standard had learned through examinations of oils, fuels, and rubber taken from Nazi planes that had been shot down, Germany had "not made extensive use" of the exchange information. He did not explain how he had had access to planes that had been shot down or how he had been able to make such determinations from mangled or exploded fuselages.

Creekmore Fath, committee counsel, prodded Farish fiercely about supplying aviation gasoline to the Nazi airlines in Brazil. He snarled, "With the Lend-Lease program in action, were you following the United States or the Almighty dollar in supplying gasoline to the Lati Line?"

"I was following the Almighty State Department," Farish retorted. "Do you question the motives of the State Department?"

Clashes between Fath, Farish, and Howard were frequent. Farish was subjected to a grueling cross-examination in which Fath frequently accused him of lying. Bone snapped at Farish, "Are you familiar with court procedure in which the plaintiff is heard first?"

Farish snapped back, "Do you mean to compare this inquiry to a court proceeding?"

Bone added, "Standard Oil may be a large outfit but it is not going to misinform the American people while I remain alive. I'm fed up with outfits like yours intimating that Congress is trying to ride them. God knows we're not. No one is big enough to ride your outfit; you're the biggest corporation in the world."

The effect of the inquiries on the Teagle and Farish families was ultimately shattering. Farish's two sons were in the Army Air Force and must have been told often that Standard was fueling the planes that they were combatting. Mrs. Teagle and Mrs. Farish had to cope with the women's clubs. As for stockholders' meetings, they were uncomfortable to say the least. Sales dropped and customers were angered. In desperation Farish's Big Board hired a top-flight public relations consultant, Earl Newsom, to improve the company's damaged image. John D. Rockefeller questioned Teagle and Farish on the matters, obviously trying to avoid direct entanglement by seeming not to know the details of the German transactions. Press conferences were held in which Farish made glowing announcements of the help that was being given the war effort. All of this failed to heal the trauma caused by the severe ordeal in Washington. Farish literally died in all except the physical sense during the Bone Committee hearings. Almost equally shattered, Teagle seldom attended a board meeting again. He was so deeply wounded that he would sleep for long hours and even showed a diminished interest in hunting. The corridors of Rockefeller Plaza seldom heard his heavy tread. Whatever he might pretend, Truman and Bone and Thurman Arnold had jointly destroyed him.

On November 29, Farish, after spending Thanksgiving with his family in New York, drove up to his hunting lodge, Dietrich Farms, near Millbrook, New York. He spent the day walking through the golden woods surrounding the farm. Those who saw him noticed that his brows were knitted in worry and that he looked pale. Shortly after two o'clock that night, he felt very ill and a doctor came to the house. At two thirty the following morning he called out to his wife in an adjoining room that he had a severe pain in his arm. A few minutes later he was dead of a heart attack. The funeral took place at St. James Episcopal Church in New York on Monday. Another service was held in Houston, where he was buried.

Among the pallbearers were Teagle and the new chairman, Ralph W. Gallagher. Others accompanying the coffin were General Motors' Alfred P. Sloan and the National City Bank's president, William G. Brady, Jr. Frank Howard was also in attendance. Harold Ickes, whose diaries daily excoriated the Standard-Nazi connection, felt compelled to deliver a hypocritical tribute for the occasion. Inspired more by propriety than honesty, the Old Curmudgeon lied:

> I feel a very real sense of loss in the death of Mr. Farish. He was a member, from the beginning, of our petroleum industry committees and

of the petroleum industry War Council. As such he gave the fullest
measure of sincere, able and patriotic service to the manifold program
which has been necessary to mobilize oil, first for national defense and
then for war. He did so even when the taking of these steps called for
a disregard of normal competitive consideration. His place in the petroleum war program will not be easily filled.

Meanwhile, on August 8, 1942, Standard was still busy. The company's West India Oil Company had shipped to the Nazi-associated
Cia Argentinia Comercial de Pesqueria in Buenos Aires on Treasury
licenses. The U.S. Embassy in Argentina and the State Department
authorized the transaction, along with members of the Petroleum Board
in Washington who were also receiving a salary from Standard.

On August 24, John J. Muccio, First Secretary of the U.S. Embassy
in Panama, wrote a letter to Cordell Hull headed "Suspicious correspondence—possible Axis control of fuel patent." The district postal
censor had intercepted a letter from Miguel Braun, a Costa Rican
inventor, to Frank Howard and H. M. McLarin of Standard, offering
for sale a newly invented fuel known as Braunite that Braun had
developed. Braun was secretary and treasurer of Chemnyco, I.G.
Farben's blacklisted New York subsidiary. The responding letter from
Howard expressed interest in purchasing the patent and soon after
proceeded to negotiate for it.

On August 28, a commercial attaché staff member in Argentina
permitted a Standard subsidiary to sell to another Farben subsidiary
of Buenos Aires despite the fact that the Argentine subsidiary was
blacklisted.

In the fall of 1942 it became clear that Germany was already in
desperate need of oil. Because of severe weather, shipment of barges
and tank cars was drastically restricted. In Africa, General Bernard
Montgomery had smashed the Germans and Italians at El Alamein.
The Russians had succeeded in their offensive against the Nazi armies.

Switzerland proved more and more valuable as a neutral country.
On the surface leaning in the direction of the Allies, that country was
in fact in a permanent state of equivocation, exchanging raw materials in Germany for precision instruments and tools. Germany used
Switzerland as a conduit for oil into France, which by mid-November

was completely in German hands. It behooved all loyal American companies to do everything in their power to stop the flow of petroleum from Rumania and Hungary through Switzerland for the trucks and armored cars and tanks. But the crumbling regime of William Farish had no such consideration for patriotism, any more than Edsel Ford had when he approved the supply of trucks for that same enemy.

In Switzerland the headquarters staff of Standard Oil was in constant touch with Rockefeller Plaza. It was not chartered to separate itself independently since it was in neutral territory. At the beginning of November 1942, Henri Henggler and David Duvoisin, the Standard bosses in Berne, paid an urgent visit to Leland Harrison and Daniel Reagan, respectively minister and commercial attaché of the United States. They asked permission to continue shipping Nazi oil from Rumania, from the oil fields that Standard had sold (or leased) to the Nazis. The oil was to be carried by tank car through Switzerland for use by, among others, the German and Hungarian embassies.

Harrison and Reagan had been given a clear mandate by the State Department on July 10, allowing them to license transactions between American concerns and enemy nationals based on the original Executive Order 8389 permitting such transactions. The procedure was that local members of the diplomatic corps had to apply to both Dean Acheson and Morgenthau for the issuing of such licenses. The meeting between Henggler and Duvoisin of Swiss Standard and Harrison and Reagan was extremely cordial. While Harrison and Reagan promised to take the matter up in Washington, they suggested that Henggler and Duvoisin should drop in and see the Swiss political department to see what the local government's attitude might be. The two Standard men went over to the government offices, where they received a characteristically Swiss reply. The officials reminded their visitors that "We shall of course, gentlemen, have to take into consideration our local laws. Article 273 of our Penal Code provides that anyone who sells to an alien with whom he is at war can be sentenced in this country to imprisonment." The officials told Henggler and Duvoisin that they would proceed as follows. The Standard men must agree not to reveal the names of the enemy companies to which they would be supplying products. Thus, Switzerland would be neatly let off the hook.

Daniel Reagan wrote to Acheson on November 4, urging him to agree to the arrangement for the oil shipment. He said that since the Swiss would not authorize the arrangements that instructions for the shipments should come directly from New York. Reagan wrote:

> Standard wants permission to store and transport in Switzerland gasoline and fuel oils imported for the use of the Nazi and Hungarian Legations. Standard will unload at the Swiss railway station from railroads controlled by the Axis. American and British oil companies are dependent upon the enemy for petroleum supplies imported by the Swiss syndicate, Petrola. To irritate the enemy by ordering Standard to discontinue the service performed for enemy legations might give the enemy *a pretext for refusing to permit oil of enemy origin to be distributed by American companies.** The U.S. Legation is heated by coal of enemy origin and the legation's automobiles are propelled by enemy gasoline. If Standard discontinues storing and transporting oil and gasoline for enemy legations, the latter can undoubtedly have this service performed by a non-American company. To compel the American concern to cease these transactions with enemy legations . . . might result in reprisals against Standard and other American and British oil companies. The legation accordingly recommends that Standard be licensed to continue this operation.

Reagan also asked for Standard to be given permission to pay a Nazi employee of Standard a monthly payment through a German-Swiss clearing account. Reagan went on to discuss Standard's ownership of the Rhine barge *Esso 4,* which was presently commandeered by Germany. DAPG, the German Standard subsidiary, had continued after Pearl Harbor to pay rental to U.S. Standard for the barge. Also, the Danube barges *Pico I* and *Pico II* were supplying I.G. Farben, Krupp, and other Nazi industrial powers, and DAPG was siphoning payments through to New York. Reagan asked if the payments could continue.

The matter of Jean Inglessi came up. He was an official of the Standard Oil office in Paris under the Nazi occupation. He was also on Swiss Standard's board in Lausanne. Reagan urged that Inglessi be kept on.

---

* Author's italics.

Furthermore, Reagan urged State to approve the matter of Standard railway tank cars carrying oil through Occupied France to Switzerland. Several of these had been commandeered by the German army. The cars were covered by Swiss war risk insurance. Standard wanted permission to assist the Swiss authorities to obtain reimbursement from the Nazis because the tank cars had been bombed by the British. On December 11, Minister Leland Harrison advised Cordell Hull and the others that the British Legation in Switzerland concurred with the recommended arrangements.

On December 26, 1941, John G. Winant, U.S. Ambassador to Britain, discussed the matter with the Chancellor of the Exchequer, Sir Kingsley Wood. Instead of stopping these transactions at once, Winant and Wood decided that it would eventually be "preferable" if a Swiss company transported oil for the enemy legations but that there was no objection to the procedure continuing and that "It is best not to incur any risk of [offending the enemy] by raising this issue." The note continued, "Embassy concurs with British view that on balance there is no reason for taking action which would at most be only minor irritant to Germans and which might complicate an already difficult situation or lead to unfortunate consequences as regards to future operations of American and British oil companies."

The embassy and the British agreed that the Nazi employee could be paid each month, that payment for the barges should be licensed, and that Jean Inglessi should be allowed to continue in office provided he did not live in Occupied France. Also, the license should be given to permit Standard to communicate with France, via the Chase Bank in Paris, to recover the tank cars or obtain war risk indemnity from the Germans, again through the Chase.

On December 29, Winant's office—he was en route to Washington—advised that all licenses should be granted as requested.

The matter was handed over to Morgenthau, who under severe pressure from State was compelled to authorize almost all of the arrangements but deferred decision on the business of supplying the enemy consulates with oil and allowing Standard to ship that oil. However, he permitted the shipments to continue until the Swiss company could efficiently take over.

On January 28, 1943, Harrison protested the decision on shipment by repeating that "to provoke enemy unnecessarily [was] highly undesirable.'' But he did promise efforts would be made to have the Swiss company transfer the services. Inglessi must surely be allowed to stay in office even though, Harrison revealed, he was working for Standard in Occupied France.

The result of all this was that Standard continued to fuel the enemy, and the enemy fueled the U.S. Legation and its automobiles, until at least mid-1943.

Other transactions continued. On March 5, 1943, a license was granted permitting Standard in Brazil to pay an enemy corporation for special apparatus. On March 22 an enemy agent on the blacklist was licensed to receive $3,668 by Standard for legal services in Rio. The licensing went on and on. On April 21, 1943, Duvoisin cabled Zurich confirming the shipment of 16.7 tons of fuel to the Axis. The message was intercepted by censorship and sent most urgently to all branches of intelligence but nothing was done about it.

On June 1, 1943, I. F. Stone of *The Nation* (who knew nothing of the aforementioned secret correspondences which were classified up to 1981) attended the Standard stockholders' luncheon at the Patrons of Husbandry Hall in Flemington, New Jersey. He reported that in an early American setting, Ralph W. Gallagher, successor to Walter Teagle as chairman, sought to reply to the angry stockholders who questioned the I.G. Farben association. Gallagher pulled two rabbits out of a hat: two meek young men who had survived torpedoed Standard Oil tankers that had been sunk (by some miscalculation). One Standard supporter asked the crowd how anyone could question the patriotism of a company that had given the lives of three hundred of its men in the war against the submarine. "At this point,'' Stone wrote, "your correspondent was taken ill.''

James W. Gerard, former ambassador to Germany, spoke in support of the company, saying that he had no knowledge of any such American-German relations. Only a handful of those present knew that he had left Germany and his post there a decade before I.G. Farben was formed.

As a grand finale to a meeting notable for its black humor, Ralph W. Gallagher said unblushingly, "We never had any cartel arrangement with I.G. Farben.'' At that moment *The Nation*'s reliable correspondent again felt unwell.

Only eight days later, in a secret document dated June 9, 1943,

C. F. Savourin of Standard Oil in Venezuela was authorized to continue trading in oil with Gustav Zingg's* company and three other Proclaimed List corporations to the tune of a total of 13,000 kilos a month.

On June 15, Joseph Flack, American chargé d'affaires in Caracas, sent to Hull an astonishing list of "sales made to Proclaimed List nationals"! Such monthly lists were sent to Washington throughout the entire war.

State Department memoranda in August 1943 show trading was permitted between a Standard subsidiary and five Proclaimed List nationals in Caracas, Venezuela, that were shipping oil to Aruba for use in Spain.

None of these transactions was ever made public. The details of them remained buried in classified files for over forty years. However, it proved impossible for Ralph Gallagher and Walter Teagle, who remained active behind the scenes, to conceal the fact that shipments of oil continued to fascist Spain throughout World War II, paid for by Franco funds that had been unblocked by the Federal Reserve Bank while Loyalist funds were sent to Nazi Germany from the vaults of the Bank of England, the Bank of France, and the Bank for International Settlements.

The shipments to Spain indirectly assisted the Axis through Spanish transferences to Hamburg. At the same time, there were desperate shortages in the United States, long lines at the gas stations, and even petroleum rationing. While American civilians and the armed services suffered alike from restrictions, more gasoline went to Spain than it did to domestic customers.

The whistle was blown by U.S. Ambassador Carlton J. H. Hayes in Madrid on February 26, 1943, who made a statement that "oil products available in this country of Spain are considerably higher than the present per capita distribution to the people of the Atlantic Seaboard of the United States." Asked by *The New York Times* how this could be explained, a spokesman for Cordell Hull declared blandly that the oil came from the Caribbean and not from the United States and was hauled by Spanish tankers. The evasiveness of the response was typical. The spokesman also neglected to mention that shipments

*Nelson Rockefeller's lessor in Caracas.

were going to Vichy and to French West Indian possessions under collaborative influence.

Hayes revealed that the gasoline and petroleum products equaled the full capacity of the Spanish tanker fleet. He neglected to add that much of that fleet proceeded regularly to Germany and helped to fuel Nazis, including their embassies and consulates and military installations, tanks and armored cars as well as Spanish troop transports on the Russian front, fighting against the Soviet Union, which was America's ally.

In addition to oil, 25,000 tons of sulphate of ammonia were shipped to Spain in 1943 along with 10,000 tons of cotton, despite American shortages in both commodities.

The economist Henry Waldman wrote to *The New York Times* on February 26, stating it accurately as it was: "Here we are, a nation actually assisting an enemy in time of war, and not only that, but stating through our Ambassador, that we stand ready to continue and extend such help . . . Spain is [an enemy] and yet we aid her."

Needled by this and other criticisms, Sumner Welles announced on March 11 that "adequate guarantees have been furnished to satisfy the British and United States governments that none of these quantities of oil will reach Germany or German territory." He evidently chose not to reveal that such guarantees from the mouth of General Franco were useless.

The flow of oil continued. On January 22, 1944, Dean Acheson said that "Oil is allowed to go to Spain as part of the bargaining done with neutral countries to keep them from supplying the enemy with what he wants from them." This statement was made on an NBC broadcast entitled "The State Department Speaks." He was telling only half the story.

The fact that this was so was revealed within less than a week. Despite opposition by Acheson, Harold Ickes overruled everybody and went to see Roosevelt. The result was that the United States suspended oil shipments to Spain. Ickes had accumulated a dossier from his special staff of investigators. The dossier showed that in fact oil was going to Germany, that German agents were operating freely on Spanish territory, and that Franco had just released 400 million pesetas of credit to Germany. This would insure the Germans a flow of all the oil it needed, plus unlimited supplies of wolfram, the ore from which tungsten, a hard substance capable of penetrating steel, was made.

Of course, all of this was known to the United States State Department long before Ickes took drastic action. Nevertheless, nothing whatsoever was done about it. For a brief period the truth emerged about Spain. Spanish ships were searched at sea, showing that oil, platinum, industrial diamonds, and liver extract, from which the Germans made a tonic for fliers, submarine crews, and even shock troops, were coming from Argentina and the Caribbean on Spanish vessels, admitted through the British blockade by American licenses.

On January 28, 1944, the British government cut off oil, gasoline, and other petroleum products to Spain. Franco protested violently. Dean Acheson remained sensibly silent.

It was a brief period of sanity. On May 2, 1944, after only three and a half months of suspension, the oil lobby won a fight to restore shipments and to allow limited wolfram exports to Germany as well. In order to secure this important move, Cordell Hull arranged for General Franco to expel Nazi agents from Spain, Tangier, and the Spanish Zone of North Africa. Although Franco more or less followed these polite requests, he continued to harbor large numbers of Nazis sheltering under diplomatic immunity. There was never any question of breaking off diplomatic relations with Germany: 48,000 tons a month of American oil and 1,100 tons of wolfram began to flow back to the Nazis.

A certain grim amusement could be extracted from an interview with R. T. Haslam, vice-president of Standard, on September 19, 1944, in *The New York Times*. Haslam said that ''Germany has succeeded in producing a fine gasoline, the equivalent of our own, but in limited quantities.'' The remark passed almost unnoticed.

On July 13, 1944, Ralph W. Gallagher of Jersey Standard sued the U.S. government for having seized the synthetic rubber patents handed over to Frank Howard at The Hague. I.G. Farben lawyer August von Knieriem flew in from Germany to testify against Standard. Gallagher's face was a picture when he saw Knieriem enter the courtroom. He knew Knieriem would reveal much of the truth of Standard's dealings with the Nazis.

On November 7, 1945, Judge Charles E. Wyzanski gave his verdict. He decided that the government had been entitled to seize the patents. Gallagher appealed. On September 22, 1947, Judge Charles Clark delivered the final word on the subject. He said, "Standard Oil can be considered an enemy national in view of its relationships with I.G. Farben after the United States and Germany had become active enemies." The appeal was denied.

4

The Mexican Connection

Even the supposed enemies of The Fraternity were connected to it by almost invisible threads. One of Jersey Standard's most powerful rivals in the field of petroleum supplies to Germany, William Rhodes Davis's Davis Oil Company, was connected to Göring and Himmler. Davis was linked to Hermann Schmitz and I.G. Farben through the Americans Werner and Karl von Clemm, New York diamond merchants (who were first cousins to Nazi Foreign Minister Joachim von Ribbentrop by marriage), and through the National City Bank.

The von Clemms were fanatical devotees of Germany, even though both had become American residents in 1932. They used a device typical in Nazi circles: a device copied, ironically, from the Rothschilds. One brother stayed in Berlin, the other remained in New York. They were connected to the Schröder banks through interlocking directorships, and on the board of a company that helped finance General Motors in Germany along with I.G. Farben.

In 1931 they financed the Gestapo with funds supplementing those supplied by Schröder's Stein Bank. Yet another Fraternity link was their involvement with the First National Bank of Boston, an associate of the Bank for International Settlements. They conceived the idea of unblocking First National's blocked German marks to build a vast oil refinery for Göring's air force and for Farben and Eurotank near Hamburg, with Karl von Clemm in charge. This oil refinery would bypass the terms of the Versailles Convention and supply Göring's so-called Black Luftwaffe, which was secretly being prepared for world conquest.

In order to secure the oil for the refinery, the von Clemm brothers had to find an American who would aid and abet them. The choice was easy. From 1926 to 1932, Werner von Clemm had financially sustained a largely unsuccessful oil prospector and confidence trickster named William Rhodes Davis.

Davis was on the face of it unprepossessing. He was short, not much over five feet, with a solid-gold left front molar and a badly bowed left leg that contained a silver plate put there after he was injured in a train wreck in 1918. His head was too large for his body, and his face sported a broken nose. Yet despite his lack of good looks he had the one indispensable quality needed for success. He had the gift of gab. He was capable of talking anyone into the ground. He spoke in superlatives. He never took no for an answer, and he would shaft anyone when the chips were down.

Davis was born in Montgomery, Alabama, in 1889. Poorly educated, he left school at sixteen and jumped a freight car. A kindly porter gave him a job as candy butcher, selling chocolate and ice cream from a tray. Railroad crazy, he graduated to brakeman, fireman, and engineer in the Southwestern states until the collision put him out of commission. Emerging from the hospital with a gimpy leg, he used his plight to his own advantage by working as a comedian on the Keith vaudeville circuit, making audiences laugh as he wiggled his distorted member in a dance. When his popularity ran out, he shipped off on tramp steamers as stoker, fireman, and engineer.

Back in the United States, he dabbled in the oil business but consistently went broke. He was under frequent investigation for a variety of swindles. People were fascinated, even hypnotized, by him; but disillusionment would always set in, followed by the inevitable lawsuit. He sold dry wells, manipulated stocks, and set up and collapsed small companies, carrying the shareholders with him.

In 1926 he was penniless. The von Clemm twins stepped into the picture in 1933. Their support of him saved him from ruin and imprisonment. As a result of this he became deeply committed to Nazism. He was fascinated by the opulence of a Germany heavily financed

by American bank loans, the handsome, healthy men in black uniforms, the pretty blond women. It all seemed a far cry from the
breadlines and pinched faces of America in the Depression.

After the deal with the German government over Eurotank, Davis
saw the way to make his fortune at last. He owned a few wells through
the von Clemms' good graces. With German money he could certainly start pumping.

He traveled to Berlin in 1933. He had to have the personal approval of Hitler before he could go ahead. He arrived at the Adlon
Hotel, where Karl von Clemm arranged a reception for him to meet
Hermann Schmitz of Farben, Kurt von Schröder, and other German
members of The Fraternity. He was welcome at once when he gave
the group the Nazi salute as he entered the room.

Next morning, two Gestapo officers delegated by Himmler arrived
at the door of his suite. They carried with them a letter from the
Führer. The former brakeman and candy butcher was overwhelmed.
He could not believe he had received so signal an honor. The letter
asked him to meet with Finance Minister Hjalmar Schacht at the
Reichsbank. When he arrived, Schacht seemed cold and uninterested
and brushed the whole matter aside. Schacht already had deals going
with Walter Teagle and Sir Henri Deterding of Shell. What did he
want with this small fry?

Furious, Davis returned to the Adlon empty-handed. He wrote to
Hitler, insisting upon better treatment. Hitler replied immediately in
person, asking him to return to the Reichsbank the following morning
for another meeting.

Davis arrived in the boardroom at 11 A.M. As FBI records show,
Schacht smiled faintly in a corner, obviously in no mood to talk. But
a door flew open and thirty directors of the bank appeared, to greet
Davis with warm handshakes. Hitler strode in. Everyone jumped to
attention and gave the Nazi salute. Hitler said, "Gentlemen, I have
reviewed Mr. Davis's proposition and it sounds feasible. I want the
bank to finance it." Then he walked out.

It was clear to Davis that the directors of I.G. Farben, along with
Kurt von Schröder, had exercised influence over the Führer.

Davis traveled to England, where he resumed an earlier business
relationship with Lord Inverforth's oil company. He obtained major
concessions in Ireland and Mexico. He traded Mexican oil for Ger-

man machinery when it proved impossible to export marks. Eurotank was built. By 1935, Davis was shipping thousands of barrels of oil a week from his wells in Texas and eastern Mexico.

Davis knew Senator Joseph F. Guffey of Pennsylvania, whose friend Pittsburgh oilman Walter A. Jones had major contacts in Washington. Through Guffey and Jones, Davis met with John L. Lewis, the labor leader of the CIO. Davis worked hard on Lewis, convincing him that national socialism was preferable to democracy and that the German worker far exceeded in health, good humor and muscular prowess the American equivalent. In 1936, Davis tried to influence Roosevelt by pouring money into the election campaign. From then on he was always able to telephone the Oval Office.

In 1937 he saw a major opportunity in Mexico. He was convinced President Lázaro Cárdenas would nationalize the oil fields. He foresaw a way to corner all the oil in Mexico. In February 1938 he started bribing high-ranking officials in the Mexican government. He made a close friend of Nazi Vice-Consul Gerard Meier in Cuernavaca, who was allegedly encouraging Cárdenas to invade and repossess California, Texas, Arizona, and New Mexico.

Davis obtained the Mexican government's cooperation. He was promised all the oil in Mexico when Cárdenas expropriated it on March 18, 1938. Cárdenas kept his promise. On April 18, John L. Lewis telephoned Cárdenas's right-hand man Alejandro Carrillo. Lewis told Carrillo that Davis would be making a deal with Germany and Italy immediately and that these two countries were the only two with which it would be safe for Mexico to deal.

Why did America's most famous labor leader support the arming of the Nazi war machine? Because Lewis had major territorial ambitions himself. He dreamed of a Pan-American federation of labor of which he would be the unchallenged leader. Through Davis, and through Cárdenas, he would be able to consolidate the unions north and south of the border. In this he had the total collusion of Vincente Lombardo Toledano, head of the Mexican labor force.

By June 1938, Davis's first tanker was steaming to Germany with thousands of tons of Mexican oil. But by 1939 he was already running into trouble. On May 31 his chief geologist, Nazi Otto Probst, was found murdered in his hotel room in Mexico City. Probst had been strangled by a clothesline that was tied to the head of his bed.

The German Embassy intervened and prevented an autopsy. FBI investigators determined Probst had been poisoned. It turned out he had bribed government officials and stimulated action against communists. It was almost certainly a communist killing.

Communist cells infiltrated Davis's growing oil empire. He used strikebreakers to vanquish the opposition and shipped millions of barrels of oil until after World War II broke out in Europe.

Meanwhile, the von Clemm brothers profited enormously from his success. Göring gave them the German franchise in hops, putting them in virtual control of the beer business.

Along with Davis, they became multimillionaires. In one of his frequent visits to Germany, Davis became close to a bespectacled, bulbous-foreheaded youth named Dr. Joachim G. A. Hertslet. Hertslet worked with Helmuth Wohlthat on Göring's economic staff and he also worked on Emil Puhl's staff with Hans-Joachim Caesar. In a series of urgent meetings with Göring, Admiral Erich Raeder, and various army chiefs, these young economists arranged for Davis to fuel the German navy, while Standard Oil fueled the air force. Davis and Joachim Hertslet arranged a German credit of $50 million to Cárdenas to be used for the reconstruction of the broken-down national railroad system, the building of irrigation and hydroelectric power projects, and the setting up of new oil-field equipment and construction. Hertslet opened the German Import-Export Corporation in Mexico City, which was to aid Mexico in stabilizing its currency. It was Göring's plan to render Mexico a debtor republic that could be relied upon to be an ally in time of war.

In meetings in Mexico City at the end of August 1939, Davis told Hertslet of his concern about what might happen to his oil shipments if Germany was involved in war. The papers were full of forebodings. Davis saw his newfound empire crumbling. Whatever happened, he had to secure permanent peace. He cabled Berlin on September 1, 1939, asking Göring if he could see Roosevelt to stave off the conflict. Needless to say, Göring's reply was enthusiastic. That same day he had sent Electrolux's Axel Wenner-Gren on a similar mission to Roosevelt.

Hitler's attack on Poland and Britain's subsequent declaration of war threw Davis into panic. He had his colleague, the beautiful secretary Erna Wehrle, help him prepare a secret code, to be approved by Himmler, which would allow him to keep in touch with Hitler and evade British censorship in Bermuda. The code designated Erna as Chrysanthemum, Hitler as Heron, and surprisingly, John L. Lewis as Dung. Roosevelt, Göring, and all other figures had their code names.

Next, Davis rushed Hertslet to Berlin to insure Göring's complete support in the future. On September 5 he had an urgent conference with Lewis, who called Roosevelt and insisted the President see the anxious oilman.

Roosevelt dared not offend Lewis because of Lewis's power over the work force on the brink of the 1940 election. However, he was afraid of what he called "entry or plot": J. Edgar Hoover and the State Department's Adolf A. Berle had handed him massive dossiers showing Davis's Nazi connections.

Like Ickes and Morgenthau, Berle was a fierce opponent of Nazi Germany. Morgenthau and Ickes were very happy to have him deal directly with the Davis matter. Busy fighting Standard Oil, they needed his assistance badly. Berle worked against Dean Acheson, whom he disliked intensely; the feeling was mutual. Berle was a maverick in the State Department, a thin, fierce, driven man who completely lacked the smooth gift of compromise normally required in Department dealings. Roosevelt trusted him completely. Indeed, he placed Berle over Hoover, preferring to have all of Hoover's reports siphoned through Berle and analyzed by him before they reached the desk of Major General Edwin M. ("Pa") Watson, the presidential secretary.

On September 13, Davis called Roosevelt for an appointment. The moment he was off the phone, Roosevelt summoned Berle to the Oval Office. He asked Berle to sit in on the meeting with Davis scheduled for the following afternoon; he was to take minutes and to give him his personal comments as soon as Davis left.

At two o'clock the following day Davis limped into the office with all of his bantam cock's outrageous arrogance. He paced about the room, spouting his line of peace with Hitler and suggesting he should go to see Göring to convey Roosevelt's peace message. He was irritated by Berle's presence in the room. He asked Roosevelt twice if Berle could leave. Roosevelt refused to accede to his request. Davis shrugged and sat down.

While Roosevelt listened through a cloud of cigarette smoke Davis unraveled a great deal of specious nonsense. Knowing Roosevelt had no time for Hitler, he tried to sell him Göring, promising that Göring would soon take over the German government and saying that Hitler had been "moved away from the main Council." He asked the President's authority to enter into peace talks with Göring on the President's behalf.

Roosevelt replied that he had often been approached to intervene in the European conflict but he could only do so through official channels. He pointed out that he had sent a message just before the war suggesting peace talks but had not received an answer until the war had begun, "which, of course, got no one anywhere."

Roosevelt did not authorize Davis to act on the American government's behalf. Indeed, as soon as Davis left, he ordered Berle to contact J. Edgar Hoover and instruct the FBI chief to report directly to Berle on Davis's movements and contacts. On no account was Hoover to report to the Attorney General Robert H. Jackson or to Cordell Hull.

Davis left the meeting with Roosevelt in a state of drastic unease. Hertslet cabled him on Göring's instruction that he and Lewis must influence Roosevelt to suppress any revision of the Neutrality Act. In his cable of September 18 he reminded Davis, who scarcely needed reminding, "selling to belligerent nations means destroying cargo boats."

Davis, afraid of falling out of favor with Göring, cabled Berlin the next day that the President wanted him to negotiate the peace. He pretended that Roosevelt had agreed Germany should keep Danzig, the Polish Corridor, Czechoslovakia, all former provinces ceded to Poland by the Versailles Treaty, and all African and other colonies that Germany had had before 1918. He asserted that Roosevelt had appointed him ambassador without portfolio. He left for Lisbon and Rome on September 20. His plane was forced down by storms in Bermuda. British Intelligence men came to the airport and questioned him closely. He refused to answer them and proceeded to Lisbon.

In Rome, Himmler sent several Gestapo men to meet Davis's plane. The oilman had a quick meeting with Mussolini, who proved welcoming. Accompanied by the SS men, he was given a special aerial tour of the German and Polish fronts.

Göring received him at the Air Ministry in Berlin on October 1,

1939. Among those present were Hertslet and Wohlthat. Göring opened the conference by expressing his admiration for Davis's efforts in providing petroleum to Germany for almost seven years through Eurotank. He asked for Roosevelt's sentiments and Davis insisted that Roosevelt was pro-German. Göring was understandably surprised. He said that he expected Davis to help secure permanent peace at the conference table, with Hitler and Roosevelt presiding.

J. Edgar Hoover and military intelligence determined that Hertslet would be returning with Davis to the United States. When Davis and Hertslet arrived in Lisbon on their way home, the local consul refused Hertslet a visa. Davis made a tremendous fuss, citing his "friendship" with Roosevelt and shouting that Hertslet was "a director of his European company." The consul cabled Berle in Washington, asking him whether he should shut his eyes to the fact that Hertslet was a high-ranking figure in the Nazi government.

In Washington, Berle had an urgent meeting with Assistant Secretary of State George S. Messersmith. They agreed Hertslet was dangerous. They cabled the consul in Lisbon to refuse Hertslet the visa. Hertslet returned to Berlin to obtain a diplomatic passport.

Back in Washington, Davis checked into the Mayflower Hotel. FBI men had difficulty in bugging his conversations and movements. A post office convention filled the hotel and the G-men were unable to find a single room from which to operate. They had to use corners, closets, fire escapes, and even the roof as bases of their operations. It was only by engaging waiters and maids to help them that they discovered the import of meetings between Davis and his reliable secretary. These indicated commitment to the Nazis whether America came into the war or not—at least on Davis's side.

Davis tried to arrange another meeting with Roosevelt. While he waited for a decision, he changed his tankers to Panamanian registry to slip them through the British blockade to Lisbon, Hamburg, and other ports of Europe. He kept up a constant flow of petroleum and vital materials to Japan, again using Panamanian registry rather than Japanese tankers because British Intelligence was boarding Japanese ships at sea and arresting their German crews. Davis entered into collaboration with a former U-boat captain who was one of the harbor staff of Brownsville, Texas, and could aid him in his blockade running.

Meanwhile, the von Clemm brothers were running into trouble. Morgenthau's Treasury agents were in Berlin, dodging the Gestapo to investigate the Davis–von Clemm deals through the Hardy Bank. Karl von Clemm cabled Davis frantically on October 11, 1940, that he saw "execution" coming, and he reminded Davis of his six and a half years of protection of the oilman. What could Davis do? Davis arranged with Göring for von Clemm to be transferred to Rome. Von Clemm and his brother diversified their company into diamond smuggling.

Following the occupation of Belgium and the Netherlands, the banks rushed their large holdings of diamonds into special vaults. But they were compelled to reveal the vaults' whereabouts. The von Clemms made a deal with the German government to obtain a corner in diamonds, importing them to North America to sell for desperately needed dollars with which to finance espionage rings and obtain industrial diamonds. Since the war was going on, these shipments were in direct contravention of the existing laws. So the von Clemms set up a complicated routing for their transactions.

The diamonds were shipped from Brussels and Amsterdam to Rome. They were put aboard the Nazi-controlled L.A.T.I. airline and flown via Lisbon and Dakar to Natal in Brazil and thence to Rio. They came by diplomatic pouch from the German Embassy to the German consulate in New York.

In 1940, with no satisfaction from Roosevelt, Davis turned violently against the President and joined with the Nazis in a desire to destroy him in the elections. John L. Lewis agreed with Davis that Roosevelt must go or the entire oil deal with Hitler might be stopped.

Davis talked with Göring and the result was that Göring actually supplied $8 million to engineer the President's downfall. The Fraternity members decided to finance Burton K. Wheeler for accession to the White House. The perfect choice of a Nazi faction, Wheeler was ceaseless in his support of Hitler. He used his senatorial franking privileges to distribute Nazi propaganda through the mail. He opposed Lend-Lease, conscription, and aid to Britain in the form of warships and munitions.

The $8 million arrived in Washington via L.A.T.I. airlines and Pan American Airways. Davis spread the money through accounts in six different banks. His first investment was $160,000 to buy forty

Pennsylvania delegates at the Chicago Democratic party convention to insure the defeat of his old friend Senator Guffey, who was threatening to expose The Fraternity. The forty Pennsylvania delegates would also vote against Roosevelt. The deal did not work. Guffey won the nomination and so did Roosevelt. Wheeler lacked the common touch and had no chance against the President.

John L. Lewis did his best. He guaranteed ten million votes for Roosevelt's Republican opponent, Wendell Willkie. He gave a radio speech on October 25, denouncing Roosevelt as a warmonger and threatening to retire from the CIO if the President was reelected. But Roosevelt remained in power. While leaving the public in no doubt of his attitude to Hitler, he promised the electorate that no American boy would die on foreign soil. He thus united the isolationist factors and assured himself the election.

Davis overcame the setback by expanding his operation. He set up U-boat refueling bases through the Caribbean and South American coastlines. He split off Eurotank into an independent body under Göring and Karl von Clemm, his profits indirectly siphoned to him through the Bank for International Settlements via Lisbon and Buenos Aires. But as America drew closer to war, the von Clemm brothers grew more and more worried about their American operation. They had to be prepared for the flow of diamonds and oil to be stopped.

In May 1941, Karl von Clemm warned Werner in a cable encoded AUNT KATE DYING FAST that Hitler was about to declare war on the Soviet Union. When Hitler invaded Russia, Davis's shipments of oil via Vladivostok and the Trans-Siberian Railroad to Berlin abruptly stopped. Hastily, he increased his Compania Veracruzana deals with Japan, and arranged for $3 million in yen to be transferred to him via the White Russian millionaire Serge Rubinstein to buy foreign exchange and finance oil wells. He also became involved in business deals with Brazil and Argentina.

Davis gave financial support to the No Foreign Wars Committee. This was financed also directly from Berlin. Meanwhile, the von Clemm brothers financed the pro-Nazi America First movement. With Verne Marshall, isolationist editor and supporter of Hitler, Davis and Werner von Clemm became involved with Charles Lindbergh and his "pacifist" campaigns against Roosevelt. On January 2, 1941, Senator Josh Lee, a Democrat from Oklahoma, charged that the formation of the No Foreign Wars Committee with Davis's backing amounted to "the diabolically cunning betrayal of the American people." He added:

> The record of this man Davis shows conclusively the great financial stake he has in a complete Nazi victory in the European war. Much of the gasoline sending showers of fiery death into the defenseless heart of London was sold to the German government by this man Davis. . . . He is still trying to promote a phony peace through the White House to pull Nazi Germany's chestnuts out of the fire. . . . The No Foreign Wars Committee is a timely object lesson in the technique of Nazi infiltration.

The truth of Lee's words could be seen in the fact that the committee included Senator Rush D. Holt of Virginia, who was alleged to be in the direct pay of the Nazi government.

On January 5, at a press conference in his offices on the fifty-fourth floor of the RCA Building in Rockefeller Plaza, Davis denied he was financing the committee. He said he would like to appear before the Senate committee that had been formed to investigate his activities. The investigative committee was headed by Senator Burton K. Wheeler!

In an attempt to bolster his case, Davis said he had not shipped oil to Germany after war broke out, knew nothing about what was happening at Eurotank (despite the fact that he had received a letter from Karl von Clemm the day before), and stated he was a direct descendant of the South African empire builder Cecil Rhodes and of Jefferson Davis. The problem was that Cecil Rhodes had had no children and that Jefferson Davis's descendants had been disowning the oilman for the past twenty years.

By May, Senator Wheeler had "cleared" Davis of all connections with the Nazi government. But this help from a fellow Fraternity figure did not ease Davis's increasing sense of fear that Roosevelt would bring America into the war. On July 26 he appeared briefly on radio to support Wheeler's all-out attack on Lend-Lease. On August 1 he was in Houston when he was stricken with a fatal heart attack in his hotel room.

In his authorized biography, *A Man Called Intrepid,* Sir William

Stevenson claims that Davis did not die from natural causes but was murdered by representatives of British Intelligence. According to the FBI files his demise was simply brought on by the terrible strain of the preceding months as his empire fell apart and his Nazi connections began to cause some of his shareholders to run for the hills.

After his death his secretary, the glamorous Erna Wehrle, became chairman of the giant corporation. Werner von Clemm became vice-president. The board was made up of Fraternity aide U.S. Secretary of Commerce Jesse H. Jones, Harry D. Collier of California Standard, and Hamilton Pell, partner of Leo T. Crowley in Standard Gas and Electric. The Fraternity had come full circle once more.

Throughout the early months of 1942, Morgenthau's team built a damning case against the von Clemm brothers. Meanwhile, they hastily sold the Davis Oil Company to Fraternity brothers Serge Rubinstein and Axel Wenner-Gren to insure its continued existence.

Werner von Clemm went on living a life of luxury on his ill-gotten gains. He became a pillar of society in the heart of the fox-hunting country: at Syosset, Long Island. No one who enjoyed his company suspected that this handsome member of the local social set was on the brink of being arrested.

On September 26, 1942, a police car containing Treasury agents rolled up at the door of the von Clemm house. The visitors rang the doorbell. A maid came to the door. The elegant von Clemm was waiting in the living room to receive the visitors. The agents apologized for the inconvenience and politely placed handcuffs on Werner's delicate wrists.

The trial caused a great stir in Syosset. Werner lied and lied, trying to hide the details of the conspiracy. But it was useless. He was sentenced to five years in prison—the only member of The Fraternity to suffer such a sentence. There is a curious footnote to the story. On October 15, 1942, the German government sent an official message through the Swiss authorities to American minister Leland Harrison in Berne. They asked for a full transcript of von Clemm's trial to be sent from Washington to Berlin. It was, of course, supplied.

At war's end, O. John Rogge, Special Assistant to the Attorney General, collected a mass of evidence in Germany to show the Davis-Lewis connection. At a speech at Swarthmore College on October 26, 1946, he told the story of the association. He also showed other questionable connections, including the activities of Burton K. Wheeler on behalf of the Nazi government. The result was that Attorney General Tom Clark fired Rogge. When the author of this book asked him in 1981 why he had been dismissed, the dying Rogge replied succinctly. "Wheeler," he said, "was closer to President Truman than I was."

5

Trickery in Texas

A partner of the Rockefeller associate, Standard Oil of California, the tall, fair-haired, and dynamic Torkild "Cap" Rieber of the Texas Company was an important link in The Fraternity. Born in Voss, Norway, in 1882, this strapping young Viking became an American citizen at the age of twenty-two. Within weeks, he was master of an oil tanker loading up from Spindletop, Texas. He joined the Texas Company at twenty-three; within twenty years he was chairman; he created a tanker fleet that gave his company enormous international power by 1933. He built the Barco pipeline in Colombia, flying suspension bridges in sections from Texas to the Andes, flinging them across 5,000-foot passes. He linked up with Standard Oil of California in Saudi Arabia and in Bahrein in the Persian Gulf, obtaining a monopoly through under-the-table deals with the local rulers and the Japanese and German interests in those areas.

"Cap" Rieber supplied Franco in the Spanish Civil War, shipping oil from Galveston to Bordeaux in France and thence to Corunna, with orders not to stop for inspection by any man-of-war, including United States gunships. He supplied polymerization techniques to I.G. Farben in the Ruhr and to I.G.-Farben–connected companies in Iran, Saudi Arabia, Egypt, and Syria with the approval of the State Department.

In December 1939 he flew with Göring in a plane piloted by Pan

American Airways pilot Pete Clausen on a personally conducted tour of the main centers of industrial Germany. He sailed his vessels through the British blockade to fuel the U-boats after 1939, and simultaneously sent more to aid Nazi corporations in South America. He told *Life* magazine in 1940, "If the Germans ever catch [any of my ships] carrying oil to the Allies they will have my hearty permission to fire a torpedo into her."

Rieber was among those, like Davis, who had high hopes for Juan Almazán's bid for the Mexican presidency to succeed in favor of the Axis. On February 12, 1940, the American Embassy in Mexico City reported that Texas Oil of Arizona was working in close collusion with affiliated oil groups including the Davis Oil Company in directing the clandestine entry of arms into Mexico. The arms were to support a possible military coup by Almazán in the event of his defeat at the polls. The report said, "Pacific Fruit Express refrigerator cars are each loaded with arms in special wooden boxes so shaped as to fit very conveniently along the sides of the wooden strips or slotted flooring that permits the drainage of the ice water to the drain pipes under the floor of these cars." The report added, "Oil company secret service operatives are ridiculing the Mexican Government for the glass-eyed vigilance on the border, as they call it, that enables them to execute adroit introduction of arms without detection." The report said, "I find that large sums of oil money are being paid out on the border for protection and I also have ascertained that Custom House officials on the American side of the line at Eagle Pass, Texas, have accepted money to facilitate the departure of arms from the U.S.A. through this American port of entry."

In 1940, Rieber worked in close collaboration with the Texas Company's German representative Nikolaus Bensmann, who was a paid spy of Hermann Schmitz's nephew Max Ilgner in Bremen. Bensmann corresponded with Rieber and Rieber's vice-president, R. J. Dearborn, in a complicated cipher that was successfully designed to evade the British censorship office in Bermuda. The cipher was so effective that, as Bensmann wrote to the Abwehr in Hamburg on January 29, 1940, "Even lengthy espionage reports can be transmitted without running the risk of discovery." By the code, Rieber was able to send information to Bensmann about gasoline shipments to the Canary Islands and secret patents being shipped clandestinely to

Berlin. These reports made their way to I.G. Farben's N.W.7. Intelligence Group, where they were examined by Ilgner. Rieber visited Roosevelt to discuss the President's attitude toward Germany; intelligence on the meetings was transferred by Bensmann's code to Berlin. Rieber's reports on every aspect of the petroleum industry in the United States rivaled those supplied by General Aniline and Film. Even restricted aircraft-production details were given, in a fifty-eight-page report that should never have left America, prepared with the cooperation of spies in the offices of Secretary of the Interior Harold L. Ickes and Secretary of the Navy James V. Forrestal. The cipher was never broken. But here is a problem. Why were these ciphers allowed to flow through Bermuda? Why were they not stopped? There is no evidence they were forwarded to London for examination.

Rieber obtained British Navicerts or certificates of authorization to send his supplies to Germany through the British blockade after Britain and Germany were at war. He bartered the shipments for nine tankers built for him in Nazi yards and delivered to him under the Norwegian flag with British consent after September 3, 1939. In 1940, Rieber sold all German interests in Texas Company's German patents for $5 million. He arranged contracts with I.G. Farben in which he supplied plans of all the motors and installations of American Navy yards and Army forts that he provided with gasoline and oil.

Some of Rieber's employees were loyal Americans. They wrote to the State Department and even the President demanding that Rieber be exposed. They alleged that he hired Gestapo agents as lubrication engineers and that emissaries of the German military authority in Norway were staying with Rieber in New York. On August 2, 1940, an employee of Rieber's Beacon Research Laboratory wrote the State Department that Rieber was "a representative of Hitler in this country." The employee added that "the entire executive staff of the Texas Co. is pro-Nazi and openly boasts of it as well as being willing to do all within its power to injure the English and help the Germans." The letter went on:

> Two men from Germany are now at the laboratory, neither one being a technical man, and as nearly as we can determine, they are here solely for the purpose of learning all they can about this country so that if an invasion is made, they will have had a chance to send to the

enemy all of the essential information about industrial plants and areas. They were "economists" in Germany and were assigned to the work in engineering in our laboratory—work they are not equipped to do. One of these men is an outright propagandist for Hitler. Contacting all the people of German extraction in America and holding meetings at his home, preparing the way for the proposed German invasion of his country. He has taken pictures of the entire area, completely mapped the district by photography and is constantly wandering over the district taking pictures of strategic areas.

The visit to New York that year of Nazi Fraternity associate Gerhardt Westrick (see Chapter 6) exposed Rieber to such unwanted publicity that several shareholders in the Texas Company demanded that there be a housecleaning and that Rieber must retire for the company's own good.

On August 20 fifteen directors of the corporation walked grimly into the Texas Company boardroom on the twenty-fifth floor of the Chrysler Building. They had to reach a decision on the future. They argued for seven hours, trying to find some way to clean up the board's image after the unwelcome attention Texas Co. had been getting. They knew that the press coverage of the Rieber-Westrick association could cause a catastrophe in business. Walter G. Dunnington, the prominent Manhattan attorney who represented the estate of railroad pioneer James J. Hill, the Texas Company's biggest single stockholder, insisted that Rieber must go. Prominent banker William Steele Gray, Jr., and stockbroker Henry Upham Harris agreed. Texas oilman John H. Lapham and Chicago banker Walter J. Cummings wanted to have Rieber take a vacation until the bad publicity blew over. But Rieber's second-in-command, the smooth, soft-voiced William Starling Sullivant Rodgers, was eager to take Rieber's place and made no bones about seeking Rieber's dismissal.

Rieber was asked to present his own point of view, which largely consisted of boomingly delivered sweet nothings. The result was that the board asked for his resignation. However, he continued to exercise influence behind the scenes. The adroit W.S.S. Rodgers took over from Rieber. He linked up with the Rockefeller empire by going into partnership with Harry D. Collier, cheerful chairman of Standard Oil of California, and the former Jersey Standard employee

Jimmy Moffett. Rodgers formed Caltex, which jointly bought up millions of dollars' worth of oil from the Arabian Sea. The banker was James V. Forrestal, of the board of the Nazi General Aniline and Film, who was about to become Under Secretary of the Navy.

Saudi Arabia had intricate economic and political links with Hitler. On June 8, 1939, Khalid Al-Hud Al-Qarqani, royal counselor of Ibn Saud, was received by Ribbentrop in Berlin. Ribbentrop expounded to Khalid his general sympathy toward the Arab world and pointed out that Germany and the Arabs were linked by a common foe in the shape of the Jews. Khalid answered that Ibn Saud attached the greatest importance to entering into relations with Germany. Ribbentrop was concerned that Ibn Saud might have a special relationship with the King of England. This had been played up in the press. Khalid set Ribbentrop's mind at ease. He stressed that the king hated the British, who hemmed him in. By contrast, Khalid stated, Ibn Saud was sympathetic toward Mussolini. The conversation ended with salaams and Heil Hitlers.

At 3:15 P.M. on June 17, 1939, Hitler received Khalid Al-Hud at the Berghof. The reception was given worldwide attention. It was agreed throughout Europe that the meeting was a blow to Britain. As a result of it Emil Puhl and Walther Funk's Reichsbank gave Ibn Saud a credit of one and a half million Reichsmarks from Hitler's personal treasury for the purchase of 8,000 rifles, 8 million rounds of ammunition, light anti-aircraft guns, armored cars, a special Mercedes for the king, and the building for a munitions factory. Soon afterward, Emil Puhl arranged a further loan of 6 million marks that was paid in installments for the rest of the war.

These arrangements were in effect on November 28, 1941, when the Grand Mufti of Jerusalem, the leading legalist of the Arab kingdoms and among the bitterest enemies of the Jews, met with the Führer in Berlin. The Grand Mufti, with the authorization of the Arab world, expressed his admiration of Hitler and named the same enemies: the English, the Jews, and the communists. He promised to guarantee assistance in war by acts of sabotage and revolution. He offered to raise the Arab Legion from all available Moslem men of military age. He indicated support for Vichy France. Hitler replied that Germany was locked in a death struggle with two citadels of Jewish power: Great Britain and Soviet Russia. It went without say-

ing that all practical aid would be given to the Arab countries in
return for Arab support. The Führer said, enjoining the Mufti to "Lock
it in the uttermost depths of your heart," that the Führer would carry
on the battle for the total destruction of the Judeo-Communist empire
in Europe, that the German armies would soon reach the southern
exit of Caucasia, and that as soon as this happened, the Führer would
give the Arab world the assurance that its hour of liberation had arrived. He would force open the road to Iran and Iraq and destroy the
British world empire.

This crucial meeting took place five months after an arrangement
had been entered into by Caltex in collusion with Roosevelt. In June
1941, jolly James Moffett of Caltex went to the President with a
proposal. Moffett stated that in order to insure that Ibn Saud remained loyal to American interests (in other words, did not hand
Caltex over to Germany or supply General Erwin Rommel with oil)
the Treasury must advance $6 million a year to Ibn Saud. Moffett
said this with the knowledge that the $6 million per annum would
not in any way affect Ibn Saud's ongoing relationship with Hitler.
Indeed, at the same time Emil Puhl was paying Ibn Saud more than
one million marks a year.

Roosevelt agreed to this deal with a Nazi collaborator. He was
greatly influenced by Jesse H. Jones, Secretary of Commerce, who
by now was part owner of the Davis Oil Company. On July 18,
1941, following a meeting with Moffett, Roosevelt wrote to Jones:
"Dear Jesse. Will you tell the British I hope they can take care of
the King of Arabia—this is a little far afield for us."

Roosevelt bypassed Congress and entered into an arrangement that
was entirely against the rule book. Saudi Arabia was emphatically
not a lend-lease country. If it were known that Ibn Saud as Hitler's
close ally in Nazi pay was being bribed by the President to protect
an oil company, there would have been a major public outcry. Roosevelt ordered Harry L. Hopkins, who was in charge of Lend-Lease,
to arrange with Britain for the money to be paid to the king under
the table. Lend-Lease to England was to be surreptitiously increased.

The arrangement continued for two years. Not only did money
flow to Arab countries but a vast range of products, many of which
were in short supply in the United States, and all of these were sent
to organizations or individual merchants who were known to have

supported pro-Axis and subversive movements from the late 1930s until then. No screening of any kind was done by the United States' Middle East Supply Center on the reshipment to the Axis of petroleum, mineral oil, fuel products, rubber, and automobiles.

When Bernard Berger, of the Board of Economic Warfare handling the Middle East, brought up complaints on shipments by Caltex's subsidiary Aramco* to the enemy, the State Department and its local consulates put every kind of obstacle in his way. At first their excuse was that the Middle East was British-sponsored territory and that it was up to the British to check the loyalty of enemy consignees. After excruciatingly slow dealings, the State Department agreed that U.S. diplomatic missions in Teheran, Baghdad, Jerusalem, Cairo, and Jidda should agree to the screening, but months after the agreement was made, Berger was complaining (on December 23, 1942) in a memorandum to his superior, H. A. Wilkinson, that "No one has lifted a finger in implementing the proposals." He continued to point out that the failure of the State Department and British Intelligence was responsible for the dangerous Fifth Column run by the Nazis in the Middle East. He urged the appointment of a trade intelligence officer in the headquarters of the American Commission in Cairo. Nothing was done about this.

Berger specifically mentioned the powerful Middle Eastern companies operating in Saudi Arabia, Syria, Iraq, and Iran; the Grand Mufti of Jerusalem; and Hitler. He also named a smuggling ring which, he discovered, was paying for imports through graft used in obtaining export licenses. Berger was only just able to avert an arrangement whereby an unnamed U.S. senator was about to pay a bribe to Henry Wallace to grant commission for licensing. Yet another company, with offices in Istanbul and New York, was also known to be trading with the enemy with State and British cooperation.

In 1943, Forrestal appointed William Bullitt as his special Assistant Secretary. They were joined by Massachusetts Senator David I. Walsh, chairman of the Senate Naval Affairs Committee, an equally extreme isolationist America Firster and supporter of Irish nationalism. These Machiavellis brought pressure to bear in Washington to change the existing arrangements. They told Roosevelt that British

---

* Arabian-American Oil Company.

influence was "becoming excessive" in Saudi Arabia and that the present deal should be stopped. Instead, the American government should invest directly in Aramco. Apart from Forrestal's financial involvement, his and Bullitt's motives were clear. Despite the fact that Ibn Saud was still closely interlocked to Hitler, they wanted the American government to aid him against British influence.

The conspirators were afraid that Harold Ickes, who was still fighting protection for the corporations, would object to these arrangements. On February 27, 1943, Bullitt dropped in to see the embattled Secretary of the Interior and tried to shake his morale by saying that State Department critics had "told me the boys took pretty sharp exception to the fact you are showing interest in oil outside of the United States. This is the exclusive function of the Department of State."

Forrestal and Bullitt were constantly in Ickes's office to enlist him in the cause. Unfortunately, he succumbed to their blandishments. The two swayed Ickes into believing that there was a British threat to American interests in Saudi Arabia. They even succeeded in having him talk to the President about the matter. Ickes listened when Bullitt said at a meeting on May 29, 1943, "The British are already laying plans to establish a branch bank in Arabia. I wouldn't put it past the British to have King Ibn Saud assassinated, if necessary, and set up a puppet who will see the oil situation through their eyes." Bullitt went on, "There is a secret agreement between Churchill and the President." (If such an arrangement indeed were envisaged, then it was because Ibn Saud was in league with the Nazis.) The result was that Ickes helped to press through the arrangement for investment in Aramco.

Meanwhile, Roosevelt, without telling Ickes, issued a document authorizing a transfer of Saudi Arabia to the status of a lend-lease country, stating, "I hereby find that the defense of Saudi Arabia is vital to the defense of the United States." But the deal for direct government investment in Aramco fell through.

Instead of giving the United States a rich supply of oil after the deal was made, W.S.S. Rodgers and Harry Collier held America to ransom. Meanwhile, the Nazi involvement in Saudi Arabia became more and more extreme. The State Department and Department of the Interior did not have to rely on Army Intelligence reports from

Britain and their own G-2 agents to discover the extent of that involvement. Details of it leaked into such liberal publications as *Asia and the Americas* and *Great Britain and the World*. From these sources, from German Foreign Office document 71/51181 (July 22, 1942) and from recently declassified secret reports prepared by British Intelligence on Walter Schellenberg of the Gestapo, it is possible to determine the extent of Nazi influence on Ibn Saud in the middle of the war. The Grand Mufti of Jerusalem was, until the time of Italy's collapse as an Axis partner, living in Rome, working with the agents of Kurt von Schröder's friend and associate Ambassador Franz von Papen in Ankara, Turkey, to send out agents through the Arab states. In Saudi Arabia fanatical Arabs were trained as Nazis at German universities and schools. From a headquarters in a carpet shop in Baghdad, Dr. Fritz Grobba, German minister to Iraq, ran espionage rings, subsidized Arabic newspapers and clubs in the Saudi Arabian capital of Jidda. The German TransOcean News Agency functioned as an espionage and propaganda agency in Jidda. The Nazi spy Waldemar Baron von Oppenheim, until recently in the United States and Syria, was headquartered in Saudi Arabia. Many Nazis flocked in disguised as tourists or technicians. They constructed roads and built factories. They formed German-Arab societies and learned Arab language so as to address crowds and whip them up into a fanatical support of Hitler. Ibn Saud, as always, played both ends against the middle, protesting admiration for Roosevelt and Churchill while authorizing his personal representative Rashid Ali El-Kilani to continue to represent him in Berlin and address the Moslem society there.

Wilhelm Keppler, founder of the Circle of Friends, friend of ITT's Sosthenes Behn, and under secretary of the German Foreign Office with substantial shareholdings in I.G. Farben, made Saudi Arabia his special provenance. He laced the country with economic agents who spread out as far as Iran and Iraq. By 1944 the United States was seriously short of oil. It cost Aramco ten cents a barrel to bring up oil in Bahrein and twenty cents in Arabia, plus a royalty of fifteen cents to the Sheikh of Bahrein and twenty-one cents to Ibn Saud in addition to the existing bribe. Suddenly, W.S.S. Rodgers of Texas Company and Harry Collier of California Standard informed Ickes that the price to America would be $1.05 a barrel, take it or leave it. With his back against the wall, Ickes had to accept. Worse, Rodgers and Collier paid no income tax on the sale because they were registered in the Bahamas. They made $120 million at the expense of the U.S. government—on an investment of no more than $1 million.

Ickes tried to buy the oil companies' stock in the interests of national defense and the economic needs of the nation. But he encountered constant resistance from Collier and Rodgers. First Collier would agree, then Rodgers would hold out; then they reversed their positions. They also said that they had doubled Aramco's royalty payments to Ibn Saud. Ickes checked with the Arabian Embassy and found that the statement was a lie; he blamed Forrestal for not having the sales figures checked.

How was this possible? Because Caltex and Aramco still had plants in the State Department.

What grievous situation existed in the State Department that allowed such infiltration? The elements of anti-Semitism and secret sympathy for the Nazis' form of government had been there since the early 1930s. In the Department's uncomfortable, crowded, and antiquated building, there were daily collisions between the embattled liberal faction and the right-wing extremists. Behind the scenes as ambassador-at-large, William Bullitt was the prime schemer in assuring that the extreme right wing in the Department retained a sophisticated neutralism in time of war. He set out to remove the single most powerful force against world fascism: Sumner Welles.

Welles was a strong opponent of The Fraternity's deals with Saudi Arabia and South America. Intelligence reports told him how deeply Hitler had penetrated Saudi Arabia, that Ibn Saud was one with Hitler despite Saudi Arabia's phony breaking off of diplomatic relations with the Axis—a sop to the public—and that much of the investment of the American government in pipelines on behalf of Caltex/Aramco would go straight into enemy hands. He was opposed to the arrangement with Vichy because he believed that in propping up Marshal Henri Pétain's regime the United States was allowing its gates to be left wide open to Hitler's commercial, political, and espionage agents.

Welles's personality was cold, authoritative, and detached. Tall, elegant, and flawlessly tailored, he came from the top of the East Coast Establishment. Wealthy in his own right, a career diplomat from the first, he had been at school with Roosevelt at Groton and frequently entertained Franklin and Eleanor in his exquisite house at

Oxon Hill. His wife was socially prominent, and he had a growing family. Despite his strongly liberal stance he was acceptable to the Establishment because he seemed to represent the finest virtues of the ruling class.

Yet he had a weakness. He was a bisexual. At night this pillar of the Washington community would disappear from his house on the excuse of working late at the office and, in disguise, make his way into parks, toilets, and places of assignation and perform intercourse with blacks. He presumably paid for sex because he was afraid that a genuine affair would expose him.

William Bullitt had long heard rumors about Welles. When Welles was ambassador to Cuba, there had been talk of relationships with young Cuban boys, some of them underage. Welles had left the Caribbean under a heavy cloud. Roosevelt had chosen to ignore the stories.

Bullitt had gone to see J. Edgar Hoover in 1940 after his return from Paris and asked him to investigate Welles. Hoover, who was himself alleged to be homosexual, knew all of the secret places where the homosexual community met. He decided to act at once.

On September 16, 1940, a solemn funeral was held in the chamber of the House for the beloved speaker William Bankhead. Two special trains left Washington for Jasper, Alabama, for the burial. On the homebound train were Roosevelt and virtually his entire Cabinet, including Welles.

As the train chugged into the night, two Pullman porters Hoover had hired went into Welles's bedroom. They first flirted with him and then blatantly offered themselves for a price of $100. Welles, who was drunk, seemed to ignore the fact that the President, Attorney General Robert Jackson, Harold Ickes, and practically everybody in the government was in the same car.

Hoover had his men stationed in the adjoining bedroom. Welles's drunken conversation, and the sexual acts that followed it, were noted down.

When the train returned, Hoover's men presented the evidence to him. Bullitt had a meeting with Hoover and went over the report. He took it to Roosevelt in the Oval Office. The President refused to read it but instructed Hoover the next day to obtain more evidence. He was evidently playing for time, worried about a confrontation with Welles.

Bullitt and Hoover spent the next three years amassing a thick dossier on Welles. "Pa" Watson, secretary to the President, was in charge of the investigation. Bullitt absurdly charged that Welles's wife was having an affair with a Russian spy and that Welles was being blackmailed by communists to leak State secrets to Russia.

On October 24, 1942, Hoover called at the Wardman Park Hotel apartment of Cordell Hull. Hull had asked to see him, saying that he was gravely concerned by stories about the improper actions of Welles. He told him that he knew Hoover had made an investigation and asked whether Hoover would give him the report so that he could evaluate the evidence. Hoover confirmed that he had made the report on behalf of Roosevelt. He suggested that Hull contact another of Roosevelt's secretaries, Marvin McIntyre, to obtain the report. Hull said he would deal with it.

Hull and Hoover kept pressing Roosevelt to look at the file. On April 27, 1943, Senator Owen Brewster of Maine called to see Hoover. He had discovered that Hoover had made the investigation and knew whom the FBI had questioned. Hoover told him that indeed an investigation had been made but that "no conclusions have been reached." Brewster went to see Hull and Biddle and decided to take the matter up with the Truman defense committee to investigate the whole affair. Biddle, evidently alarmed by the potential of such a public inquiry, decided to go to the President.

Faced with the fact that his long cover-up for Welles might be revealed, Roosevelt was forced to bow to pressure from Biddle and his supporters and ask for Welles's resignation. A delighted Bullitt suggested coolly to Roosevelt that perhaps Welles should be sent to Russia as a diplomatic representative. Roosevelt was not impressed. Not only did he disconnect all contact with Welles, he verbally thrashed Bullitt and never spoke to him again. It was the ruination of Welles's career, but Bullitt never recovered from the results of his exposé.

The catastrophe wrecked the State Department overnight. Welles's carefully built-up policy of opposing appeasement in time of war was shattered at a blow. The Department fell apart.

The exposure of Welles distracted attention from the fact that Aramco supporter David I. Walsh of Massachusetts was exposed in a similar scandal.

The scandal broke when Naval Intelligence officers and city detectives raided a homosexual brothel in Brooklyn and arrested the proprietor, Gustave Beekman. District Attorney William O'Dwyer and Naval Intelligence officers discovered that the brothel was a nest of Nazi agents. One of those who mingled with those agents was Senator Walsh. In an affidavit made in Raymond Street jail following his arrest, Beekman gave detailed testimony about Walsh. He said that Walsh used to come to his bordello on Sunday afternoons—at least ten times between July 1941 and March 1942. Beekman reported that he saw the senator in close conversation with another customer, described only as "Mister E," who was known as "the Nazi's ace spy in the U.S." Mister E would arrive with sailors and would question them on their ships, their comings and goings and destinations. Mister E was accompanied by a number of Germans who were also acting as espionage agents. The spies specialized in luring soldiers and sailors and determining information from them.

According to Beekman's attorney, Harvey Strelzin, who is still in practice in New York, Roosevelt decided to use the episode. Since Walsh was restricting supplies of ball bearings, oil, and other strategic products to the Navy in the interests of isolationism, Roosevelt decided to make a deal with Walsh. If he let Walsh off the hook, Walsh must aid the war effort. Walsh agreed instantly. Strelzin says Roosevelt asked Hoover to have Beekman reverse his testimony. Hoover grilled Beekman cruelly and impersonally with several of his toughest men for several hours around the clock until Beekman cracked and changed his story. Later he tried to change it back on the offer of a substantial check from the *New York Post*, but it was too late. At Beekman's trial under the famous Judge Samuel Leibowitz, Beekman told the truth.

The isolationist clique protested the accusations and demanded that there be a full public exoneration for Walsh. At a stormy meeting of the Senate, Burton K. Wheeler and two other isolationists, Gerald P. Nye and Bennett C. Clark, jumped to their feet and called in concert for a sweeping investigation with a view to punishment of all persons who had conspired to smear Walsh.

Wheeler shouted, "This is a diabolical attempt on the part of certain individuals . . . to smear every member of the Senate who has disagreed with them on matters of foreign policy." Senator Clark urged that Mrs. Dorothy S. Backer, "the old hussy who runs the New York *Post*," should be "brought before the bar of the Senate."

Wheeler attacked Judge Leibowitz: "If I were a Federal judge, I would have him impeached," and, ironically in the context, he called for a cancellation of the financing of the *Post* by the Federal Reserve Bank. Senator Nye urged, "Let this matter not be dropped here. An investigation will reveal a secret society which for two years have [sic] been engaged in gathering such information as would permit the smearing of individual members of the Senate."

The Nation investigated the matter and found that indeed Walsh had been seen in conversation with suspected Nazi spies who lured soldiers and sailors to the "house of degradation" for the purpose of obtaining military secrets. The magazine discovered that the FBI had made Beekman recant his original statement after hours of high-pressured questioning. *The Nation* wrote, "So summary an attempt to bury an unpleasant affair may involve the sidetracking of a full and open investigation of the house in Pacific Street." The editorial added, "We can't afford to encourage [Nazi Fifth Columnists] by covering up the case . . . *The Nation* strongly supports the *Post*'s demand for a full and public inquiry."

It goes without saying that the "full and public inquiry" never took place and that Walsh remained chairman of the Naval Affairs Committee. The following year he was in part responsible for the Aramco swindle.

On October 5, 1942, Judge Samuel Leibowitz sentenced Beekman to five to twenty years in Sing Sing. In March 1947, James Moffett of Caltex, gravely ill and in agony in his hospital bed following a major operation, decided that with death facing him, he should unburden himself of the details of the Aramco affair. He had another motive that was slightly less altruistic: Caltex owed him $6 million for his rake-off on the deal.

He went to Welles's nemesis, Senator Owen Brewster, and asked for a full-scale inquiry into Aramco. He made such a stink in the press that Brewster had to go ahead. Inevitably, since Walsh had been deactivated, Brewster appointed Burton K. Wheeler to investigate

Moffett's charges. Barely audible, Moffett gave a halting address on May 5 in which he outlined the plan. The committee called for Roosevelt's files in the matter. President Truman declined to permit a search of the late President's papers at Hyde Park. On May 7, 1947, the executors of Roosevelt's estate explicitly denied permission for a search, citing a July 16, 1943, directive by the President that all his letters of a sensitive character should be locked up for between ten and fifty years.

On May 25, because of overwhelming public pressure, part of the file showing Moffett's original correspondence with the White House was revealed. But the executors of the Roosevelt estate blocked the bulk of the appropriate documents.

The only ray of light for Moffett in this harrowing ordeal was that Truman was forced by public pressure to remove Wheeler from the special investigative council on June 4.

Moffett was unable to push Aramco to produce the text of the oil concession agreement with Ibn Saud. The council ruled that the request for the document should be quashed "to protect the defendant, the government of Saudi Arabia and the government of the United States from annoyance and embarrassment."

As the facts gradually came to light despite every effort to suppress them, Congress was rent apart by violent debates.

On April 25, 1948, Senator Brewster delivered a broadside to an almost empty and notably indifferent Senate. He described the Aramco action as "an amazing picture of corporate greed when our country was in its most bitter need." Senator William Langer of North Dakota said, "The men who have put over this oil deal ought to be in the penitentiary. These men, who have called upon American boys to go into foreign lands to protect their oil interests, are traitors to America. They ought to surrender their citizenship or have it taken away from them." Brewster and Langer charged that three former Navy Department aides in the Justice Department were at that moment blocking a new investigation into the scandals. The investigation was indeed blocked.

On February 1, 1949, Moffett brought suit in federal court in New York for $6 million in damages against Caltex's Aramco on the ground that he had made the original arrangements between Roosevelt and

Secretary of Commerce Jesse Jones and that he had not been given his promised rake-off.

Jones tried to avoid appearing at the hearing. The matter was so embarrassing to him that he feigned illness. But Moffett had connections. He arranged for a friend of his in the FBI to follow Jones to the Twenty-Nine Club on East Sixty-first Street on the night that Jones was supposed to be having a heart attack. The FBI report read: "The witness Jones played poker on the night of November 16, 1948, until 2 A.M. and in the course of the evening the stakes ranged as high as $4,000 a hand and on one occasion the said Jones backed a straight in a pot involving approximately $4,000 against four 4's." The report continued, "No doubt backing a straight against four 4's with $4,000 in the pot has been the cause of many a heartache, but to my knowledge it never has been recommended as a cure for heart trouble."

Next day, Federal Judge Samuel H. Kaufman said that Mr. Jones must be compelled to appear and that "if Mr. Jones indicated signs of fatigue as a result of his poker game" he could retire from the proceedings for a few moments during the course of the day.

Jones appeared on November 26. Asked for records of the transactions for Aramco, he said jovially, "I don't keep a diary because I don't plan to write a book like Mr. Morgenthau and some others and I kept no Dictaphone in my desk—I'd like to put that into the record, too!" Moffett's attorney, William Power Maloney, who had been the scourge of Nazi agents until Senator Wheeler had him dislodged from the Nazi Sedition Trials of the 1940s, pressed Jones for more details. Jones answered that his memory was "vague of the entire matter" and that he had "even forgotten the name of his secretary" whom Maloney was trying to find as a material witness. Asked about Roosevelt's note suggesting to him that the British should "take care of the King of Arabia," Jones gave a calculated reply. He said, "I scribbled the note during a Cabinet meeting, handed it to the President and asked him to write it down in his own handwriting, so I could let them know it was his decision as well as mine."

Jones claimed he had no legal authority to grant the loan and had had no intention of doing so, but that he wanted to let "a Mr. Moffett and a Mr. Rodgers" who had discussed the loan with him know that they "could not get any help from the United States Government." This curious example of perjury was presumably intended to absolve Jones of any complicity in the illicit measure. The implication was that Moffett and Rodgers* had gone ahead on their own.

Suddenly, Jones added, "Judge Kaufman, I'd like to ask the bench a question off the record."

The judge told him to go right ahead.

Jones said, "I've been given $195 by Mr. Maloney and $225 by the other side to come here in January to testify. I want to know whether I have to return the money because I think I ought to keep it."

Judge Kaufman told Jones, "You will have to return the money if the subpoena is dismissed."

"Oh, don't do that, Judge, don't do that," Jones replied, to loud laughter in court.

It was in this spirit of levity that the entire case was conducted. Inevitably, Aramco came out the winner. Moffett was awarded one million one hundred dollars by the jury in settlement of his claims. But the judgment was set aside by the trial judge.

*W.S.S. Rodgers of the Texas Company.

6

The Telephone Plot

During the early days of 1942, Karl Lindemann, the Rockefeller–Standard Oil representative in Berlin, held a series of urgent meetings with two directors of the American International Telephone and Telegraph Corporation: Walter Schellenberg, head of the Gestapo's counterintelligence service (SD), and Baron Kurt von Schröder of the BIS and the Stein Bank. The result of these meetings was that Gerhardt Westrick, the crippled boss of ITT in Nazi Germany, got aboard an ITT Focke-Wulf bomber and flew to Madrid for a meeting in March with Sosthenes Behn, American ITT chief.

In the sumptuous Royal Suite of Madrid's Ritz Hotel, the tall, sharp-faced Behn and the heavily limping Westrick sat down for lunch to discuss how best they could improve ITT's links with the Gestapo, and its improvement of the whole Nazi system of telephones, teleprinters, aircraft intercoms, submarine and ship phones, electric buoys, alarm systems, radio and radar parts, and fuses for artillery shells, as well as the Focke-Wulf bombers that were taking thousands of American lives.

Sosthenes Behn, whose first name was Greek for "life strength," was born in St. Thomas, the Virgin Islands, on January 30, 1882. His father was Danish and his mother French-Italian. He and his brother Hernand, later his partner, were schooled in Corsica and Paris.

In 1906, Behn and his brother took over a sugar business in Puerto

Rico and snapped up a small and primitive local telephone company by closing in on a mortgage. Realizing the potential of the newfangled telephone, Behn began to buy up more companies in the Caribbean. He became a U.S. citizen in 1913. In World War I, Behn served in the Signal Corps as chief of staff for General George Russell. He learned a great deal about military communications systems, and his services to France earned him the Légion d'Honneur. Back in the United States, Behn became associated with AT&T, of which Winthrop Aldrich was later a director. In 1920, Behn's work in the field of cables enabled him to set up the ITT with $6 million paid in capital. Gradually, he spun out a web of communications that ran worldwide. He soon became the telephone king of the world, making deals with AT&T and J. P. Morgan that resulted in his running the entire telephone system of Spain by 1923. His Spanish chairman was the Duke of Alba, later a major supporter of Franco and Hitler. In 1930 Behn obtained the Rumanian telephone industry, to which he later added the Hungarian, German, and Swedish corporations. By 1931 his empire was worth over $64 million despite the Wall Street crash. He became a director of—inevitably—the National City Bank, which financed him along with the Morgans.

Behn was aided by fascist governments, into which he rapidly interlocked his system by assuring politicians promising places on his boards. He ran his empire from 67 Broad Street, New York.

His office was decorated with Louis XIV antiques, rich carpets, and portraits of Pope Pius XI and various heads of fascist states. He traveled frequently to Germany to confer with his Nazi directors, Kurt von Schröder and Gerhardt Westrick. On August 4, 1933, he and his representative in Germany, Henry Mann of the National City Bank, had a meeting with Hitler that established a political relationship with Germany that continued until the end of World War II. The Führer promised aid and protection always.

Through Mann, Behn was closely connected with Wilhelm Keppler, who formed the Circle of Friends of the Gestapo and introduced him to Schröder and Westrick. Not only did Keppler, Schröder, and Himmler see to it that Behn's German funds and industries were untouched by forfeit or seizure, but Schröder arranged for Emil Puhl at the Reichsbank to pay off ITT's bills.

Behn became an important aid to his friend Hermann Göring. In

1938 he and Schröder obtained 28 percent of the Focke-Wulf company; they greatly improved the deadly bomber squadrons that later attacked London and American ships and troops. When Austria fell in 1938, Behn organized his Austrian company under the management of Schröder and Westrick and aided in the expulsion of Jews. Some Nazis tried to take over the Austrian offices, but Behn again visited Hitler at Berchtesgaden and made sure that ITT would be allowed to continue in business.

In Madrid during the Spanish Civil War, Behn supplied telephones to both sides, gradually shifting over his commitments to Franco when it was obvious that Franco was winning. He spent months in the shell-shattered Madrid headquarters known as the Telefónica, playing both ends against the middle and driving, with immunity given by both sides, to and from the Ritz. He gave lavish parties for both the British and American press, while negotiating through the Bank for International Settlements so that Franco could buy up ITT's Loyalist installations.

When Hitler invaded Poland, Behn and Schröder conferred with the German alien property custodian, H-J Caesar. The result was that the ITT Polish companies were protected from seizure for the duration.

Another protector of Behn's in Germany was ITT's colorful corporation chairman, Gerhardt Westrick. Westrick was a skilled company lawyer, the German counterpart and associate of John Foster Dulles. Westrick's partner until 1938, the equally brilliant Dr. Heinrich Albert, was head of Ford in Germany until 1945. Both were crucially important to The Fraternity.

At the beginning of 1940, Behn decided to have Westrick go to the United States to link up the corporate strands that would remain secure throughout World War II. German Foreign Minister von Ribbentrop was equally concerned that Westrick undertake the mission. Westrick represented in Germany not only Ford but General Motors, Standard Oil, the Texas Company, Sterling Products, and the Davis Oil Company.

Since Behn had to be engaged in business in Lisbon, he arranged that Westrick would be hosted by Torkild Rieber in the United States. Behn also called up the Plaza Hotel in New York where he kept a permanent suite, and he had it placed at Westrick's disposal.

Westrick traveled via San Francisco in March 1940, where he handed $5 million of Farben-ITT money on Behn's and Ribbentrop's joint authorization to Nazi Consul General Fritz Wiedemann. The money was to insure the cooperation of small American businessmen with the Third Reich.

Rieber met Westrick at the Plaza on April 10, 1940, and arranged a press conference for him. The reporters were delighted with the German. Burly and bullnecked, with a strong, guttural voice, he had lost his right leg to British shells in World War I. He had an aluminum leg attached to his body by complicated webbing and a silver rod. And he had with him a mysterious and glamorous secretary, the Baroness Ingrid von Wallenheim.

After a series of meetings with the Fraternity leaders, Westrick gave an interview to *The New York Times* on April 12. He echoed precisely the views of Emil Puhl and Dr. Walther Funk. He said that America must release its vast holdings in gold, amounting to $7,500 million in notes and $18 billion in coinage, to the Nazi government and its conquered territories. Westrick insisted that the loan should be made at a mere one and a half percent interest. He urged that the money be shipped to the Bank for International Settlements for transfer to the Reichsbank. He wanted an end to the economic friction that caused wars and he sought peace forever—presided over by the Triumvirate of Wall Street, the Reichsbank, and the Bank of Japan, sustained on a river of gold. Indeed, as the *Times* correspondent pointed out rather sharply, Westrick's views of free trading instead of barter were remarkably similar to those of Secretary of State Cordell Hull.

There was, of course, no mention of such inconvenient subjects as Austria, Czechoslovakia, and Poland in Westrick's visionary pronouncement.

A letter appeared in the *Times* on April 15, written by Karel Hudek, acting consul general representing the Czechoslovakian republic in exile, saying, inter alia, "I think that all downtrodden nations—Austria, Czechoslovakia, Poland, Denmark, Norway and some others, who may join us in a short time, will thank Dr. Westrick for his kind endeavors. . . . Dr. Westrick is right when he says that wars come from economic causes. I can speak here for my country: they invaded us and promptly took over all industry—yes, that is economic cause.''

On June 26, 1940, his Fraternity associates gave a party for Westrick at the Waldorf-Astoria Hotel to celebrate the Nazi victory in France. This was, of course, only appropriate. Fraternity guests at this scorpions' feast included Dietrich, brother of Hermann Schmitz of General Aniline and Film; James D. Mooney of General Motors; Edsel Ford of the Ford Motor Company; William Weiss of Sterling Products; and Torkild Rieber of the Texas Company. These leaders of The Fraternity agreed to help in the free-trade agreements that would follow a negotiated peace with Germany.

Westrick leased a large house in Scarsdale, New York, from one of Rieber's Texas Company lawyers. He was seen entering and leaving the house in the company of prominent figures of the Nazi government and American industry. The New York *Daily News* sent reporter George Dickson to investigate the meaning of a big white placard with a large *G* on it in a window of a front second-floor bedroom. The press generally was suggesting this formed some kind of code for use by Nazi agents. Dickson wrote in his column: ''Phantom-like men in white have been responding by day and night to mysterious signalling from a secluded Westchester mansion—now disclosed as the secret quarters of Dr. Gerhardt A. Westrick—invariably they carry carefully wrapped packages . . . they salute with all the precision of Storm Troopers, deliver the packages, salute again—and silently depart . . . super-sleuthing finally solved the mystery just before last midnight.'' Then Dickson delivered his death blow to the story: The *G* sign was an invitation to the Good Humor man to deliver his famous ice cream on a stick!

J. Edgar Hoover of the FBI determined that Westrick had illegally obtained his driver's license by lying that he had no infirmities. The purpose was achieved: Walter Winchell, Drew Pearson, and other patriotic columnists blew up Westrick's Nazi connections out of all proportion, and Westrick was asked by German Chargé d'Affaires Hans Thomsen to return to Germany at once.

But before he was ordered home, Westrick had been extremely busy. He had gone to see Edsel and Henry Ford at Dearborn on July 11 at the Fords' urgent invitation, conferring with the Grand Old Man and his son on the matter of restricting shipment of important Rolls-Royce motors to a beleaguered Britain that urgently needed them. He also visited with Will Clayton, Jesse Jones's associate in the Department of Commerce, who went with Westrick to see Cordell Hull to plead for the protection of German-American trade agreements on behalf of his friends in the Texas cotton industry.

Clayton was the chairman of the U.S. Commercial Company, and he helped protect Fraternity interests during World War II. Others of Westrick's circle included, interestingly enough, William Donovan, who became head of the OSS (precursor of the CIA) on its formation in 1942. Westrick also made significant contacts with good and true friends at Eastman Kodak and Underwood before returning home via Japan and Russia.

After Pearl Harbor, at meetings with Kurt von Schröder and Behn in Switzerland, Westrick nervously admitted he had run into a problem. Wilhelm Ohnesorge, the elderly minister in charge of post offices, who was one of the first fifty Nazi party members, was strongly opposed to ITT's German companies continuing to function under New York management in time of war. Behn told Westrick to use Schröder and the protection of the Gestapo against Ohnesorge. In return, Behn guaranteed that ITT would substantially increase its payments to the Gestapo through the Circle of Friends.

A special board of trustees was set up by the German government to cooperate with Behn and his thirty thousand staff in Occupied Europe. Ohnesorge savagely fought these arrangements and tried to obtain the support of Himmler. However, Schröder had Himmler's ear, and so, of course, did his close friend and associate Walter Schellenberg. Ohnesorge appealed directly to Hitler and condemned Westrick as an American sympathizer. However, Hitler realized the importance of ITT to the German economy and proved supportive of Behn.

The final arrangement was that the Nazi government would not acquire the shares of ITT but would confine itself to the administration of the shares. Westrick would be chairman of the managing directors.

Thus, an American corporation literally entered into partnership with the Nazi government in time of war.

Westrick and Behn appointed Walter Schellenberg as a director with a nominal salary in return for his protection and for his assistance in insuring the company's continuing existence. General Fritz Thiele, second-in-command of the signal corps, was added to the directorial board because army stock orders were crucial in keeping the company afloat. Hitler was gravely suspicious of Thiele for drawing money from an American corporation in time of war and sought to dislodge him, but Himmler stepped in as a protector.

Ohnesorge did not give up. In 1942 he again tried to induce Himmler to sign a warrant of arrest against Westrick for high treason. His idea was to keep Westrick in a concentration camp while he disposed of the shares of ITT. Once again, Schröder stepped in and there was no further trouble.

Not only did Behn own all of the German companies of ITT outright through the war but he also ran ITT factories in the neutral countries of Spain, Portugal, Switzerland, and Sweden, which continued to buy, sell, and manufacture for the Axis. Behn and his directors made repeated and persistent efforts to obtain licenses for dealings with the enemy. When Morgenthau refused the licenses, they proceeded anyway. They also exported materials to their subsidiaries in neutral nations producing for the enemy.

After Pearl Harbor the German army, navy, and air force contracted with ITT for the manufacture of switchboards, telephones, alarm gongs, buoys, air raid warning devices, radar equipment, and thirty thousand fuses per month for artillery shells used to kill British and American troops. This was to increase to fifty thousand per month by 1944. In addition, ITT supplied ingredients for the rocket bombs that fell on London, selenium cells for dry rectifiers, high-frequency radio equipment, and fortification and field communication sets.

Without this supply of crucial materials it would have been impossible for the German air force to kill American and British troops, for the German army to fight the Allies in Africa, Italy, France, and Germany, for England to have been bombed, or for Allied ships to have been attacked at sea. Nor would it have been possible without ITT and its affiliates for the enemy to have kept contact with Latin American countries at a time when Admiral Raeder of the German Navy contemplated an onslaught on countries south of Panama. It is thus somewhat unsettling to note the following memorandum sent by the State Department lawyer R. T. Yingling to Assistant Secretary of State Breckinridge Long on February 26, 1942. It read in part:

It seems that the International Telephone and Telegraph Corporation which has been handling traffic between Latin American countries and Axis-controlled points *with the encouragement or concurrence of the Department of State* * desires some assurance that it will not be prosecuted for such activities. It has been suggested that the matter be discussed informally with the Attorney General and if he agrees the Corporation can be advised that no prosecution is contemplated . . . if the International Telephone and Telegraph Corporation feels that activities of the nature indicated above which it may be carrying on at the present time in Latin America are within the purview of the Trading with the Enemy Act it should apply to the Treasury Department for a license to engage in such activities.

Whether or not the license was issued, the trading was continued with the assurance that neither the State Department nor the Department of Justice would intervene. Armed with this convenient endorsement, Sosthenes Behn was constantly flying in and out of Spain during the war for transactions with the enemy. He owned not only a telephone operating company in Spain, but a major manufacturing company as well: Standard Electrica. In the middle of 1942, after a visit to Madrid, Behn had the audacity to go to the State Department and talk to Dean Acheson's staff to obtain permission for his Spanish subsidiary to purchase materials in Germany for use in Spain. When this was questioned, Behn said that there was a likelihood of the Franco government's taking over the Spanish properties unless they complied. It was a familiar argument, but Behn, who had tried to sell the Spanish company to that same government a year earlier, knew perfectly well that Franco had no intention of running the complex corporation. With a unique gift of understatement, U.S. Ambassador to Spain Carlton J. H. Hayes wrote to the State Department on August 15, 1942, "The Embassy . . . feels that the ITT may not have always placed our war efforts above its own interests." The letter was written at a time when ITT was manufacturing military equipment for the German army in Spain.

On September 28, 1942, Ambassador John G. Winant in London telegraphed Washington urgently recommending that the ITT Swiss and Spanish subsidiary, Telephone and Radio, "be issued licenses to

* Author's italics.

trade with Nazi Germany.'' State Department officials had a meeting with Morgenthau and Harry Dexter White saying that it was essential ITT be allowed to trade with enemy territory. Morgenthau and White flatly refused to countenance any such trading.

In January, February, and March 1943, Behn was back in Barcelona and Madrid for conferences with Colonel Wilhelm Grube of the German army signal corps on the question of forming the German Standard, or European Standard (as it was later known), Corporation amalgamating all ITT companies throughout the whole of Western Europe. Grube carried out Behn's instructions to the letter.

Shortly after Pearl Harbor, Roosevelt had asked Nelson Rockefeller to prepare a study of the communications systems of South America. On May 4, 1942, the President had sent a memorandum to Henry Wallace in his role as chairman of the Board of Economic Warfare, ordering him to insure disconnection of all enemy nationals in the radio, telephone, and telegraph fields. He had urged Wallace to eliminate all Axis control and influence in telecommunications in Latin America, acquire hemisphere interests of all Axis companies, insure loyalty in employees, and disrupt direct lines to the enemy. He had asked for a corporation to be set up to handle the financial aspects of the program with the assistance and advice of an advisory committee.

Wallace approached Secretary of Commerce Jesse H. Jones to make the necessary arrangements. Jones set up the U.S. Commercial Company to take charge of the matter. It was a characteristic choice. The company's second-in-command was none other than Robert A. Gantt, vice-president of ITT itself. Gantt continued to receive salary from ITT while holding his position with the U.S. Commercial Company. The rest of the board was largely composed of directors of ITT or RCA (also a wartime partner in Nazi-American communications companies).

The Hemisphere Communications Committee sat with a mixed Treasury, State, Army, Navy, and U.S. Commercial Company board throughout World War II, doing little more than discussing possible actions against Axis-connected companies.

A pressing issue from Pearl Harbor on was the matter of ITT amalgamating the telephone companies of Mexico. One of these, Mexican Telephone and Telegraph, was owned by Behn outright. The other was owned by the Ericsson Company, of which Behn had a 35 percent share in Sweden. The Ericsson Company was partly owned by Nazi collaborator Axel Wenner-Gren and by Jacob Wallenberg, Swedish millionaire head of the ball bearings firm, which played both sides of the war. Behn was in and out of Europe in the early 1940s discussing a merger of the two Mexican companies under his guidance.

He made the reason for the take-over the need to remove Axis influence in Mexico—though he failed to explain how ITT could in any way reduce such influence. Indeed, it would almost certainly have enhanced it. C. J. Durr, acting chairman of the Federal Communications Commission, was drastically opposed to any such take-over. Durr was correctly worried that some $15 million of money that would be advanced to Behn by the Export-Import Bank would make its way directly into German hands.

Durr was also concerned over the fact that ITT retained a contract with the Nippon Electric Company in Japan that provided that Behn could place Japanese employees in Mexico in time of war.

On October 29, 1942, the Export-Import Bank agreed to pay $36 million for the merger. When Durr asked point-blank why this was the case, Hugh Knowlton said, "The ITT will supply a listening post." Durr replied, "Isn't that a two-way affair?" Commander Willimbucher of the U.S. Navy said, "The question of which side gets most value from the listening post depends on the relative shrewdness of the particular people in the company." "Who gets the information?" Laurence Smith of the Department of Justice asked. "The company," Francis DeWolf of the State Department said. *"The Government gets what the company wants it to.* The company has to be careful lest competitive information gets into the hands of the Government and then reaches its competitors."

Statements of this kind infuriated Durr. He was aggravated also by the fact that all the circuits to the Axis remained open throughout the war. The real truth of the matter emerged at a meeting on January 6, 1943. There was an argument between Durr and Hugh Knowlton of the board. Knowlton said that "The army has investigated ITT thoroughly and . . . ITT is presently engaged in confidential manufac-

* Author's italics.

turing work for the army so I assume they're all right." Durr stated he wasn't so much worried about their operations in the United States "as they could be watched, but rather their operations outside this country and particularly their Axis connection." Knowlton kept up his defense. So did DeWolf, who said, "It might be well to put a finger on just what the Committee is afraid of. ITT has factories in Germany, it has a company in Spain, it is in correspondence with Belgium, in fact, it is in correspondence with the enemy. *What this Committee is afraid of is public opinion. . . . That the corporation might not play our game."* *

Knowlton said he had never heard anyone express any doubt as to Colonel Behn's patriotism. ("Col. Behn certainly knows his way around but he is a loyal American citizen.") Laurence Smith (of Justice) said he had not yet had from the U.S. Commercial Company "an adequate appraisal of possible dangers." He mentioned Westrick and Nazi cooperation in South America and DeWolf answered, "ITT is a loyal American corporation." Smith disagreed. Lawrence Knapp of Justice asked if the Tokyo circuit was still operating. Knowlton said, "Not if the U.S. Government asked them not to." DeWolf said, correctly, "If they are doing it, it is with the license of the State Department!"

While these meetings were going on, CIDRA, ITT's Argentine subsidiary, handled a constant flow of phone calls to Buenos Aires, Germany, Hungary, and Rumania. Another ITT subsidiary, the United River Plate Telephone Company, handled 622 telephone calls between the Argentine and Berlin in the first seven months of 1942 alone.

There was constant dealing with Proclaimed List firms. Licenses were issued by authorization of the local embassies. At Behn's instructions Brazil and Peru were supervised from Argentina since Argentina had not declared war on the Axis.

In Brazil the ITT obtained a license from the embassy to buy equipment from a leading German-owned Proclaimed List electrical company, Industria Electre-Ace Plangt, which supplied tungsten and cobalt to ITT. The mailing lists of ITT were filled with enemy names. In Venezuela, in June 1942, ITT bought many consignments of radio

---

* Author's italics.

tubes from the firm Armanda Capriles and Co., which was contributing heavily to the Nazi Winter Help Fund, designed to pay for Germany's troops in Russia and Poland. In Uruguay, Behn's manager was himself on the Proclaimed List.

By the second half of 1942, ITT sent telephone apparatus to its offices in South America without licenses. Discounts were permitted and the Export-Import Bank loan continued. In July 1942 the ITT All-America Cables Office in Buenos Aires obtained secret information on tungsten ore through handling cables and passed this on to the enemy-controlled Havero Trading Company of Buenos Aires.

On December 4, 1943, P. E. Erickson of the ITT subsidiary in Sweden wrote to H. M. Pease of the head office in New York consulting with him on a 400 million kroner plan to automatize the telephone system in Nazi-occupied Denmark. The Danish ITT subsidiary employed two hundred people in its Copenhagen factory. It was of vital importance to the Germans in its North European network of communications.

In South America, Sosthenes Behn was in partnership (as well as rivalry) with an even more powerful organism: the giant Radio Corporation of America, which owned the NBC radio network. RCA was in partnership before and after Pearl Harbor with British Cable and Wireless; with Telefunken, the Nazi company; with Italcable, wholly owned by the Mussolini government; and with Vichy's Compagnie Générale, in an organization known as the Transradio Consortium, with General Robert C. Davis, head of the New York Chapter of the American Red Cross, as its chairman. In turn, RCA, British Cable and Wireless, and the German and Italian companies had a share with ITT in TTP (Telegráfica y Telefónica del Plata), an Axis-controlled company providing telegraph and telephone service between Buenos Aires and Montevideo. Nazis in Montevideo could telephone Buenos Aires through TTP without coming under the control of either the state-owned system in Uruguay or the ITT system in Argentina.

Messages, often dangerous to American security, were transmitted directly to Berlin and Rome by Transradio. Another shareholder was ITT's German "rival," Siemens, which linked cables and networks with Behn south of Panama.

The head of RCA during World War II was Colonel David Sarnoff, a stocky, square-set, determined man with a slow, subdued
voice, who came from Russia as an immigrant at the turn of the
century and began as a newspaper seller, messenger boy, and Marconi Wireless operator. He became world famous in 1912, at the age
of twenty-one, as the young telegraph operator who first picked up
word of the sinking of the *Titanic:* for seventy-two hours he conducted ships to the stricken vessel. He rose rapidly in the Marconi
company, from inspector to commercial manager in 1917. He became general manager of RCA in 1922 at the age of thirty-one and
president just before he was 40. Under his inspired organization NBC
inaugurated network broadcasting and RCA and NBC became one of
the most colossal of the American multinational corporations, pi-
oneers in television and telecommunications.

After Pearl Harbor, Sarnoff cabled Roosevelt, "All of our facilities
and personnel are ready and at your instant service. We await your
command." Sarnoff played a crucial role, as crucial as Behn's, in
the U.S. war effort, and, like Behn, he was given a colonelcy in
the U.S. Signal Corps. He solved complex problems, dealt with a
maze of difficult requirements by the twelve million members of the
U.S. armed forces, and coordinated details related to the Normandy
landings. He prepared the whole printed and electronic press-cover-
age of V-J day; in London in 1944, with headquarters at Claridge's
Hotel, he was Eisenhower's inspired consultant and earned the Medal
of Merit for his help in the occupation of Europe.

Opening in 1943 with a chorus of praise from various generals, the
new RCA laboratories had proved to be indispensable in time of
war.

But the public, which thought of Sarnoff as a pillar of patriotism,
would have been astonished to learn of his partnership with the enemy through Transradio and TTP. The British public, beleaguered
and bombed, would have been equally shocked to learn that British
Cable and Wireless, 10 percent owned by the British government,
and under virtual government control in wartime, was in fact also in
partnership with the Germans and Italians through the same companies and proxies.

Immediately after Pearl Harbor, Hans Blume, manager of Transradio in Chile, set up an arrangement in connection with his related

clandestine station, PYL, to transmit Nazi propaganda, coordinate espionage routes, give ship arrivals and departures, supply information on U.S. military aid, U.S. exports, the Latin American defense measures, and set up communications with German embassies throughout South America. Transradio was equally active in Rio and Buenos Aires.

In Brazil, Transradio was known as Radiobras, its mixed American, British, Nazi, and Italian shares permanently deposited in—of course—the National City Bank of New York in Rio. Its directors were American, Italian, German, and French. Transradio's London bank transferred as much as a quarter of a million shares of Transradio stock from Nazi-controlled banks to the National City Bank branch in 1942.

In Argentina the board was again a mixture of Nazi, Italian, and Allied members. Like the members of the Bank for International Settlements, though with even less excuse, the directors sat around a table discussing the future of Fascist alliances. So extreme was the situation that many messages could not be sent to Allied capitals by U.S. embassies or consulates without going through Axis hands first.

On March 15, 1942, Transradio in London instructed its Buenos Aires branch to open a radio-photograph circuit to Tokyo. Since British post office authorities were in charge of British Cable and Wireless's wartime operations, the British government was presumed to have authorized this act. On March 16 the U.S. Embassy in Buenos Aires reported to the State Department in Washington that the opening of the radio-photograph circuit "would appear to offer the Japanese opportunity of transmitting news photos unfavorable to the united nations to Buenos Aires for distribution here and in other countries."

On March 16, Thomas Burke of the State Department sent a note to State's Breckinridge Long saying, over three months after Pearl Harbor, "Now that we are at war and parties to Resolution XL of the Rio Conference, it seems proper to require our companies to desist from carrying any Axis traffic in the other American republics. It is our understanding in this connection that the Treasury Department in the future will require licenses of American communications companies desiring to carry traffic of this nature. . . . As far as the past is concerned, it is believed that we can give oral assurances to the companies that they will not be prosecuted against." It is of interest to note that those assurances extended into the future and that indeed the companies were not prosecuted against at any time.

At the same time, London allegedly authorized Transradio to transmit messages from South American capitals direct to Rome. The British authorities had cut off Italcable's line to Rome at Gibraltar in 1939, but Transradio now took over its Italian partner's transmissions at a 50 percent discount.

Simultaneously, the Transradio stations, according to State Department reports with the full knowledge of David Sarnoff, kept up a direct line to Berlin. The amount of intelligence passed along the lines can scarcely be calculated. The London office was in constant touch with New York throughout the war, sifting through reports from Argentina, Brazil, and Chile and sending company reports to the Italian and German interests.

In a remarkable example of the pot calling the kettle black, Nando Behn, the nephew of Sosthenes Behn, cabled his uncle from Buenos Aires to New York on June 29, 1942: "It is about time something is done down here to cut out the sole communication center in the Americas with Berlin. Our competitors, Transradio, have a direct radio circuit with Berlin and you can be pretty sure that every sailing from Buenos Aires is in Berlin before the ship is out of sight."

General Robert C. Davis never seemed to question the fact that his Swedish fellow board members were proxies of an enemy government. Nor that secret documents, charts, and patents were being transferred with speed, accuracy, and secrecy, with the authorization of the Japanese Minister of Communications, to South America direct.

On July 10, 1942, adhering to terms of the Rio Conference at which Sumner Welles had succeeded in obtaining agreements for discontinuing communications with the Axis, the Argentine Minister of the Interior addressed an official letter to the Director General of Posts and Telegraphs, seeking to suspend such connections for the duration. Despite that fact, Transradio and RCA, like their counterparts in ITT, pretended they feared that if they did not discontinue the circuits, the Argentine government would retaliate by nationalizing them.

By blaming the Argentine, Chilean, and Brazilian cabinets, Sarnoff and his own board proved conclusively that they were interested in business as usual in wartime.

On July 12, two days after Argentina's intention to disconnect the circuits was made clear, an urgent meeting was held in the office of Breckinridge Long, Assistant Secretary of State in charge of communications and visas, and a former ambassador to Italy, admirer of Mussolini, and notorious block to Jewish refugee immigration. Among those present were Sarnoff, Sir Campbell Stuart, New York representative of British Cable and Wireless, RCA vice-president W. A. Winterbottom, and General Davis. It was graciously decided that Davis should go to Argentina and Chile and "have a look see." The ostensible purpose of Davis's mission was to do everything in his power to close down the circuits. He would travel with an engineer, Phillip Siling, of the FCC (and ITT) and Commander George Schecklin of the Office of War Information (and RCA).

At a further meeting on July 20, setting out details of the mission, Breckinridge Long calmly referred to the importance of the question, pointing out without anger the unfortunate fact that "a stream of information is being sent out by the consortium stations with resulting losses in our shipping." Sir Campbell Stuart of British Cable and Wireless coolly promised to keep his government "advised of the decision of this meeting." It was agreed that the State Department would take care of all costs of Davis's mission and arrange the necessary priorities in terms of passports and visas.

Davis traveled to the South American cities and began interviewing the local directors and chiefs of staff. He either was completely blind to the facts, or lied to cover his associates. Despite the fact that every branch of Transradio was bristling with Nazis, he dislodged only two: Henri Pincemin, the Vichy manager in Buenos Aires, and Hans Blume in Valparaiso. Ernesto Aguirre, president of the board of directors of Transradio in Buenos Aires, was kept on despite the fact that he was also on the board of the Nazi branch of General Electric as well as of Italian, Japanese, and German companies.

In Buenos Aires, Rio, and other cities, Davis retained important Nazis. One of these, Jorge Richter, an official of Siemens who moved from branch to branch, was reported by the FBI to be an espionage agent of the Nazi High Command.

On August 18, 1942, Davis cabled Long from Santiago, Chile, stating that he could give Transradio there "a clean bill of health," and that the company was "entirely under Allied control." Yet in January 1943 the FBI was to supply its own report based on an independent investigation saying that Transradio there still had four receivers tuned in to Tokyo, Berlin, London, and New York and that Hans Blume's brother, Kurt, was now in charge. Similar reports reached Washington on Buenos Aires and Rio.

On August 25, 1942, Davis, Sarnoff, Winterbottom, and Breckinridge Long met in Long's office to hear General Davis give RCA a complete whitewash in South America. He said, "There is a satisfactory condition now existing. . . . The communication facilities of Transradio . . . are in friendly hands." Friendly to whom? one might ask; but Long conveyed to Cordell Hull his own satisfaction with the situation, even confirming such an outrageous statement as, "Dr. Aguirre is entirely pro-Ally and cooperative."

On August 31, Davis presented his report to an understandably delighted RCA shareholders' meeting. He read messages that the State Department had conveyed to the Italian and German proxies in the middle of the war. The French and Germans urged Davis via the board not to make any further changes in South America. None was made except that an American, George W. Hayes, took over in Buenos Aires. He found himself as managing director of a mixed Axis and Allied board. He also allegedly did not enforce the suggestion that Aguirre resign from his Nazi companies—until October 6, 1943.

Despite pretensions to the contrary, and promises to close down the circuits, they continued. Breckinridge Long proved incapable of vigorously enforcing the disconnections or unwilling to do so. The British government seemed to be prepared to let the matter drift on indefinitely. Whenever it was suggested by Long that the British should disconnect, Sir Campbell Stuart indicated he was waiting for the Americans to act. Sarnoff waited for Stuart and Sosthenes Behn for Sarnoff. The buck was passed to South American governments, from London to New York and back again, while the profits and the espionage continued.

The U.S. Commercial Company sat on the matter on September 25, 1942, as part of the FCC special board in charge of hemispheric communications. Hugh Knowlton reported that RCA had instructed

Transradio in Argentina and Chile to close the circuits of the Axis "when the British did so." The British ambassador in Washington had advised FCC Acting Chairman C. J. Durr "that the British government expects daily to be able to report that the British representatives in these two companies have been so instructed." ITT "would also close their circuits when the British did."

By October 1942 the matter was still dragging on. At a meeting at the State Department on October 7, Sarnoff took the view that he would "generously waive consideration" of the commercial interests at stake. Such "generosity" was surely mandatory in wartime. Ignoring the fact that the British directors had said that it was up to him to discontinue the South American circuits if he wanted to, and that much of South America had turned against the Axis, he repeated that the British directors had still to concur in the action, and he questioned whether the order to close would be obeyed by the local managements in each case—ignoring the fact that he had the power through Davis to fire anybody who disobeyed such orders.

By February 1943, Transradio was still in business. On February 10, RCA's W. A. Winterbottom cabled Martin Hallauer of British Cable and Wireless in London that he was making sure that RCA received all dividends and interests of Transradio, supervised all accounts, and helped maintain its offices in London. Even as the war deepened, RCA and British Cable and Wireless continued to own a substantial proportion of Transradio's stocks. In Brazil in March 1943, seven months after Brazil was at war with Germany, RCA's Radiobras held 70,659 German shares: part of the 240,000 voting shares held by the National City Bank of New York in Rio. On March 22 a British Cable and Wireless executive wrote from London to State that the Swedes, who represented the Nazi interests, had received the minutes of the latest board meeting and had sent them to Berlin and Paris.

On May 24, 1943, Long called Sarnoff with a mild complaint "that we have reason to believe that more messages than the agreed 700 code groups a week are being sent from Buenos Aires by the Axis powers for their Governments." Long added, "There may be sound reasons why your man George W. Hayes refuses to disclose the exact number of messages sent in code groups by each of the Axis representatives to their Governments. But I don't see any reason why Hayes shouldn't ask for a report on all code groups being sent day by day and to include a report on all belligerents. If you would obtain the information we would be appreciative. Don't do it by telegraph or telephone. We'll make our diplomatic pouch available to you.'' Sarnoff replied, ''I'll talk to Winterbottom. I don't see why we shouldn't do it.'' The documents do not show that he did.

As it turned out, the final disconnection of the circuits only took place because the South American governments willed it. There is no evidence that ultimate action was taken by the State Department, RCA, or British Cable and Wireless.

Sosthenes Behn, like Sarnoff, paradoxically showed great dedication to the American war effort. On May 15, 1942, Behn announced to *The New York Times* that the United States government could have free use of all ITT patents and those of its subsidiaries, both in the United States and abroad, for the duration of the war and six months thereafter. He would not charge manufacturers engaged in the production of war equipment.

With a touch of black humor he told the *Times* that ''We have 9,200 patents and more than 450 trademarks in 61 countries, and about 5,100 patents and 40 trademark applications pending in 38 countries. These figures do not include patents to German subsidiaries of the corporation since information about them is not available.'' This barefaced lie was published without demur in the *Times*.

Behn coolly announced that profits and losses of his international corporations ''and the accounts of German subsidiaries, Spanish subsidiaries, the Shanghai telephone company . . . and Mexican subsidiaries'' had not been included in the annual financial statements for the same reason of ''lack of information''—information that was, in fact, reaching him daily.

Amazingly, on April 21, 1943, Behn let the cat at least peep out of the bag. He said, at an ITT shareholders' meeting in New York, ''More than 61 percent of ITT's operations are in the Western hemisphere, almost 24 percent in the British Empire and neutral nations in Europe and less than 13 percent in Axis or Axis-controlled countries. Most of the cash available to the corporation originated with 'subsidiaries in the Western hemisphere.' ''

The announcement to the shareholders that 13 percent of ITT was held in enemy territory caused not a ripple of surprise.

Despite the fact that all branches of American Intelligence were monitoring Colonel Behn at every turn, intercepting his messages, supplying unflattering memoranda marked "Confidential," and in general knowing exactly what he was up to, nothing whatsoever was done to stop him. As the war neared its end, whatever mild internal criticisms were voiced within the American government were quickly silenced by the prospects of peace with Germany and future plans to confront Russia. The FBI released through its internal organization a number of detailed reports on Behn forwarded to Navy, Army, and Air Force Intelligence. J. Edgar Hoover linked Behn to Nazi sources, including agents in Cuba and other parts of the Caribbean. Yet, despite the overwhelming evidence of Behn's collusion in his files, Hoover was pleased to receive from Behn the book *Beyond Our Shores the World Shall Know Us,* written with Behn's cooperation in 1944 and dealing with the problem of providing adequate American international broadcasting facilities. On June 17 of that year Hoover wrote to Behn: "Your letter of June 10 . . . has been received and the book entitled *Beyond Our Shores the World Shall Know Us* has arrived. I do want to express to you my heartfelt appreciation for your thoughtfulness in making this splendid volume available."

Ironically, Behn's wartime headaches came not from Roosevelt but from Hitler. During that last period of the war Behn's work on behalf of the German army had deeply intensified. His communications systems for the OKW, the High Command of the Nazi armed forces, had become more and more sophisticated. The systems enabled the Nazis under Schellenberg's special decoding branch to break the American diplomatic code. They also allowed the building of intercept posts and platoons in the defensive campaign against the British and American invasion of France. At the same time, Behn was indispensable in making that invasion possible.

The problem was that the forces of anti-Behn were moving in under Postminister Wilhelm Ohnesorge. Behn's associate, General Erich Fellgiebel of the OKW, was prodded by the determination to bring about a negotiated peace, and Schellenberg's efforts undoubtedly abetted him. With Behn moving behind the scenes, and the assistance of John Foster Dulles's brother, Allen Dulles, of the Schröder

Bank and the OSS, the famous generals' plot of July 1944 was hatched to assassinate Hitler. When Fellgiebel hesitated in cutting off communications to Hitler's headquarters after the bomb went off that almost killed the Führer, conversations were overheard by Hitler's spies that revealed the plot's purpose. Ohnesorge's hour had arrived. In a desperate effort to save himself from ruin or worse, Schellenberg turned against his fellow conspirators and Himmler—who had all along tacitly half-encouraged Behn and the plotters—was compelled to feed Fellgiebel to the wolves. Fellgiebel and his associate in ITT General Thiele were executed, and Karl Lindemann of Standard Oil went to prison, narrowly escaping the gallows. Only ITT's Gerhardt Westrick's hold over his fellow ITT board member Schellenberg and close contacts with I.G. Farben saved Westrick from a similar fate. Again, Behn's German empire very nearly was confiscated by Postminister Wilhelm Ohnesorge, but Schellenberg took a great risk and protected it once more.

On the day Paris was liberated, August 25, 1944, Behn drove in a jeep down the Champs-Élysées in a new role: He was "special communications expert for the Army of Occupation." His right-hand man, Kenneth Stockton, who had remained joint chairman with Westrick of the Nazi company throughout the war, was with him in the uniform of a three-star brigadier general. Behn made sure in Paris that his collaborating staff were not punished by Charles de Gaulle and the Free French. He was helped at high army levels to protect his friends.

When Germany fell, Stockton, with Behn, commandeered urgently needed trucks to travel into the Russian zone, remove machinery from ITT-owned works and aircraft plants—and move them into the American zone.

In 1945 a special Senate committee was set up on the subject of international communications. Completely unnoticed in the press, Burton K. Wheeler, "reformed" now that Germany had lost the war, became chairman. An immense dossier showing the extraordinary co-ownership with German and Japanese companies of RCA and ITT was actually published as an appendix to the hearings, but almost nobody took note of this formidable and fascinating half-million-word transcript. Least of all were its contents noted by the committee itself, which wasted the public's money by simply discussing for days (with Fraternity figures like James V. Forrestal) the possibility, quickly ruled out, of centralizing American communications systems. There was not a mention from beginning to end of the discussions of the questionable activities of RCA and ITT chiefs. Yet, in a curious series of exchanges between Wheeler and Rear Admiral Joseph R. Redman, who had been in charge of Naval Communications during the early part of the war, the cat leaped out of the bag in no uncertain manner. Apparently under the impression that the hearings would never be published, Wheeler seriously sat and talked of some of the reasons that such events had taken place. He asked Redman the question, already knowing the answer, "To what extent has American ownership of communications manufacturing companies in foreign countries, such as Germany, Sweden, and Spain, been of advantage, if any, to this country?" Redman replied, "Of course, from an economic point of view, I am not qualified to say, but I would say this from possibly a technical or research point of view, you get a cross-exchange of information in the research laboratories."

This amazing revelation by a high personage won the response from Wheeler, "And what about the disadvantages to us?" Redman replied blandly, "While you are working on things here that are developed for military reasons, there may be a certain amount of leakage back to foreign fields."

Wheeler asked, "How could you keep a manufacturing plant in Germany or in Spain or in Sweden, even though controlled by Western Electric from exchanging information as to what they were doing?"

Redman replied, "Well, we have had to rely a great deal upon the integrity of our commercial activities. Of course, if a man is a crook, he is going to be a crook regardless of whether you set up restrictions or not."

Wheeler said, "Let us suppose that you have a manufacturing company in Germany and also one here, and they are owned by the same company, aren't they exchanging information with reference to patents and everything else? . . . Admiral Redman, you are not naive enough to believe, if a company has an establishment in Germany and another in America, they are not both working to improve their patents, are they?"

Redman admitted, "No, sir."

Warming to his theme, Wheeler said, "Consequently, if there are private companies that have factories over there and also here, they're bound to exchange information. It seems to me this has been going on in all kinds of industry. And that would be true of the electronics industry, or any other manufacturing industry, and whether they have a medium for such exchange in the nature of cartels or something else, they exchange information. What check has the Navy made to find out whether or not information is exchanged in that manner?"

Redman said, "We get a certain amount of information from captured equipment, captured documents, and things like that, and can find out if there is a leakage. . . . Of course we have depended somewhat on our foreign attachés to get us some information on these things. . . . I do not like here to get into a discussion of intelligence because I fear we might get ourselves into trouble."

Wheeler said, "You might, but some of us don't feel that way about it."

"Perhaps not," Redman replied.

Wheeler continued, "We might get into trouble in the Senate, but they cannot do anything about it. They cannot chop our heads off at the moment."

Senator Homer Capehart added, "For at least six years."

On February 16, 1946, Major General Harry C. Ingles, Chief Signal Officer of the U.S. Army, acting on behalf of President Truman, presented the Medal of Merit, the nation's highest award to a civilian, to Behn at 67 Broad Street, New York. As he pinned the medal on Colonel Behn, Ingles said, "You are honored for exceptionally meritorious conduct in the performance of outstanding service to the United States." A few years later Behn received millions of dollars in compensation for war damage to his German plants in 1944. Westrick had obtained an equivalent amount from the Nazi government.

7

Globes of Steel

Throughout World War II, Sosthenes Behn was an investor in the Swedish Enskilda Bank, chief financier of the colossal ball-bearings trust known as SKF. Göring's cousin Hugo von Rosen and William L. Batt, vice-chairman of the War Production Board, were directors of SKF in America throughout the war, dedicated to keeping South American companies on the Proclaimed List supplied with ball bearings.

Tiny ball bearings were essential to the Nazis: The Luftwaffe could not fly without them, the tanks and armored cars could not roll in their missions of death. ITT's Focke-Wulfs, Ford's autos and trucks for the enemy, would have been powerless without them. Indeed, World War II could not have been fought without them. Focke-Wulfs used at least four thousand bearings per plane: roughly equivalent to those used by the Flying Fortresses. Guns, bombsights, electrical generators and engines, ventilating systems, U-boats, railroads, mining machinery, ITT's communications devices—these existed on ball bearings.

With its 185 sales organizations throughout the world, SKF could have contributed a fine example of Sweden's economic democracy at work. However, SKF was concerned only to make profits, trade on both sides of the fence in wartime, and act as a front for German interests. It was in part an arm of the Swedish government since its representatives abroad were often ambassadors, ministers, or consuls, who represented Swedish policy all over the world. SKF represented virtually every industrial combine in Sweden and every member of the board was part of the companies that controlled the entire Swedish economy. Founded in 1907, SKF, with its subsidiaries, was the largest manufacturer of bearings on earth. It controlled 80 percent of bearings in Europe alone. It also controlled iron ore mines, steel and blast furnaces, foundries and factories and plants in the United States, Great Britain, France, and Germany. The largest share of its production until late in World War II was allocated to Germany: 60 percent of the worldwide production of SKF was dedicated to the Germans. Some indication of SKF's attitude toward the Allies can be gauged from the fact that while the German factory at Schweinfurt produced 93 percent of capacity, the U.S. company in Philadelphia produced less than 38 percent, and the British less than that.

And ball bearings were among the most powerful weapons of The Fraternity's sophisticated form of wartime neutrality. Their inventor and the power behind their production and distribution as SKF chairman was Sven Wingquist, a dashing playboy friend of Göring and the Duke and Duchess of Windsor. He was a prominent partner in Jacob Wallenberg's Stockholm Enskilda, the largest private bank in Sweden—a correspondent bank of Hitler's Reichsbank. Wallenberg was large, athletic, impeccably Aryan—comptroller of mining, shale oil, electrical goods, munitions, iron mines—virtually the whole industrial economy of his native country. Sosthenes Behn and Wingquist were in partnership with Axel Wenner-Gren of U.S. Electrolux in the gigantic Bofors munitions empire: Bofors supplied Germany with a substantial part of its steel production in World War II.

As stated, American directors for the duration were Göring's second cousin by marriage Hugo von Rosen, and William L. Batt. A hard-bitten and driving individualist, Batt was born in Indiana; he began in railway shops, where he learned a machinist's trade from his father. He earned his engineering degree at Purdue in 1907; next year he was employed in the ball-bearing plant of Hess-Bright Manufacturing Co. of Philadelphia. When Hess-Bright amalgamated with SKF in 1919, he rose rapidly to become president of the company in 1923.

A big man, with the hands of a lumberjack, black patent-leather hair, a prominent nose and a jutting cleft chin, Batt dressed in high fashion, and sported monogrammed silk handkerchiefs and Sulka ties. His SKF factory in Philadelphia rivaled the giant sister factories in Göteborg in Sweden and Schweinfurt in Germany. SKF Philadelphia was the subject of glowing articles in *The Wall Street Journal* and *Fortune* magazine, its products reaching a staggering $21 million a year by 1940.

With war approaching, and the fear of America entering the conflict, Hugo von Rosen and fellow board members traveled to their German and Italian plants, which were jointly owned with Germany and Italy, and promised their managers that if it proved difficult to ship ball bearings to Nazi or Italian affiliates in Latin America through the British blockade, Philadelphia would take over whether or not Roosevelt declared war. Simultaneously, the SKF directors protected their associated chemical company, I.G. Farben's Bosch, with the aid of John Foster Dulles. Batt was president of American Bosch. Dulles, the Bosch/General Aniline and Film attorney, set up a voting trust to protect the company with himself and Batt as trustees after Pearl Harbor. He was thus enabled to save the company from being seized until the spring of 1942, five months after America was at war.

Dulles also proved helpful in setting up similar protections for SKF: protections that lasted until the end of the war. He helped organize a deal whereby Batt became the nominal majority shareholder with trustee voting rights. Since American-owned companies could not be seized by Alien Property Custodian Leo T. Crowley, this proved to be a protection.

With the outbreak of war, Roosevelt appointed Batt vice-chairman of the War Production Board, whose chairman was Sears, Roebuck's Donald Nelson. Batt worked from 8 A.M. until after midnight, so busy that his lunch consisted of apples and milk eaten in the middle of meetings while he kept relighting his cold pipe with a lighter in the form of a cannon.

From the moment he took up his position on the War Production Board, Batt instituted the famous motto "Patch and pray." Ignoring the fact that his fellow Fraternity members had caused these very shortages, and that he was wartime majority trustee shareholder for companies collaborating with the enemy, he blasted the public on the radio for being extravagant with rubber and scrap metal. He insisted that housewives turn in their tin cans, old tires, tubes, leaky hot water bottles, rubber gloves, and aprons. He called for all old newspapers to be sent for packing ammunition; he enforced voluntary surrender of rags, used wool, and even fats for glycerin. At the same time, he cheerfully overlooked the fact that scrap had gone to build the bombs that were rained on Pearl Harbor. He moved smoothly between that whited sepulcher of Republicanism, the Union League Club of Philadelphia, and the New Dealers on Capitol Hill. He was smart enough to express admiration of the Red Army when he went to Russia on the famous Averell Harriman mission. It was convenient for him to be called a "pink" while maintaining his Nazi connections.

During his period with the War Production Board, which lasted for the duration, Batt's behavior was largely in the interests of The Fraternity. He was ideally situated to turn a blind eye to von Rosen's trade with Proclaimed Listees, given his immense influence and the fact that he had innumerable government employees on his staff throughout North and South America and neutral Europe. Because of war and the blockade, it was difficult for SKF in Sweden to supply its Proclaimed List customers south of the Panama Canal. As a result, von Rosen saw to it that those same companies were supplied direct from Philadelphia.

Von Rosen was under direct orders from Stockholm to supply the Latin American Nazi-associated firms irrespective of the fact that there was an overwhelming demand for all available ball bearings in the United States. He was to base his sales on the principle of Business as Usual rather than on the needs of the war effort. Batt, accepting these arrangements, could not use the excuse that he was in effect working for a Swedish company and therefore had to obey neutral rules, since he himself as an American owned 103,439 shares of capital stock.

Under von Rosen's directorship and Batt's trusteeship, SKF production in wartime failed to reach even the minimum of American expectations. This fact infuriated Morgenthau, who designated the stocky, feisty Canadian-born Lauchlin Currie of the White House Economics Staff to hammer away at the government to stop this outrageous circumstance. Currie was seconded by a very determined and thorough official of French extraction, Jean Pajus of the Office of Economic Programs, who prepared millions of words in reports on the doings of Batt and von Rosen until as late as 1945.

Delving deep into records, Currie found that the all-important Curtiss-Wright Aviation Corporation was unable for fifteen months after Pearl Harbor to secure sufficient ball bearings from SKF and came close to closing down. Worn-out ball bearings caused crashes that cost American lives. At a time when every plane in the country was desperately needed for the war effort, large numbers of planes were grounded because of the lag in supply.

In June 1943, one loyal, patriotic executive of SKF finally lost all patience with von Rosen and went to Washington to see Batt in his role of vice-chairman of the War Production Board to complain bitterly of the SKF shortages that were hampering America's fight in the air. Batt listened coldly and then said, "Nothing can be done. Nor will it be done." That was the end of the matter. The executive resigned.*

Someone on the SKF staff even doctored the inventories in Philadelphia so that it seemed only a few million ball bearings were ground out, when in fact vastly more had been produced. Sometimes, for American use, von Rosen manufactured an outer bearing part without its inner component and vice versa. It exasperated Currie and Pajus that the incomplete bearings were useless.

While holding up orders, causing bottlenecks (with the collusion of the indispensable Jesse H. Jones), and causing shortages, von Rosen did not only ship to South America. He also sent to Sweden secret patents, detailed charts, and private production details. Knowing that these might be intercepted by British or American censorship in Bermuda, members of his staff placed the precious documents in the diplomatic bags of the Swedish embassy in Washington. Neutral diplomatic bags were precluded from seizure or search in time of war. Currie wrote, in a memorandum summing up Batt's collusion, on May 3, 1944: "Batt was busy . . . pulling all wires he could in the U.S. Office of Censorship and with the British Purchasing Commission."

At the same time these activities were continuing, the SKF Phila-

* Name not given in government reports.

delphia operation was issued a general license to deal internationally throughout the war. And Batt's retention in his official position during World War II can only be ascribed to Roosevelt.

Treasury even allowed SKF to get away with posing as an American-owned corporation, despite the fact that Treasury had records of the Swedish-German ownership in its possession. When Lauchlin Currie became too inquisitive, Batt deliberately burned all of the appropriate SKF correspondence and accountancy files.

On April 10, 1943, a loyal and patriotic American, J. S. Tawresey, chief engineer on the SKF board of directors, resigned following a furious quarrel with Batt. He charged that SKF was "destructive to the war effort," that SKF had failed to meet orders for 150,000 deliveries per month to the all-important Pratt-Whitney fighter airplane engine company, and that Batt was flagrantly working against America despite his WPB role. In disgust with the company, Tawresey joined the Air Corps. He contacted Treasury. Franklin S. Judson of the Foreign Economic Administration flew to see him at an Air Force base in Florida. The men had a charged meeting in which Tawresey poured out his heart on the doings of SKF. Angrily he charged von Rosen and many of his staff with anti-Semitism and pro-Nazi feelings, and said that they blatantly held the United States up to scorn at board meetings and in private conversations. Currie was horrified. He wrote Morgenthau a blistering report on the meeting, followed by an equally damning SEC report, but nothing happened to the company as a result.

Throughout the war an old reliable of The Fraternity proved to be helpful. The National City Bank of New York siphoned through money to Sweden: the SKF profits from Latin American dealings. Officially, all National City Bank's Swedish accounts were frozen on Roosevelt's orders. Somehow, Batt managed to use his government influence to have the funds specially unblocked by license for transfer across the Atlantic.

As war went on, it became necessary to cloak SKF shipments to South America in case members of the FBI should discover what was going on. As a cover, von Rosen set up a subsidiary that took a leaf out of the Standard Oil book. Registered in Panama, it was protected by Panamanian laws from American seizure. Ball bearings traveled from American ports on Panamanian registered vessels. Over

600,000 ball bearings a year traveled in this manner to Nazi customers in South America including Siemens, Diesel, Asea, and Separator, as well as Axel Wenner-Gren's Electrolux and Behn's ITT. Transfer was made of purchasing funds through the Nazi Banco Aleman Transatlantico. Von Rosen used a crude code in his telegrams, all of which were passed through the diplomatic bag. "Wild duck glacé arrived, also Schnapps" meant that ball bearings had arrived along with their component parts.

When Germany began to run short of ball bearings in 1943, despite the vast shipments from Sweden and its own local production, more were needed from South America. So von Rosen arranged for reshipment from Rio and Buenos Aires via Sweden. The British, utterly dependent on SKF for their own ball bearings, appeased the dubious corporation by issuing special Navicerts allowing vessels to pass unsearched through the blockade to Sweden. Even the Russians concurred—they, too, needed SKF.

A curious series of events took place in 1943. Early in October, Batt flew to Stockholm in an American Army bomber accompanied by Army representatives. The ostensible purpose of the mission was to secure further supplies of ball-bearing production machinery, despite the fact that there was quite sufficient in Philadelphia. Details of his meetings with Jacob Wallenberg and Wingquist were not disclosed. However, on October 14, when General Henry H. ("Hap") Arnold, U.S. Army Air Force chief, commanded a raid on SKF's giant Schweinfurt factory, he was shocked to discover that news of the supposed bombing had been leaked to the enemy. The result was that America lost sixty planes in the attack. Arnold told the London *News Chronicle* on October 19, "I don't see how they could have prepared the defense they did unless they had been warned in advance."

For the first time since Pearl Harbor there were some signs that action might be taken by the American government. The energetic Jean Pajus spearheaded a drive to expose SKF.

Meanwhile, General Carl Spaatz of the U.S. High Command in London was furious because the Swedes were tripling their shipments to Germany with British and American official authorization after the raid on Schweinfurt. He called U.S. Ambassador John G. Winant to his headquarters on March 13, 1944, and blasted him about his handling of the matter, claiming that Winant was "playing along with the British." Spaatz screamed, "Our whole bomber offensive is being nullified!" Winant, red-faced and smarting from the dressing down, asked his assistant Winfield Riefler to look into the matter. Riefler found that the British Ministry of Economic Warfare, which was supposed to enforce the restrictions of shipments, was failing to do so because Britain was as dependent on Swedish SKF as Germany—following Luftwaffe raids on the SKF subsidiary's plant in Luton.

On March 20, Lauchlin Currie wrote to Dean Acheson that he was drastically concerned by the gravity of the situation: "During the past few months our air forces have made sixteen heavy and costly raids for the sole purpose of destroying the ballbearing production capacity of the Germans. But while we are eliminating German production at tremendous sacrifice in planes and men, Swedish production continues to be available to the enemy. Swedish shipments to Germany in 1943 were at an all-time peak." Acheson did not reply.

On April 13, 1944, U.S. Ambassador Herschel Johnson had a meeting with Swedish Foreign Minister Christian E. Günther in Stockholm. Günther pointed out that negotiating the three-way pact between the United States, Britain, and Germany had been immensely difficult and that if Sweden should break the pact now, Germany could react violently. Günther added sharply, "American public opinion would see the justice of the position taken by Sweden if Sweden should publish the entire correspondence in which it would appear that trade between Sweden and Germany was on a contract basis known to the Allied governments and based on prior agreements with them." Thus it was clear the Swedish Foreign Minister was threatening the United States: if it didn't play along, Sweden would disclose to the American public that its government was making deals with the enemy.

Lord Selborne, Minister of Economic Warfare, gave his views to Riefler of Winant's staff in London. He was responding to a U.S. government proposal that SKF should be put on the blacklist if it refused the request for an embargo. Selborne totally disagreed with the proposal. He felt that such a threat would be a fatal blunder. He begged Riefler to dissuade the U.S. government from such a course. Instead, the British government felt that the entire output of SKF should be bought by the United States outright: a sure source of dollars for the Nazis. It was clear that Selborne was concerned that in the event of blacklisting, Britain would be left without its vast influx of ball bearings. Not only were bearings immediately expected by ship, but there were 350 tons being held at Göteborg by British supply authorities. He felt that these would be held hostage, and seized by the Swedes in reprisal if Swedish property in the United States or Britain should be seized. There was also the danger of thousands of tons of bearings loaded on two British cargo ships, *Dicto* and *Lionel*, being hijacked at sea.

On April 25, Under Secretary of War Robert P. Patterson advised Secretary of War Stimson that Sweden had rejected the U.S. demand to stop shipments to Germany in excess of those agreed to in 1943. He wrote, "Sweden, I am sure, will try to drag the matter out by discussions, holding out hopes to us that exports to Germany will be reduced in the future. This has been her policy in the past, and she'll try it again." Patterson pointed out that Sweden was furnishing Germany with munitions that killed American soldiers, that 20 percent of the shells fired at Americans came from Swedish iron ore, and that the Swedes were getting large quantities of petroleum when the British and U.S. were short of it for war purposes. He added, "I . . . believe that the government should make the facts public." It was a futile hope.

On April 27, Lieutenant James Puleston, Navy liaison in the Foreign Economic Administration, wrote to Lauchlin Currie that "no confidence whatsoever" should be placed in Jacob Wallenberg, that the idea of the embargo was a "mirage" and "a pleasant dream." He felt that a much more effective way to secure cooperation was for the State Department to threaten cutting off oil supplies to Sweden; he disliked Swedish ships "hanging around" American and Caribbean ports "because we believe that there are enough pro-German crews [in the Swedish navy] to act as spies." He added in his report to Currie:

> If we dilly-dally or accept the half measures proposed by Wallenberg and the State Department we abandon the last battle before it begins. . . . If we go through the [oil embargo] we can at least put the additional loss of American lives where it belongs—squarely in the State Department. If we do not, we will share this responsibility and, person-

ally, I don't want to think that a single American soldier died because I did not press the State Department for the proper action.

Pressing the State Department was no easy matter. However, in April 1944, Treasury was finally able to induce Dean Acheson to agree to hire someone to fly to Sweden and try to buy off the Enskilda Bank from supplying Germany.

The choice of special emissary fell on a curious figure. Instead of sending Currie or Harry Dexter White, Acheson and Morgenthau selected a banker and movie executive of Paramount Studios, Stanton Griffis, who was better known as a socialite than as an expert in economics. He flew to London, where he was joined by a smooth young economist and Red Cross vice-chairman named Douglas Poteat. The two men squeezed into a cramped Mosquito aircraft and flew through violent electrical storms to Stockholm. There, at the gloomy and overpowering Grand Hotel, they met with Ambassador Johnson and with Jacob Wallenberg.

On the second morning of his stay at the Grand, Griffis woke up to see a waiter standing with a breakfast. The man said in a heavy Balkan voice, "I am an American secret agent. I will be working for you and will keep you informed. In Room 208, where you will be meeting with [the Swedes], the Germans have installed listening devices. In Room 410 is Dr. Schnurre of the Nazi government, who is hoping to outbid you in the ballbearings negotiations." Griffis was astonished by this little speech. He assumed the man was a jokester or a plant. But from that moment on the waiter, who was working for the OSS, kept him informed of every movement of Wallenberg and the Nazis.

The negotiations in the gloomy Enskilda Bank boardroom dominated by Wallenberg family portraits were slow and tedious. Griffis obviously knew nothing of the links between Batt and the Axis, because in the course of his discussion he said to one of the SKF executives, Harald Hamberg, "You can hold out as long as you like, but the U.S. is not going to stand by while you make machines to kill American boys." Hamberg, no doubt hiding his knowledge of the matter, replied, "How do you know that our ballbearings help kill American boys?" Whereupon, Douglas Poteat took out a handful of ball bearings and laid them on the table. "Where were these made?'' Poteat asked. The executive examined them. ''In Sweden,'' he said. And Poteat added, looking the executive in the eye, ''Every one of these was taken from a German plane shot down over London.''

At last, after several weeks, an agreement was reached. Griffis authorized $8 million to be paid to the credit of the Enskilda Bank. When the war was over, Griffis guaranteed, there would be no antitrust action against SKF. SKF would keep all of its German properties forever, and all SKF Nazi connections in the United States would be forgiven, forgotten, and—more importantly—unexposed.

Meanwhile, public criticism was beginning to surface. SKF workers in Philadelphia got wind of the dealings with the Nazis. An article appeared in the liberal newspaper *PM*, charging von Rosen and Batt with gross malfeasance and trading with enemy collaborators. Various disaffected SKF executives, troubled by the nature of the corporation to which they belonged, began to snitch.

Batt gave *The Washington Post* an interview on May 14, 1944, saying that production in Philadelphia would be hurt if the company were nationalized or Proclaimed Listed in response to press criticism from the Left. He insisted he was not a Nazi front and he denied that Göring's relative was his partner. He described von Rosen as ''a salesman.'' He admitted that he voted 95 percent of the stock without revealing that his ownership was to protect the company from seizure as an alien concern.

But the loyal American executives, and workers on the assembly lines in Philadelphia, grew increasingly restless. There was a series of union meetings, in which shop stewards talked angrily of a strike. Many workers went home to their wives and children, muttering about collaboration with the enemy. It seemed that what the U.S. government had lamentably failed to do—put SKF out of business—the workers might.

Batt didn't lose control. On May 16 he called a mass meeting of the eight thousand employees of SKF in the large truckyard of the factory. His wavy black hair, strong face, and powerful broad-shouldered figure always inspired confidence in the workers, who tended to trust him no matter what the evidence against him. He delivered a speech, standing on a high platform flanked by four American flags flapping in the wind. He shouted, "None of our production is reaching the enemy! I assure you of that, my friends! All these rumors about Nazis influencing our company in Sweden are sheer nonsense! These kinds of rumors are just Hitler propaganda to pull us down!"

This outrageous lie was greeted with cheers by eight thousand gullible workers. They were hugely relieved and almost ran back to the assembly lines. Somebody in the government got to *PM* and forced it to issue a retraction. On May 18 the Treasury and the Office of the Alien Property Custodian issued a joint statement to the press to the effect that following an investigation of SKF, it was "totally absolved of all alleged collusion with the enemy." The statement went on, "Both the War and Navy departments have advised the Treasury Department and the Alien Property Custodian that all of the production of SKF Industries and SKF Steel contributes to the war effort of the United States . . . SKF Industries and SKF Steel have excellent records for war production, and state that any serious loss of production would have an immediate and serious effect on production of war munitions needed for plant operations."

On June 13 the agreement was concluded between SKF and the governments of the United States and the United Kingdom regarding reduced bearings exports to the enemy. Despite the expert example of public relations shown by William L. Batt, it was clear that the government was uneasy about advertising the fact that Nazi Germany was still being benefited by the Allies. A note on the top of the State Department memorandum dated June 13 and listing the amount of shipments reads: "It has been agreed to keep this arrangement secret not only during the period of its operation, but also after its termination."

In July a series of memoranda of the Foreign Economic Administration was shuffled between government departments alleging that so far from adhering to the $8 million agreement, SKF was indulging in a so-called triangular trade, shipping via Spain, Portugal, and Switzerland to the enemy to avoid charges that they were shipping directly. Every effort possible was made to get around the agreements. Unfortunately, the memoranda show, since the U.S. government had whitewashed SKF, it could scarcely expose these new activities. Under Secretary of War Patterson kept hammering away at the issue, but nothing was done about it. A helpless Lauchlin Currie could merely try to reassure everyone that everything would be all right in the end.

On behalf of the Foreign Economic Administration, Jean Pajus prepared a devastating indictment of William Batt, Hugo von Rosen, and SKF as a whole on September 15, 1944. Following a pocket history of the corporation up to date, he summarized the key matters as follows. He stated that Batt had been "under SKF orders to supply the Latin American market, irrespective of current war orders in the United States, and to base all sales in the United States primarily on the long-term business interests of the company rather than the needs of the war effort." He pointed out that directives from the Swedish plant came through the Swedish Legation in Washington, thus escaping the normal channels of censorship. These directives showed that a company collaborating with the enemy could exercise control of a vital U.S. industry.

Pajus reiterated that SKF production had not reached even minimum expectations; that there had been great lapses in ball-bearings deliveries to vital war industries; that as a result planes had been grounded; that William L. Batt could have corrected the situation but had not done so. He summarized the deliberate tying up of raw materials, the associations with enemy corporations, and the overall disgrace of a so-called American company controlled by enemy interests. SKF remained unpunished.

The Norwegians, who had suffered enough from Swedish collusion with the enemy, struck out in the only way possible. They showed their protest on December 4, 1944. Norwegian workers at the SKF plant in Oslo destroyed the entire factory by explosion and fire, disposing of $1.5 million worth of ball bearings.

Meanwhile, Dean Acheson failed to put SKF Philadelphia on the Proclaimed List, as he was empowered to do. Instead of taking new action against SKF as new public criticism began to surface, he simply urged Morgenthau and Currie to keep up a series of public relations statements that SKF was loyal and decent—in order not to hamper the war effort.

Lauchlin Currie's belief that matters would improve as the war neared its end proved to be unfounded. On December 9, 1944, Jean Pajus wrote to U.S. Ambassador Johnson in Stockholm that he was shocked at the continuing trade. He wrote, "After the losses in men and planes sustained in the attack on Schweinfurt, what would the American people think if they learned that SKF is still supplying the German war machine with ballbearings?"

By early 1945 it was painfully obvious that Stanton Griffis's $8 million was largely useless. Not only did it absorb merely a part of the ball-bearings shipment, and a small part at that, but the Swedes were infringing on the agreed maximum shipments all down the line. It was only when it was obvious that Hitler was about to lose the war that Sweden finally showed some signs of adhering to its agreements.

The war ended as Griffis had arranged, without punishment for William L. Batt or any of his circle. Hugo von Rosen was, of course, protected by his "neutrality." In the weeks at the end of the war, Batt suddenly turned up in Germany and visited the military decartelization branch in Berlin. He conferred with Brigadier General William H. Draper, in charge of decartelization, making sure that the secret promises made by Griffis to Wallenberg would be kept: that nothing would be done to disrupt the Swedish interests in SKF in Germany, that none of the plants in Germany would be broken down or removed, and that he and his American colleagues would not be subject to antitrust action. It goes without saying that the promises were kept.

8

The Film Conspiracy

I.G. Farben's joint chairman Hermann Schmitz was crucial to the activities of The Fraternity. Born in 1880 in the grim industrial city of Essen, Schmitz was the child of impoverished parents. He was driven from the first by a desire to obtain immense power. He started work at the age of fifteen, slaving as a leather-sleeved clerk at ledgers in a metals corporation. He studied at night school, learning about chemistry, fuels, and gases. Gifted with an extraordinary memory, he obtained a brilliant grasp of many branches of science by age twenty. As with millions of Germans, his nationalism flared during World War I. After service in the army this muscular, broad-shouldered, short-necked young man forced his way to the top of one of Germany's biggest steel corporations at the age of thirty-three. Secretive, difficult, mistrustful yet dynamic he used his government connections to the limit, bludgeoning his way into the Economics Ministry in 1915.

He became a close friend of Hjalmar Horace Greeley Schacht, who introduced him to the idea of a world community of money that would be independent of wars and empires. He became a dominant figure in the chemicals trust that he helped his friend and colleague Carl Krauch forge into I.G. Farben in 1925. Encouraged by Schacht, he developed a series of crucial friendships in England and the United States, always aiming unerringly for the greatest powers. One of his earliest allies was Walter Teagle of Standard Oil, who shared his views on international financial solidarity. Another was Edsel Ford, son of Henry Ford.

In 1929, Schmitz, his nephew, Max Ilgner, Walter Teagle, Edsel Ford, and Charles E. Mitchell of the ever-reliable National City Bank jointly set up the American Farben organization known as American I.G./Chemical Corp. Hermann Schmitz became president, with his brother Dietrich delegated to take over in his absence in Europe. It was an identical arrangement to that made by the von Clemm brothers, giving the family a foothold on both sides of the Atlantic that would survive any possible future war.

In 1931, President Herbert Hoover received Schmitz at the White House. Hoover shared Schmitz's attitude toward Russia: that it must be crushed. Hoover had lost extensive Russian oil holdings during the communist revolution.

So great was the enthusiasm of the German-American population for a recovering Germany that Schmitz's $13 million worth of debentures were sold by the National City Bank in one morning. The wealth and power of German-American I.G. were almost beyond calculation. The international company was the chief economic instrument of the German government. It produced a vast range of chemicals and chemical products, including artificial oil, synthetic rubber, aviation gasoline, plastic, nylon, and numerous poison gases, including the deadly insecticide later used at Farben's combined rubber factory and concentration camp, Auschwitz, where the SS murdered some four million Jews. Schmitz helped to found the Bank for International Settlements and was a member of the board until the end of World War II; he also launched an investment policy whereby American I.G. had, by 1941, $5,042,550 invested in Standard Oil of New Jersey, $838,412 in Du Pont/General Motors, and $155,000 in Standard Oil of California.

With Krupp, I.G. Farben was an executor of Göring's Four-Year Plan to make Germany militarily self-sufficient by 1940. By 1939, I.G. provided the Nazis with 90 percent of their foreign exchange, 95 percent of their imports, and 85 percent of all the military and commercial goods provided for by the Plan.

In 1932, Schmitz joined forces with Kurt von Schröder, director of the BIS and the enormously wealthy private bank, J. H. Stein,

of Cologne, Germany. Schröder was a fanatical Nazi. On the surface
he was suave, elegant, impeccably dressed, with a clean-cut face. In
private he was a dedicated leader of the Death's Head Brigade. During the war he could be seen driving from his office in his sober
pinstripe, changing into a black and silver uniform covered in decorations, and continuing to a meeting by torchlight of his personal
storm troopers. It was this SS man who was most closely linked to
Winthrop Aldrich of the Chase Bank, Walter Teagle of Standard Oil,
Sosthenes Behn of ITT, and the other American members of The
Fraternity. In 1933, at his handsome villa in Munich, Schröder arranged the meeting between Hitler and von Papen that helped lead
to Hitler's accession to power in the Reichstag.

Also in 1932, Hitler's special economic advisor Wilhelm Keppler
joined Schröder in forming a group of high-ranking associates of The
Fraternity who could be guaranteed to supply money to the Gestapo.
They agreed to contribute an average of one million marks a year to
Himmler's personally marked "S" account at the J. H. Stein Bank,
transferable to the secret "R" Gestapo account at the Dresdnerbank
in Berlin.

This group became known as the Circle of Friends of the Economy. Schmitz was the largest contributor to the Circle, which included representatives of ITT and Standard Oil of New Jersey. Schmitz
supplied considerable funds to Himmler separately, partly to secure
his properties from seizure by the Gestapo, and to insure contracts
for the concentration camps.

In the late 1930s, Schmitz began to conspire with the young and
hard-bitten Walter Schellenberg, who was rapidly rising to become
head of the SD, the Gestapo's counterintelligence service. Army Intelligence documents declassified in 1981 show that Schellenberg
discussed Schmitz as head of a Council of Twelve. The council would
place Hitler under the protection and rulership of Himmler while the
Führer remained a prisoner of Berchtesgaden. Knowing that Schmitz
was dedicated to Himmler and the Gestapo cause, Schellenberg plotted constantly toward this end. However, Himmler vacillated constantly. He could not bring himself to depose the Führer, nor did he
expose Schellenberg to the Führer.

The underlying purpose of the Schellenberg plan, revealed in the
same recently declassified Army Intelligence report, was clearly to

bring about the negotiated peace between Germany and the United States that was the overriding dream of The Fraternity.

As that war approached, Schmitz's brother Dietrich, acting on instructions from Berlin, moved from there to Manhattan and went into action to undermine any prospective American war effort. Despite the fact that he was an American citizen, enjoying all of the privileges of a glamorous social life in New York, he had involved himself in espionage with Farben's N.W.7. intelligence network. American I.G. owned the General Aniline and Film works and the huge film corporation Agfa and Ansco. It also owned Ozalid, the multimillion-dollar blueprint corporation. The General Aniline works supplied khaki or blue dyes for army, air force, or naval uniforms, which gave Schmitz's army of salesmen spies access to every military, naval, and air force base before and after Pearl Harbor. These "salesmen" talked the forces into using Agfa/Ansco for their private instruction films and having their photographs of secret installations developed in American I.G.'s laboratories. They also arranged to have every Ozalid print of secret military and naval plans copied and filed at their headquarters in Berlin.

The person responsible for this remarkable espionage stunt was Hermann and Dietrich Schmitz's nephew, plump, jolly Max Ilgner. Ilgner's motivation was to infiltrate at the top of Farben and prove himself indispensable to the company. He allied N.W.7. with the A.O., the Organization of Germans Abroad, an intelligence network which came directly under Walter Schellenberg. He set up an army of five thousand secret agents headed by Nazi Consul Fritz Wiedemann, operating through American I.G., which penetrated North and South America, weaving through military, naval, and air force bases as staff to supplement the information supplied by the I.G. salesmen. Between the two sets of spies Germany had a very clear picture of American armaments before Pearl Harbor.

Like Hermann Schmitz, Max Ilgner sent his brother to carry out his purposes in the United States. Rudolf Ilgner, an equally pushy, greedy, grasping opportunist, became a leading executive under Dietrich Schmitz in New York. He set up Chemical Co.— a "Statistical Branch" of I.G. dedicated to espionage. He made contact with a famous priest, Father Bernard R. Hubbard, known as the Glacier Priest because of his work as missionary and explorer in the frozen wastes of Alaska. The friendship had a purpose. In 1939, just weeks after war broke out in Europe, U.S. Secretary of War Henry Stimson asked Hubbard as a special favor to undertake a tour of strategic U.S. Army bases in Alaska. On the pretext of giving a lecture tour, he was to make a complete movie and still photographic survey of the bases for use at military headquarters at the War Department in Washington.

Innocently if recklessly, Father Hubbard told Rudolf Ilgner of his assignment. Ilgner told him that in the goodness of its spirit, American I.G. (now known as General Aniline and Film) would present him with free cameras and film from its finest Agfa color wholesale supplies. Naturally, Ilgner pointed out, Hubbard would want to process the film in General Aniline and Film's laboratories. Hubbard agreed. Apparently no one in military intelligence bothered to consult FBI or State Department files that showed the GAF-Nazi connection. Hubbard undertook his long and difficult expedition, through blizzards and rainstorms, returning with a priceless record of the whole United States northwestern defense system. This, Rudolf Ilgner naturally forwarded to his brother at N.W.7. in Berlin.

Simultaneously, the Army began to photograph the Panama Canal for defense purposes. Rudolf Ilgner offered the Army Agfa film at a very low price. The films were processed and shipped to Berlin. Ilgner had a sense of humor. He gave the American government copies of the movies and still photographs and kept the originals, which were shipped via the Hamburg-America steamship line in 1941. The president of this company was Julius P. Meyer, head of the Board of Trade for German-American Commerce, whose chairman was—Rudolf Ilgner.

In September 1939 the Schmitz brothers and the Ilgners realized that with the outbreak of war in Europe, the name I.G.—as in Farben—might put off some of the scores of thousands of American smaller shareholders who were unwittingly helping to finance Hitler.

Rudolf Ilgner burned all of his incriminating records. The directors instructed their publicity team to lay off any further plugging of Nazi superefficiency as a selling point. It was thus that the company had become General Aniline and Film. The I.G. Farben subsidiary I.G. Chemie in Switzerland, run by the Schmitzes' brother-in-law, owned 91.5 percent of the stock through—need one add?—the National City Bank of New York and the Chase National Bank. The board still included William E. Weiss of Sterling Products and Edsel Ford; Teagle had resigned in 1938 following much unwelcome publicity. In his place James V. Forrestal was appointed to the board. Forrestal was a partner in the part-Jewish banking company of Dillon, Read, which had helped to finance Hitler in the earlier days. He was soon to become Under Secretary, and later Secretary, of the Navy. Another on the board was former Attorney General Homer S. Cummings. Cummings, who had done much to protect American I.G. when he was in his official post, now became the leading defense lawyer for the corporation. Just how qualified he was for the job may be judged by the fact that he slipped secret intelligence to Hans Thomsen, Nazi chargé d'affaires in Washington. In a telegram marked Top Secret sent to Germany on June 11, 1940, Thomsen revealed that Cummings had supplied him with details of a private conversation with Roosevelt. Cummings told Thomsen's special contact that the President would make use of every legal trick in order to circumvent neutrality and help Britain in the Atlantic; that should the war last long enough for American armaments to be built up, he would give them to England, and that should the war end with Hitler defeating England and France, America would be "sweet and polite and gracious" toward Germany for two years, during which she would build up her armed forces regardless of cost. Roosevelt said Germany would be crushed if she tried to attack Canada or the Caribbean. Thus, a former attorney general in the pay of a known Nazi corporation supplied Hitler with secret intelligence on the private thoughts of the President.

General Aniline and Film could not have functioned as a branch office of N.W.7. the German Secret Service and The Fraternity without help in the Senate and in the House. Hans Thomsen's private memoranda allege that GAF, in addition to financing N.W.7. agents and the A.O. in America, supplied funds to significant figures of the House to secure propaganda arrangements. A telegram from Thomsen to Joachim von Ribbentrop, the Foreign Minister in Berlin, dated June 12, 1940, read:

> A well known Republican Congressman who works in close collaboration with the special official of Press Affairs will invite some 50 isolationist Republican Congressmen on a 3-day visit to the Party Convention, so that they may work on the delegates of the Republican Party in favor of an isolationist foreign policy. $3,000 are required.

In addition, the Republican in question is prepared to form a small ad hoc Republican committee, which, as a counterblast to the full-page advertisement by the [William Allen] White committee, "Stop Hitler Now," would, during the Party Convention, publish in all of the leading American newspapers a full-page advertisement with the impressive appeal "Keep America Out of War." The cost of this would be about $60,000 to $80,000, of which half will, in all probability, be borne by his Republican friends. In view of the unique opportunity I have accepted the proposal. I request telegraphic instructions as to whether [the project] is of interest and if it is, that the funds referred to be transferred.

Ribbentrop's office cabled back on June 16: "The Foreign Minister agrees to the adoption of the countermeasures against pro-Ally propaganda activities in the U.S.A." The money was released and paid to the congressman.

Who was he? Representative Stephen A. Day, a pro-Nazi from Illinois, in partnership with a group of ardent admirers of Hitler including Senator Rush D. Holt of West Virginia and Senator Ernest Lundeen of Minnesota.

On July 19, 1940, Thomsen reported the success of the mission. He telegraphed Berlin: "As I have reported, isolationist Republican Congressmen at the Republican Convention succeeded in affixing firmly to the Party platform the language of an isolationist foreign policy that will not let itself become entangled in a European war. Nothing has leaked out about the assistance we rendered in this. . . . For travel assistance and costs of the advertisements, $4,350 have been disbursed, which please refund to the Embassy."

As the international situation drew America to the brink of war, Max Ilgner and his Uncle Hermann became increasingly nervous about the future of their New York operation. They summoned two crucial directors of GAF to a meeting in Milan, on May 2, 1941, to discuss how best they could function if Hitler and Roosevelt clashed in war. These men were Alfredo E. Moll and Ernest K. Halbach—both of whom were Americans. Moll and Halbach agreed that they would slip drugs and patents to South America through an American export firm called Fezandie and Sperrle, which had an impeccable background and would not be seized in time of war. Hugh Williamson, a director of General Aniline, allegedly handled materials and agents. Meanwhile, Halbach arranged to have his own subsidiary, General Dyestuffs, reconstructed as an American company that also would not be subject to seizure. In New York, Dietrich Schmitz bundled all the incriminating Chemnyco documents into a furnace and watched them burn.

On May 9, 1941, Attorney General Robert H. Jackson yielded to pressure from Roosevelt. He seized American I.G.'s deposits at the National City Bank of New York. But it turned out that only $250,000 of the half-billion-dollar corporation account was in the bank vault. Evidently, Ilgner had good contacts, because only six weeks later all except $25,000 of the money was unfrozen. It looked as though I.G. had gotten away with everything, but Morgenthau and Roosevelt froze all Swiss holdings in the United States and with them, American I.G. Its Swiss cloak had proved its undoing for the time being.

Sosthenes Behn of ITT proved to be a useful Fraternity member when he stepped in on Göring's suggestion to try to buy General Aniline and Film, thus Americanizing it, and removing the Swiss freeze order, and preventing it from seizure in time of war. He would make a neat exchange of ITT's German properties so that these, too, would escape seizure. The inescapable National City Bank naturally encouraged the transaction, but Hermann Schmitz was convinced that Behn was trying to outfox him and instead he decided to sell the company to one of its own subsidiaries. Schmitz outsmarted himself. The deal nearly went through but it was too much for Morgenthau, who stopped it. Schmitz tried again. Part of the American I.G. shares were owned by a Dutch subsidiary. He tried to have that subsidiary buy out GAF, but Morgenthau stopped that arrangement, too.

With the advent of Pearl Harbor, Morgenthau set his sights on an outright seizure of GAF for the duration. He had already closed down or nationalized fifty related firms of which he was suspicious. Shortly after Pearl Harbor, Morgenthau begged Roosevelt to let Treasury run GAF instead of the Department of Justice or the Office of the Alien Property Custodian, which was then in the process of being formed. He was strongly opposed to Roosevelt's suggestion that the tycoon Leo T. Crowley, a bête noire of his, should take over General Aniline and Film as Alien Property Custodian. He didn't trust Crowley, an appointee of the weak and vacillating Attorney General Francis Biddle. He knew that Crowley, a big, bragging, loudmouthed man, was a close friend of the corporations: a protector of big money in the Jesse H. Jones mold. Crowley had begun as a Wisconsin delivery boy, had fought his way up through the electrical business. A prominent Roman Catholic, Knight of Columbus, and recipient of the Order of St. Gregory, the Great Order of Knights, from Pope Pius XI, he was a pillar of the business establishment and, Morgenthau felt, the last person on earth to take over General Aniline and Film.

While the Crowley matter remained undecided, Morgenthau, on January 13, 1942, invaded General Aniline and Film and began sacking some obviously pro-Nazi personnel. Roosevelt was 100 percent behind him and told him that "in case anybody asks you, you can say that the President [says] 'Kill the son-of-a-bitch.' "

However, Roosevelt almost simultaneously undermined Morgenthau's power over the company by putting in temporary charge of it a servant of big business, the wealthy lawyer John E. Mack. Mack brought in the ever-scheming William Bullitt as chairman of the board. Mack opposed the removal of Nazi officers and flatly refused Morgenthau's demand that he stop using them in a consulting capacity. Morgenthau was disgusted by the huge salaries Mack and Bullitt were drawing for simply covering for Nazis. Mack even tried to set up a so-called "plant management committee," staffed in its entirety by hardcore former I.G. Farben executives.

On February 16, 1942, Morgenthau won a round against Mack by seizing 97 percent of the shares of GAF. Bullitt resigned at once. Mack stayed on, furiously arguing with Morgenthau and his policy. Meanwhile, Roosevelt kept mentioning that Crowley was waiting in the wings. Frustrated, angry with the President, Morgenthau wrote to Harry Hopkins on February 26, "Roosevelt wants to be in the position that if I go ahead and clean all of this up, he doesn't know anything about it, and he can say he doesn't know anything about it."*

Hopkins conveyed his fury to the President, who on March 5 at last told Morgenthau to "proceed at once with Aniline." However, scarcely a week later, Roosevelt suddenly appointed Crowley the head of General Aniline and Film! It was typical of Roosevelt's equivocation that he would do this. Within twenty-four hours of taking of-

*Blum, John Morton: *From the Morgenthau Diaries: Years of War, 1941–1945:* Boston: Houghton Mifflin.

fice, Crowley put Ernest K. Halbach, perhaps the most committed pro-Farben executive in the whole organization, in as chairman. He declined to fire him even when Halbach was indicted three times for dealing with Farben after Pearl Harbor. To Morgenthau's intense disgust he hiked his salary from $36,000 to $82,000 a year and with shocking boldness reappointed Alfredo E. Moll, Halbach's collaborator, as GAF head of sales in South America. Both men were given back shares that Morgenthau had seized, and their bank accounts at the National City Bank were unfrozen on Crowley's specific instruction. Nor was Crowley content with this. His partner in the multimillion-dollar firm Standard Gas and Electric was the immensely wealthy Victor Emanuel, who had obtained control of SGE with the aid of the Schröder banks. Crowley continued to receive a salary from SGE and from the J. Henry Schröder Bank of New York while remaining Alien Property Custodian! John Foster Dulles, a close friend of Crowley's and Halbach's, became special legal counsel for Crowley. He was also Halbach's attorney, suing the government for the recovery of funds.

By 1944, after Crowley had been in charge of GAF for two years, he and Francis Biddle had still failed to try three antitrust indictments returned against General Aniline and Film on December 19, 1941, accusing the corporation of being part of the world trade conspiracy for Hitler. They had failed to enforce its acceptance of consent decrees that would bar it permanently from resuming its ties with I.G. Farben. They had failed to merge it with General Dyestuffs, which still got 10 percent of all GAF sales. They had not released GAF's patents, nor had they prepared a report showing which of those patents had been given it by the Nazi government for protection from seizure during the war.

I. F. Stone led a storm of criticism against Crowley in *PM* and *The Nation*. Crowley "resigned"—only to find himself in the even more important position of Foreign Economic Administrator. In an editorial in *PM*, on February 10, 1944, Stone wrote: "'Crowley's resignation is not enough. . . . We hope that, in picking a new Alien Property Custodian, the President will pick a man who, unlike Crowley, is not dependent on private salaries for the bulk of his income. . . . [We suggest the government] remove from the board of General Aniline and Film any men associated with Victor Emanuel, the

Schröder banking interests, Standard Oil or any company linked by business ties with I.G. Farben before the war.'' The article continued, ''Throw open to American business all the dyestuffs, chemical, pharmaceutical and other patents owned by General Aniline directly or through its subsidiary, Winthrop Chemical . . . break up General Aniline into smaller companies under permanent American ownership, each handling a different one of General Aniline's business interests, so that we may be rid of the monopolistic power this German-controlled firm exercised in so many products.''

It goes without saying that none of these ideas were followed by the President.

It was three months after Crowley left his post in March 1944, that further details of his iniquities came to light. William La Varre of the Department of Commerce charged before a Senate Postal Committee meeting on June 1, 1944, that censored information was being distributed by Crowley through the U.S. government against the nation's best interests. He said that two men representing themselves as salesmen for General Aniline and Film sought from him data from a censored message about Eastman Kodak for use in a film sales campaign in Latin America. He refused to give the information. La Varre told the committee that instead of freezing General Aniline, Crowley was running it in competition with Kodak. The GAF reps had returned to Crowley and then gone back to La Varre with letters saying they were working for the Alien Property Custodian and they must have the secret data. In view of the fact the instruction came from the government, La Varre had felt obliged to hand it over. General Aniline had beaten Kodak hollow below Panama.

Worse, La Varre found out that when the Mexican government made a deal with American Cyanamid for the operation of seized Nazi chemical companies, two of Crowley's officials flew to Mexico City in 1944 and bribed everyone in sight to break the arrangement in favor of General Aniline.

Crowley was not punished. Meanwhile, John Foster Dulles represented Mrs. Ernest Halbach in suing the Alien Property Custodian's office for the return of her husband's remaining Nazi shares. Crowley had been replaced by his assistant, James E. Markham, as Custodian. Markham was also a director of Standard Gas and Electric! It is scarcely surprising that Dulles had no problems with Markham in winning the case. Halbach received a total of $696,554,000 for properties that the government had seized—plus the compound interest paid by the U.S. Treasury.

One of the multitudinous branches of I.G. Farben before and during World War II was the General Aniline and Film associate Sterling Products, Inc., the colossal drug empire partly financed by the National City Bank, that manufactured in connection with its subsidiaries, the Winthrop Chemical Company and the Bayer Company. Sterling, Winthrop, and Bayer distributed the famous pharmaceutical products known as aspirin and Phillips Milk of Magnesia. Millions of Americans would have been shocked to learn that by their use of these familiar nostrums they were helping to finance an army of secret agents north and south of Panama who supplemented the Max Ilgner N.W.7. spy network in supplying information on every aspect of American military possibilities.

A close friend of Hermann Schmitz's, a director of American I.G. and General Aniline and Film, William E. Weiss was chairman of Sterling. He was a tough, stocky, aggressive German-American from Wheeling, West Virginia. Episcopalian, pillar of the community, expert chemist, he built his flourishing business from the base of a small drugstore. He early formed an intimate friendship not only with Schmitz but with Wilhelm Mann, director of Farben's pharmaceutical division.

American Bayer, the developer of the aspirin, had been seized by the World War I Alien Property Custodian in 1918 and closed down. In buying the company in 1919, Weiss had to sign a pledge that he would never let anyone obtain control of it who was not "one hundred percent loyal to the United States."

Within six months of signing the agreement, Weiss got in touch with Hermann Schmitz of Farben to find methods of entering into collusion with America's former enemy and circumventing the Versailles Treaty, which did not permit Germany to build up its drug industry. His first move was characteristic. Another Pennsylvanian—the brisk, no-nonsense Pittsburgh Scots-Irish attorney Earl McClintock—had been second-in-command to the Alien Property Custodian in charge of the German properties. Weiss hired this bright, smooth, fast-talking young man away from the Custodian office at

$13,000 a year, $10,000 more than he had been getting, and made him a junior partner. In 1920, McClintock traveled to Baden-Baden in Germany. In meetings with Carl Bosch and Hermann Schmitz, he reestablished the very links with German Bayer that he himself had legally broken off on behalf of the U.S. government a mere nine months before.

He helped to set up a clandestine network of agents in South America, threading through cities and small towns in order to form one of the most powerful drug cartels in the world. In the 1920s, Sterling wholly owned Bayer in the United States. The two companies operated in separate offices and factories, but were bound together as closely as twin threads.

In 1926, Herbert Hoover as Secretary of Commerce set up a Chemical Advisory Committee with Frank A. Blair of Sterling, Walter C. Teagle of Standard Oil, and Lammot du Pont, brother of Irénée, on the board. Two years later Sterling Dyestuffs was sold by Weiss to the old and well-established American firm of Grasselli, which merged with Du Pont and finally became part of General Aniline and Film. Thus, The Fraternity strands were knitted together almost from the beginning.

During the 1920s, Weiss and I.G. had signed a fifty-year agreement in which they literally carved up the world into market areas, with each assuming control of specific regions as far as New Zealand and South Africa. They jointly set up Alba Pharmaceutical Co. I.G. controlled 50 percent of Alba. And Winthrop, Alba, Sterling, and I.G. interchanged board members in a thirty-year game of economic musical chairs.

In 1928 a Nazi agent joined the company. This man was Edward A. Rumely, an independent financial consultant to Henry and Edsel Ford—those founder members of The Fraternity.

In World War I, Rumely had been a leading German propagandist, working with Westrick's partner, Fraternity lawyer Dr. Heinrich Albert, later head of German Ford. Rumely had spent $200,000 on an advertising campaign urging the readers of 619 newspapers to protest sending war supplies to the Allies. He had bought the New York *Evening Mail* as a German front. In 1918 he was arrested on charges of trading with the enemy but, although convicted, he only served one month in jail. Henry Ford had used influence with President Calvin Coolidge. The day Rumely left prison, Ford, with a touch of black humor, handed him a parcel of Liberty Bonds as a stake.

Rumely remained a fanatical German nationalist and an early Nazi party member. He proved to be Sterling's chief advisor, working closely with Weiss to set up nascent Nazi organizations below Panama. He was greatly aided by Alfredo E. Moll, who continued to function in World War II under the malign aegis of Leo T. Crowley. To make the picture complete, Weiss used the Dulles brothers as one set of lawyers and, as another, Edward S. Rogers and partners, connected to the Rogers Standard Oil family and formerly legal advisor to the Alien Property Custodian.

Yet another valuable connection came in 1929, when Weiss gave the vice-presidency of Sterling to Edward Terry Clark, secretary to President Coolidge and later to President Hoover.

Clark headed a Washington lobby in I.G.'s favor that continued to function in various forms until after World War II. Ten years later, after Clark's death, his papers were sold by his wife to an obscure hobby shop on Seventeenth Street in Washington, just around the corner from the White House. The owner, Charles Kohn, specialized in rare documents, stamps, coins, and autographs. A tiny item announced in the press that the Clark letters, which contained details of the I.G. Farben connections, were in the shop. Within two hours of reading the announcement, a representative of the German government pretending to be a document collector turned up with $100,000 in crisp new banknotes. Kohn refused to part with the letters at any price: a Jewish veteran of World War I, he had a nose for German spies. Next day a beautiful young woman appeared, offering money and physical inducements. Again, Kohn refused. However, when he handed the letters over to the Library of Congress, the incriminating documents had disappeared. They have never been traced.

Throughout the 1930s, Weiss used every avenue for political propaganda, collection of strategical information, and efforts to suppress equivalent drug production by loyal American companies. On March 29, 1933, Farben's Max Ilgner—by now a Nazi officer in Gestapo uniform—sent a message to Max Wojahn, Sterling export manager for South America, which read, in part: "You are asked to refrain from objecting to 'indecencies' committed by our [Nazi] government. . . . Immediately upon receipt of this letter, you are to contribute to the spread of information best adapted to the conditions of your country and to the editors of influential papers, or by circulars to physicians and customers; and particularly to that part of our letter which states that in all the lying tales of horror [about Germany] there is not one word of truth.''

It was agreed that no anti-Nazi newspaper would receive advertisements from Sterling. Indeed, an advertising contract would be canceled if the paper changed to an anti-Nazi attitude.

In 1933, after the accession of Hitler, Weiss in his correspondence with Farben's Rudolf Mann, indicated that he was ''worried about the condition of Germany.'' However, Mann, who had embraced the Nazi doctrine with alacrity from the start, reassured Weiss that in Germany things would be very much better under the Nazi party. Weiss stated that he was not inclined to believe the ugly rumors of things that were happening in Germany but he wanted a more substantial report. Mann replied, completely endorsing the National Socialist government. Noting that there had been ''a few unfortunate cases'' he quoted as an excuse the German proverb *''Wo Gehobelt Wird, Da fallen Spane''* (''Where one shaves, the shavings fall''), which had become popular in Germany a few days before when Göring used it in the course of a speech. There was further correspondence of the same type between Weiss and Mann.

In the fall of 1933, Weiss made a trip to Germany. His thirty-second wedding anniversary was celebrated with great pomp among Gestapo leaders in Munich. After his return, in a letter of November 17, 1933, Weiss assured Rudolf Mann that his ''American friends were naturally very much interested in our trip and we made many inquiries as to existing conditions in Europe. I have informed them of the remarkable strides made in Germany and you may rest assured that I will help to give an enthusiastic report of the conditions as I viewed them in Germany and the splendid progress that the country has made under Herr Hitler.''

A young and feisty former employee of I.G., Howard Ambruster, constantly hammered away at Sterling's pro-Nazi activities. Football coach at Rutgers, engineer, liberal journalist, chemist, editor, builder, and contractor, he was a robust, muscular jack-of-all-trades who spent a lifetime trying to strip bare Sterling's influences in Washington. But he had little chance of success. His numerous memoranda to congressmen and senators were ignored. Every effort was made to silence him.

Ignoring such small fry, Weiss and Earl McClintock maneuvered through the Depression years to insure Sterling's rise to the most important pharmaceutical corporation in the United States. In 1936, McClintock almost pulled off a major coup. Irritated by the Securities and Exchange Commission's investigations into Sterling's activities, he pulled several strings to take over as SEC chairman. Fortunately for American security, he did not achieve his purpose. As Europe moved toward war, he found other protections. He and Weiss poured a large sum of money into the Democratic National Committee—and the Republican National Committee as well—to make sure that whoever won the presidency would prove supportive. In May 1938, McClintock traveled to Basle to confer with Hermann Schmitz and Kurt von Schröder during meetings of the Bank for International Settlements. The subject of the discussion was the best way of handling Sterling if Roosevelt brought the United States into the war. The conference members agreed that the vast funds earned by Sterling from distributing Bayer products in Latin America would be held in the J. Henry Schröder Bank of New York until the end of the war. In return for this arrangement, Sterling Products in Germany and in the countries Germany would occupy would be held in the Stein Bank of Cologne for the duration. As for the all-important Bayer patents, which could easily be seized by the U.S. government if they were German-controlled, they would be sanitized by transferal to Sterling as American patents for the duration.

I.G. was to continue its Latin American operation under the Sterling cloak. Goods would be stockpiled for the duration or relabeled in order to disguise their origin to avoid the freezing of their distribution as enemy products. A further meeting took place in Florence, Italy, in February 1940, with Europe at war. Schmitz and Schröder again met with McClintock and reconfirmed the arrangements. In an addendum to the original agreement, funds earned in South America would be held in local banks for use by Nazis in exile.

It would have been impossible to achieve these arrangements without powerful contacts in Washington. Thomas Corcoran, the famous

"Tommy the Cork," became first the unofficial, then the official lawyer for Sterling. Eventually, he became a director of the corporation.

In 1934, Corcoran introduced his brother David to Weiss. David wanted a job. He was an automobile salesman with no other experience to speak of, but Weiss hired him on the spot to take over Sterling's South American operation.

That operation became a fabulous resource for Nazi Germany. In his 15,000-word report to the Truman defense committee in 1942, the young and keen-witted Assistant Attorney General Norman Littell stated: "When the Nazi government pressed I.G. Farben for money in 1938, it drew on Sterling Products Inc. or its subsidiaries."

The shipments to South America continued from Germany until the outbreak of war in September 1939. The British blockade created the same problems that it had for Davis and for Standard. Therefore, Hermann Schmitz was compelled to hand over his South American distribution to Sterling. The drug supply continued uninterrupted, emanating more and more from New York.

On September 11, 1939, ten days after war broke out in Europe, Weiss took over the operation of the Latin American businesses in order to avoid seizure if the United States should enter the war. In addition he made arrangements to stockpile products for the German agencies to last for at least five years. With $2 million in stock and $30 million in investments in actual medication in South America, Weiss and Earl McClintock fought desperately to save their Nazi association. In February 1940, McClintock flew to Rome to confer with I.G.'s Rudolf Mann to tell him once again that the alliances would continue whether or not the United States came into the war. Mann refused initially on the ground he might be executed for trading with Germany's potential enemy. He was evidently more afraid of Hitler than McClintock was of Roosevelt.

Mann said that providing Sterling took care of the German businesses south of Panama, it would be possible to continue the association without actual contact visible to the Nazi government. The National City Bank characteristically agreed to protect the arrangement indefinitely and not show on any statements that any of the dealings took place. The reason for this was a fear not of the U.S.

government finding out but of the information slipping into the hands of German agents.

Max Wojahn of Sterling dealt with the National City Bank loan that would help finance dealings with the enemy: "To avoid the appearance of this loan on the balance sheet at the end of each year, we would cancel it late in December and renew it early in January."

On May 31, 1941, I.G. began to make the transfers. It handed over 75 percent of its Argentine operation to Sterling in return for money advanced in helping I.G. to finance an Argentine laboratory helping the Nazis in Buenos Aires. This reached the attention of the U.S. Department of Justice, which ordered the money transferred to "miscellaneous income of the Bayer Company" on the ground that transactions with I.G. were illegal and that the matter might reach the attention of the public.

Under pressure from Henry Morgenthau, on August 15, 1941, Weiss signed a consent decree in return for minimal fines in which Sterling and Bayer would cease their association for the duration. By now most of the Bayer operation was tucked under the Sterling cloak. Weiss promised he would not sell Bayer products in South America under German names. He broke the promise within twenty-five days of signing the agreement. On September 10 SFI, a Sterling subsidiary in Rio, advised New York that it was handling its aspirin product under the old German name. Instead of instructing his agent to discontinue the distribution, Wojahn told him to proceed as usual.

Again under pressure from Morgenthau, who ceaselessly hammered away at the board, Weiss left the company on December 3, 1941, and returned to his home in Wheeling, West Virginia. However, he continued to exercise an influence behind the scenes. He made two trips to Albany to attend board meetings at which he sought to state his case for being reinstated, but this was out of the question: the company's image was tarnished enough already. Back in Wheeling, he refused to remove his effects from his office. During the Christmas vacation he wrote asking for information on products from the Sterling secret laboratory. Even as late as February 1942 he still had done nothing to clean out his office. He suggested to his successor, James Hill, that he should have a separate entrance built and his office could be kept in the building. Hill explained that this would not be acceptable to Treasury. Hill warned Weiss that Morgenthau might treat him as harshly as he was treating some of the board of General Aniline and Film. On February 23, Hill returned again and Weiss was still installed. Hill screamed at Weiss that for the company's own good he must leave at once. On March 10, Hill made a fourth trip to Wheeling and nothing had been done. Weiss had taken off to Arizona on a vacation, leaving his office intact. Hill shouted at Weiss's secretary, who refused to move her boss's belongings. Hill thereupon ordered the plant superintendent to remove the secretary and the remainder of Weiss's effects from the premises in twenty-four hours. His instructions were carried out.

When Weiss returned, he was devastated to see what had happened. Completely blackballed, he became a kind of ghost, walking or driving meaninglessly around Wheeling for eighteen months. In March 1943 he drove his car head on into another and was killed instantly.

The new management of Sterling was almost as unsatisfactory— except for James Hill. Earl McClintock, who had so coolly fed his own colleague to the wolves, stayed on. Meanwhile, some three weeks after Weiss's resignation, on December 31, U.S. Military Intelligence had intercepted a cable from the Sterling headquarters to Mexico City and Venezuela stating under the heading Top Secret, "In order that shipments . . . be afforded greater security, it is requested that you designate different consignees which are perfectly neutral, and to whom we will ship the goods in lots of 40 or 50 cases after repacking in neutral packing cases following a period of storage in a warehouse. It is possible for us to obtain consignments in the Western coast ports to avoid having U.S. espionage be able to ask in pursuing the matter the transportation route of the consignment.''

The cable was examined in Washington, but the consignments were not discontinued. On February 4, 1942, J. Edgar Hoover sent a private memorandum to Under Secretary of State Adolf Berle with a report on the Sterling operation in Chile. He revealed that Werner Siering of the local operation was head of the espionage service in that country. Hoover wrote, ''Not only does this group keep careful files on the principal opponents of Nazism, but checks on each German citizen to test his loyalty to Hitler. This organization has agents in all American-controlled copper mines, the American and British-controlled night raid works, as well as in large chemical and financial houses. Through these agents they keep check on all important economic developments.'' The report continues at great length to disclose that Siering and his corporation had aided German crewmen of the scuttled German battleship *Admiral Graf Spee* to escape from prison and go by Japanese ship to Japan.

Siering also worked with local Nazi officials to collect information on the political and economic situation, the activities of Chile's leaders, the production of minerals in Chile and Bolivia, general conditions in industry and commerce, maritime and military movement.

In April 1942, Morgenthau's staff investigated Sterling's headquarters in Manhattan. The investigative team found that a man who for sixteen years had worked for I.G. Farben was still employed as an executive. The team found that an attorney who had been executive vice-president of General Aniline and Film had continued to represent Sterling on its legal staff until February.

On May 28, 1942, the Lima, Peru, manager of Sterling wrote to his Buenos Aires office stating that the Peruvian government was suspicious of Sterling's operations and wanted to control its business dealings. The letter stated that no such control would be permitted. No interference with Sterling's dealings with Proclaimed List nationals would be tolerated.

On August 27, 1942 Phillip W. Thayer, senior economic assistant of the American Embassy at Santiago, Chile, wrote to Mario Justiniano, manager of the Sterling laboratories in that city, urging Sterling to collect ''the sum of 500,827 pesos, the equivalent of $14,861.81 which is owed you by Quimica Bayer, of Santiago, a branch of I.G. Farben.'' Thus, an official of the U.S. government authorized a branch of a New York company to collect money from a Nazi corporation in time of war. The note continues with the words: ''It would also be very much appreciated if you will inform us as to the steps which are now being taken by your firm in the United States to obtain the necessary commission and the license to effect this cooperation.''

On August 30, 1942, Justiniano wrote to the Securities and Exchange Control Commission in Washington to seek the license. He informed the SECC that there would be a problem in getting the money. He would have to obtain it through the German-owned Banco Aleman Transatlantico in Buenos Aires. He wanted to avoid this transference because of the unfavorable attention that a disclosure of it might cause. He advised SECC that his lawyer had approached Bayer to obtain payment in Chilean pesos and cash. The money came from the Banco Aleman Transatlantico and was transferred to a Chilean bank.

Justiniano sent McClintock a copy of the letter to the SECC. McClintock immediately cabled him that the arrangement was unacceptable and that Sterling *must approach the Banco Aleman direct*. Thus, McClintock personally authorized an arrangement with the enemy.

There was some delay in getting a response from Washington. The detailed interoffice memoranda between Treasury and State make interesting reading. Justiniano was complaining that he was having difficulties getting letters through to New York so that the long delay could be checked on by head office. He seemed to think that some foreign intelligence service must have intercepted the mail. Treasury checked into the matter and found that in fact letters were coming through safely but perhaps Justiniano was afraid of their being seen. State wavered, then finally agreed to the transaction.

On November 4, 1943, Dudley G. Dwyre, legal counsel of the U.S. Embassy in Montevideo, Uruguay, reported to State that Sterling in that country was utterly failing to meet its agreements with the U.S. government to desist from trading with the enemy. Sterling's local branch was still using Nazi trademarks and retaining Nazi employees, every one of whom had worked for Bayer, in defiance of the Consent Decree. Indeed, a local Sterling executive had been hired from Bayer, which he also had run. The Sterling laboratories were still part-owned by Proclaimed List firms. A local lawyer for Sterling's subsidiary was a known Nazi.

Various dispatches from embassies throughout 1943 assert that McClintock actually bribed Chilean government officials to enable him to continue business connections with the Nazis. That same year a Treasury team arrived in South America to investigate Sterling from Panama to Cape Horn. In many areas Sterling had done much to clean house, transferring patents and products to American ownership from Bayer management. But the pockets of collusion and collaboration—chiefly in Uruguay and Chile—survived.

Norman Littell, antitrust lawyer in the Attorney General's Department, spent most of the war years fighting Sterling and its protections within the U.S. government. He was appalled by the infringements of the Consent Decree and he was upset by the fact that the famous Tommy Corcoran was handling Sterling. He felt that Corcoran exercised too great an influence on Attorney General Francis Biddle. He was aggravated by a statement Biddle made to *The New York Times* on September 6, 1941, a statement that Littell felt showed Biddle's weakness and vacillations and lies to protect the corporation: "Sterling Products has always been a wholly American company, and none of the profits of the sale of Bayer Aspirin has been shared among foreign investors. Similarly, none of the domestic American products or achievement of the Bayer Company was involved in relations with I.G. Farben nor is there any foreign interest in the numerous other subsidiaries of Sterling Products engaged in the proprietary medicine field."

Another bugbear of Littell's was Alien Property Custodian Leo T. Crowley, who, as part of the "house cleaning" of Sterling, took over the Bayer patents for Atabrine. This substitute for quinine was indispensable during quinine shortages caused by the Japanese seizure of Malaya and the Dutch East Indies. Without quinine, or Atabrine, thousands of young Americans died of malaria on the tropical warfronts.

Through 1942, Littell tried desperately with the help of the former American I.G. employee Howard Ambruster to persuade Crowley to release Atabrine for use by American soldiers. Crowley refused. Meanwhile, as hitherto classified documents show, the Atabrine was freely distributed from heavy stockpiles or even from new supplies through Proclaimed List customers in South America.

The Atabrine story leaked to I. F. Stone and others of the press, who backed Littell and Ambruster in an all-out assault on Crowley. Owing to their pressure Senator Homer T. Bone, chairman of the Senate Patents committee, announced that there would be a full-scale hearing on Atabrine. But the hearing was postponed again and again. Despite the fact that Biddle had thousands of documents proving the suppression of Atabrine, he refused to move on the evidence. The matter dragged on until August, when at last a hearing began; but it was quickly suspended when five members of the patents committee refused to discuss the matter.

In August 1942, Thurman Arnold of the Department of Justice Antitrust Division wrote in *The Atlantic Monthly:* ''The spectacle of the production of this essential drug, left so long to the secret manipulation of a German-American combination during a period when Germany was preparing for war against us, is too shocking to need elaboration.''

In March 1943, Ambruster went to see Earl G. Harrison, new head of the Immigration and Naturalization Service. He brought with him a list of every American simultaneously connected to Sterling Products and Proclaimed List companies. He demanded to know why none of these people had been interned, denaturalized, or deported. Harrison told him that Immigration was forbidden to discuss the subject. Ambruster asked for a regulation upon which that refusal might be based. He was told that no such regulation would be supplied.

Ambruster now wrote to Assistant Attorney General Wendell Berge. Berge was in charge of the Criminal Division of the Department of Justice. He asked the same questions. There was no reply. Berge said later on the telephone, ''I am not permitted to reply to your inquiries.''

Assistant Attorney General Littell became so persistent a gadfly that on November 18, 1944, Roosevelt, under pressure from Littell's enemies, called for the young man's resignation. Instead of tendering it, Littell wrote a 15,000-word blast, exposing the intricate connections between Sterling, Tommy Corcoran, and the enemy. Biddle insisted Roosevelt fire Littell. Roosevelt hesitated. He dreaded personal confrontations of any kind. But Biddle finally won. Roosevelt dismissed Littell for insubordination, saying, ''When statements made by Norman Littell [criticizing the government] first appeared in the papers I put it to him . . . that I hoped for his future career he would resign. . . . Under the circumstances my only alternative is to remove him from office which I have done today.''

In 1945, Littell at last found support in Congress. Representatives Al Smith of Wisconsin, and Jerry Voorhis of California entered Littell's charges against Sterling in the Congressional Record on January 22 of that year, demanding a full-scale investigation. The investigation never took place. Within a few days of the resolution being entered, it was removed from the agenda, and Biddle quietly resigned, ironically taking up the post of prosecutor at the Nuremberg Trials immediately afterward.

Just before Roosevelt died, the ailing President asked to see Littell, who recalls that in a charged meeting in the Oval Office he told the young man he would like to have seen Biddle impeached for treason but the difficulties were too great in his grievous physical condition. Littell asked Roosevelt why Biddle, of all people, was a judge at Nuremberg. Roosevelt did not reply.

9

The Car Connection

William Weiss's partner in General Aniline and Film, Edsel Ford, whose father, Henry Ford, was chairman of the Ford empire, played a complex part in The Fraternity's activities before and during World War II. The Ford chairman in Germany, in charge of all Ford operations after Pearl Harbor, was Dr. Heinrich Albert, partner until 1936 of Gerhardt Westrick in the law firm associated with the Dulles brothers—Sullivan and Cromwell.

Henry Ford was once ranked in popular polls as the third greatest man in history: just below Napoleon and Jesus Christ. His wealth may be gauged by the fact that when young Edsel turned twenty-one, the father took the boy into a private vault and gave him $1 million in gold. Henry Ford controlled more than half of the American automobile market by 1940: in the early years of the century, his famous Model T, the chariot of the common man, revolutionized the nation.

Lean and hard as a Grant Wood farmer, Henry Ford was a knotty puritan, dedicated to the simple ideals of early-to-bed, early-to-rise, plain food, and no adultery. He didn't drink and fought a lifetime against the demon tobacco.

He admired Hitler from the beginning, when the future Führer was a struggling and obscure fanatic. He shared with Hitler a fanatical hatred of Jews. He first announced his anti-Semitism in 1919, in the

New York *World,* when he expressed a pure fascist philosophy. He said, "International financiers are behind all war. They are what is called the international Jew: German-Jews, French-Jews, English-Jews, American-Jews . . . the Jew is a threat."

In Germany, Hitler was uttering identical sentiments. In 1920, Ford arranged for his *Dearborn Independent,* first published in 1918, to become a platform for his hatred of the Jews. Week after week the newspaper set out to expose some horror of Jewish misbehavior. The first anti-Semitic issue on May 22 carried the headline THE IN-TERNATIONAL JEW: THE WORLD'S PROBLEM. The leading article opened with the words "There is a race, a part of humanity, which has never been received as a welcome part . . ." and continued in the same vein to the end. A frequent contributor was a fanatical White Russian, Boris Brasol, who boasted in one piece: "I have done the Jews more injury than would have been done to them by ten pogroms."

Brasol was successively an agent of the Czar and of the U.S. Army Intelligence; later he became a Nazi spy.

Ford's book *The International Jew* was issued in 1927. A virulent anti-Semitic tract, it was still being widely distributed in Latin America and the Arab countries as late as 1945. Hitler admired the book and it influenced him deeply. Visitors to Hitler's headquarters at the Brown House in Munich noticed a large photograph of Henry Ford hanging in his office. Stacked high on the table outside were copies of Ford's book. As early as 1923, Hitler told an interviewer from the Chicago *Tribune,* "I wish that I could send some of my shock troops to Chicago and other big American cities to help." He was referring to stories that Ford was planning to run for President.

Ford was one of the few people singled out for praise in *Mein Kampf.* At Hitler's trial in 1924, Erhard Auer of the Bavarian Diet testified that Ford had given Hitler money. Ford formed crucial links in The Fraternity at an early stage. He appointed Gerhardt Westrick's partner Dr. Heinrich Albert as chairman of the Ford Company. Other prominent figures in that company were fanatically pro-Nazi. They included a grandson of the Kaiser and Carl Bosch, Schmitz's forerunner as head of I.G. Farben. Later, Carl Krauch of I.G. Farben became a director and Kurt von Schröder, as one might have predicted, handled the banking.

Carl Krauch testified in an interrogation in 1946:

I myself knew Henry Ford and admired him. I went to see Göring personally about that. I told Göring that I myself knew his son Edsel, too, and I told Göring that if we took the Ford independence away from them in Germany, it would aggrieve friendly relations with American industry in the future. I counted on a lot of success for the adaptation of American methods in Germany's industries, but that could be done only in friendly cooperation. Göring listened to me and then he said: "I agree. I shall see to it that the German Ford Company will not be incorporated in the Hermann Göring Company." So I participated regularly in the supervisory board meetings to inform myself about the business processes of Henry Ford and, if possible, to take a stand for the Henry Ford Works after the war had begun. Thus, we succeeded in keeping the Ford Works working and operating independently of our government's seizure.

Edsel Ford had a great deal to do with the European companies. He was different in character from his father. He was a nervous, high-strung man who tried to work off his extreme tensions and guilts over inherited wealth in a furious addiction to tennis and other sports. Darkly handsome, with a whipcord physique, he was miserable at heart. He could not relate to his father, who despised him, and his inner distress caused him severe stomach ulcers that developed into gastric cancer by the early 1940s. Nevertheless, he and his father had one thing in common. True figures of The Fraternity, they believed in Business as Usual in time of war.

Edsel was on the board of American I.G. and General Aniline and Film throughout the 1930s. He and his father, following their meetings with Gerhardt Westrick at Dearborn in 1940, refused to build aircraft engines for England and instead built supplies of the 5-ton military trucks that were the backbone of German army transportation. They arranged to ship tires to Germany despite the shortages; 30 percent of the shipments went to Nazi-controlled territories abroad. German Ford employee publications included such editorial statements as, "At the beginning of this year we vowed to give our best and utmost for final victory, in unshakable faithfulness to our Fuehrer." Invariably, Ford remembered Hitler's birthday and sent him 50,000 Reichsmarks a year. His Ford chief in Germany was responsible for selling military documents to Hitler. Westrick's partner Dr. Albert continued to work in Hitler's cause when that chief came to the United States to continue his espionage. In 1941, Henry Ford delivered a bitter attack on the Jews to *The Manchester Guardian* (February 16, 1941) saying inter alia, that the United States should make England and Germany fight until they both collapsed and that after that there would be a coalition of the powers.

And in 1941 he hired Charles Lindbergh as a member of his executive staff. Lindbergh had been one of the most vocal supporters of Hitler. Indeed, the advent of Pearl Harbor made no difference to Lindbergh's attitude. On December 17, 1941, ten days after the Japanese attack, Lindbergh said to a group of America Firsters at the home of prominent businessman Edwin S. Webster in New York,

> There is only one danger in the world—that is the yellow danger. China and Japan are really bound together against the white race. There could only have been one efficient weapon against this alliance. . . . Germany. . . . the ideal setup would have been to have had Germany take over Poland and Russia, in collaboration with the British, as a bloc against the yellow people and Bolshevism. But instead, the British and the fools in Washington had to interfere. The British envied the Germans and wanted to rule the world forever. Britain is the real cause of all the trouble in the world today.*

While Lindbergh took over as consultant, Edsel Ford began to concentrate on insuring that his interests in France would not be affected following the German invasion. Management of the Ford interests was in the hands of the impressively handsome and elegant Paris financier Maurice Dollfus, who had useful contacts with the Worms Bank and the Bank for International Settlements. Although he had little knowledge of manufacturing processes, Dollfus supplied much of the financing for the new sixty-acre Ford automobile factory at Poissy, eleven miles from Paris in the Occupied Zone. Under Dollfus the Poissy plant began making airplane engines in 1940, supplying them to the German government. It also built trucks for the German army, as well as automobiles. Carl Krauch and Hermann Schmitz were in charge of the operation from their headquarters in Berlin along with Edsel Ford at Dearborn.

After Pearl Harbor, Edsel Ford moved to protect the company's

*FBI report, December 18, 1941.

interest in Occupied France, even though this would mean collaboration with the Nazi government. Edsel and Dollfus decided to consolidate their operation in conjunction with Carl Krauch, Heinrich Albert, and Gerhardt Westrick in Germany. The problem they had was how to keep in touch, since their two countries were at war. In order to overcome this difficulty, Edsel traveled to Washington at the beginning of 1942 and entered into an arrangement with Assistant Secretary of State Breckinridge Long, who simultaneously was blocking financial aid to German-Jewish refugees by citing the Trading with the Enemy Act. Long agreed that it should be possible for letters to travel to and from Occupied France via Lisbon and Vichy. Since it would be too dangerous to risk the letters falling into the hands of the press or foreign agents, they would have to be carried by a Portuguese courier named George Lesto who, with clearance from the Nazi government, was permitted to travel in and out of Paris.

On January 28, 1942, Dollfus sent the first letter after Pearl Harbor to Edsel Ford in Dearborn, Michigan, via the Portuguese courier Lesto. Dollfus wrote that, "Since the state of war between U.S.A. and Germany I am not able to correspond with you very easily. I have asked Lesto to go to Vichy and mail to you the following information." He added that production was continuing as before, that trucks were being manufactured for the occupying Germans and the French, and that Ford was ahead of the French automobile manufacturers in supplying the enemy. Dollfus said he was getting support from the Vichy government to preserve the interests of the American shareholders and that a company in North Africa was being founded for the Nazis with ground plots in Oran. Amazingly, the letter concluded by saying, "I propose to send again Mr. Lesto to the States as soon as all formalities and authorizations are accomplished."

Edsel replied at length on May 13: "It is interesting to note that you have started your African company and are laying plans for a more peaceful future." He went on, "I have received a request from the State Department to make a recommendation for issuance of a visa to Mr. Lesto." However, the letter went on, Ford was uneasy about making the request; it was clear that he was nervous about the matter being disclosed.

The Royal Air Force, apparently not briefed on the world connections of The Fraternity, had just bombed the Poissy plant. Ford wrote on May 15 that photographs of the plant on fire were published in our newspapers here but fortunately no reference was made to the Ford Motor Company. In other words, Edsel was relieved that it was not made clear to the American public that he was operating the plant for the Nazis.

On February 11, 1942, Dollfus wrote again—that the results of the year up to December 31, 1941, showed a net profit for Ford's French branch of 58 million francs including payment for dealings with the Nazis.

On June 6, Dollfus wrote Edsel enclosing a memorandum prepared by George Lesto. The memo stated that the RAF had now bombed the plant four times, and that all machinery and equipment had been taken from the plant and scattered all over the country. Lesto was pleased to state that the Vichy government "agreed to pay for all damages." The reparation was "approved by the German government." Ford replied to this letter on July 17, 1942, expressing pleasure with this arrangement, congratulating Lesto on organizing the repayment, and saying that he had shown the letter to his father and to Charles E. Sorenson, and that they both joined him in sending best wishes to Dollfus and the staff, in the hope that they would continue to carry on the good work that they were doing.

Meanwhile, Dollfus and Heinrich Albert set up another branch of Ford in North Africa, headquartered in Vichy Algiers with the approval of I.G. Farben. It was to build trucks and armored cars for Rommel's army. In a lengthy report to the State Department dated July 11, 1942, Felix Cole, American Consul in Algiers, sent a detailed account of the planned operation, not complaining that the headquarters was located in the Occupied Zone of France or that Dollfus was prominent in the Pucheu* group of bankers that financed the factory through the Worms Bank, the Schröder Bank, and BIS correspondent in Paris. Cole remarked en passant, "The [Worms] firm is greatly interested in the efforts now being made to effect a compromise peace on behalf of Germany." Cole had put his finger on something: Dollfus was more than a mere Nazi collaborator working with Edsel Ford. He was a key link in The Fraternity's operation in Europe, scheming

---

*Pierre Pucheu, Vichy Minister of the Interior, who helped to leak the secret of Eisenhower's North African invasion plan to the Nazis and was executed by the Free French for treason in 1944.

with Pucheu, the Worms Bank, the Bank of France, the Chase, and the Bank for International Settlements.

The letter from Cole went on: "It is alleged that the main outlets for the new works [in Oran] will be southwards, but the population which is already getting plenty of propaganda *about the collaboration of French-German-American capital and the questionable (?) sincerity of the American war effort* * is already pointing an accusing finger at a transaction which has been for long a subject of discussion in commercial circles."

Dollfus wrote again on August 15, 1942; the letter reached Edsel Ford two weeks later. Dollfus stated that following the RAF bombing, production had been resumed in France at the same rate; that he was not permitted to say where the new plants were to which production had been disbursed but that they were four of the principal plants. He went on, "Machinery has been overhauled and repaired and some new machinery purchased so that the capital in machinery and equipment is completely restored to its pre-bombing status. I have named a manager in each plant and the methods and standards are the same as they were in Poissy. Essential repairs have been started at Poissy but work is slow because of the difficulty in obtaining materials."

In the rest of a very long letter, Dollfus pointed out that at this stage the Poissy and other works came directly under Dr. Heinrich Albert and a German officer named Tannen, in trust, "Mr. Tannen has in turn given me back most of the powers that I used to have previously to run our business, with the exception of certain ones that he does not hold himself, and some others which I believe should have been given me but anyhow they are not indispensable for me to continue to run the business normally." Dollfus added that Dr. Albert was clearly anxious to play a part "so as to appear a Good Samaritan after the war in the eyes of the Allies."

On September 29, 1942, Breckinridge Long wrote to Edsel enclosing a letter from Dollfus saying that Vichy's compensation payment to Ford to the tune of 38 million francs had been received. On October 8, Ford sent a letter of thanks.

In April 1943, Morgenthau and Lauchlin Currie conducted a lengthy investigation into the Ford subsidiaries in France, concluding that

* Author's italics.

"their production is solely for the benefit of Germany and the countries under its occupation" and that the Germans have "shown clearly their wish to protect the Ford interests" because of the "attitude of strict neutrality" maintained by Henry and Edsel Ford in time of war. And finally, "the increased activity of the French Ford subsidiaries on behalf of Germans receives the commendation of the Ford family in America."

Despite a report running to hundreds of thousands of words and crammed with exhaustive documentation including all the relevant letters, nothing whatsoever was done about the matter.

Meanwhile, Ford had gone on making special deals. On May 29, 1942, the Ford Motor Company in Edgewater, New Jersey, had shipped six cargoes of cars to blacklisted José O. Moll of Chile. Another consignee was a blacklisted enemy corporation, Lilienfeld, in Bolivia. On October 20, 1942, John G. Winant, U.S. Ambassador to London, coolly reported to Dean Acheson that two thousand German army trucks were authorized for repair by the Ford motor works in Berne. On the same day, Winant reported that the British Legation and the U.S. authorities recommended the Ford Motor Company of Belgium be blacklisted because its Zurich branch, on U.S. orders, was repairing trucks and converting the use of gasoline for trucks and cars of the German army in Switzerland.

In December 1943 a further report from Minister Leland Harrison in Berne said, "The Ford Motor Company in Zurich, acting for Cologne, supplies spare parts for the repair of Ford trucks and passenger cars to U.S. Ford Motor Company agents in Switzerland. Some of these parts are imported, which provides the enemy with clearing funds." Thus, one year after these matters were reported in Washington, trading with the enemy was continuing. All Swiss operations functioned under the guidance of Ford's Charles E. Sorenson.

Edsel died of cancer in 1943, but Sorenson went on with the dealings. On November 6, 1945, Maurice Dollfus, enemy collaborator, traveled to New York (by U.S. Army Air Transport Command) and gave an interview to *The New York Times* at the Ritz-Carlton Hotel. He discussed his operation during the war, but apparently nobody on the *New York Times* staff thought to question him on the nature of that operation, which remained a complete secret to the American public.

*   *   *

General Motors, under the control of the Du Pont family of Delaware, played a part in collaboration comparable with Ford's. General Aniline and Film had heavy investments in the company.

Irénée du Pont was the most imposing and powerful member of the clan. He was obsessed with Hitler's principles. He keenly followed the career of the future Führer in the 1920s, and on September 7, 1926, in a speech to the American Chemical Society, he advocated a race of supermen, to be achieved by injecting special drugs into them in boyhood to make their characters to order. He insisted his men reach physical standards equivalent to that of a Marine and have blood as pure as that in the veins of the Vikings. Despite the fact that he had Jewish blood in his own veins, his anti-Semitism matched that of Hitler.

Between 1932 and 1939, bosses of General Motors poured $30 million into I.G. Farben plants with the excuse that the money could not be exported. On several visits with Hermann Schmitz and Carl Krauch of Farben in Berlin in 1933, Wendell R. Swint, Du Pont's foreign relations director, discovered that I.G. and the gigantic Krupp industrial empire had arranged for all Nazi industry to contribute one half percent of its entire wage and salary roll to the Nazis even before they rose to power. Thus, Swint (who testified to this effect at the 1934 Munitions Hearings) admitted under oath that Du Pont was fully aware it was financing the Nazi Party through one half percent of its Opel wages and salaries as well as through its deals with I.G. and its building of armored cars and trucks.

Simultaneously with the rise of Hitler, the Du Ponts in 1933 began financing native fascist groups in America, including the anti-Semitic and antiblack American Liberty League and the organization known as Clark's Crusaders, which had 1,250,000 members in 1933. Pierre, Irénée, and Lammot du Pont and John Jacob Raskob funded the Liberty League, along with Alfred P. Sloan of General Motors. The League smeared Roosevelt as a communist, claimed the President was surrounded by Jews; and despite the fact that they were Jewish, the Du Ponts smeared Semitic organizations.

The connections between General Motors and the Nazi government began at the moment of Hitler's rise to power. Göring declined to annex General Motors and indeed received with pleasure William S. Knudsen, General Motors' president, who returned on October 6, 1933, to New York telling reporters that Germany was "the miracle of the twentieth century."

Early in 1934, Irénée du Pont and Knudsen reached their explosion point over President Roosevelt. Along with friends of the Morgan Bank and General Motors, certain Du Pont backers financed a coup d'état that would overthrow the President with the aid of a $3 million-funded army of terrorists, modeled on the fascist movement in Paris known as the Croix de Feu. Who was to be the figurehead for this ill-advised scheme, which would result in Roosevelt being forced to take orders from businessmen as part of a fascist government or face the alternative of imprisonment and execution? Du Pont men allegedly held an urgent series of meetings with the Morgans. They finally settled on one of the most popular soldiers in America, General Smedley Butler of Pennsylvania. Butler, a brave hero, had been awarded two Congressional Medals of Honor and his brilliant career as commandant of the Marine Corps had made him a legend. He would, the conspiratorial group felt, make an ideal replacement for Roosevelt if the latter proved difficult. These business chiefs found great support for their plan in Hermann Schmitz, Baron von Schröder, and the other German members of The Fraternity.

The backers of the bizarre conspiracy selected a smooth attorney, Gerald MacGuire, to bring word of the plan to General Butler. MacGuire agreed Butler would be the perfect choice. Butler had attacked the New Deal in public speeches.

MacGuire met with Butler at the latter's house in Newton Square, Pennsylvania, and in a hotel suite nearby. With great intensity the fascist attorney delivered the scheme to the general. Butler was horrified. Although there were many things about Roosevelt he disliked, a coup d'état amounted to treason, and Butler was nothing if not loyal to the Constitution. However, he disclosed nothing of his feelings. With masterful composure he pretended interest and waited to hear more.

When MacGuire returned, it was with news of more millions and more extravagant plans, which included turning America into a dictatorship with Butler as a kind of Hitler. Once more Butler was infuriated but kept quiet. After MacGuire left on the second occasion, the general got in touch with the White House. He told Roosevelt of the entire plan.

Roosevelt's state of mind can scarcely be imagined. He knew that in view of the backing from high banking sources, this matter could not be dismissed as some crackpot enterprise that had no chance of success. He was well aware of the powerful forces of fascism that could easily make America an ally of Nazism even that early, only one year after Hitler had risen to power.

On the other hand, Roosevelt also knew that if he were to arrest the leaders of the houses of Morgan and Du Pont, it would create an unthinkable national crisis in the midst of a depression and perhaps another Wall Street crash. Not for the first or last time in his career, he was aware that there were powers greater than he in the United States.

Nevertheless, the plan had to be deactivated immediately. The answer was to leak it to the press. The newspapers ran the story of the attempted coup on the front page, but generally ridiculed it as absurd and preposterous. When Thomas Lamont of the Morgan Bank arrived from Europe by steamer, he was asked by a crowd of reporters to comment. "Perfect moonshine! Too utterly ridiculous to comment upon!" was the reply.

Roosevelt couldn't quite let the matter rest. Under pressure from liberal Democrats he set up a special House committee to investigate. Butler begged the committee to summon the Du Ponts but the committee declined. Nor would it consent to call anyone from the house of Morgan. Then Butler dropped a bombshell. He gave interviews to the press announcing that none other than General Douglas MacArthur was a party to the plot. This again was dismissed by the press, and MacArthur laughed it off.

The committee hearings were a farce. MacGuire was allowed to get away with saying that Butler had "misunderstood" his intentions. Other witnesses lamely made excuses, and there the matter rested.

It was four years before the committee dared to publish its report in a white paper that was marked for "restricted circulation." They were forced to admit that "certain persons made an attempt to establish a fascist organization in this country . . . [The] committee was able to verify all the pertinent statements made by General Butler."

This admission that the entire plan was deadly in intent was not accompanied by the imprisonment of anybody. Further investigations disclosed that over a million people had been guaranteeed to join the scheme and that the arms and munitions necessary would have been supplied by Remington, a Du Pont subsidiary.

The Du Ponts' fascistic behavior was seen in 1936, when Irénée du Pont used General Motors money to finance the notorious Black Legion. This terrorist organization had as its purpose the prevention of automobile workers from unionizing. The members wore hoods and black robes, with skull and crossbones. They fire-bombed union meetings, murdered union organizers, often by beating them to death, and dedicated their lives to destroying Jews and communists. They linked to the Ku Klux Klan. Irénée du Pont encouraged General Motors foremen to join the Legion. In one episode a Detroit worker, Charles Poole, was brutally murdered by a gang of Black Legionists, several of whom belonged to the sinister Wolverine Republican League of Detroit. This organization had as its members several in big business. However, their names were kept out of the papers during the Poole case trial. It was brought out that at least fifty people, many of them blacks, had been butchered by the Legion, which swept through General Motors factories and had 75,000 members.

At the same time, the Du Ponts developed the American Liberty League, a Nazi organization whipping up hatred of blacks and Jews, love of Hitler, and loathing of the Roosevelts. Financed by Lammot and Irénée to the tune of close to $500,000 the first year, the Liberty League had a lavish thirty-one-room office in New York, branches in twenty-six colleges, and fifteen subsidiary organizations nationwide that distributed fifty million copies of its Nazi pamphlets. In September 1936, while Hitler at Nuremberg expressed his grand design for the Four-Year Plan, the Du Ponts and the American Liberty League poured thousands into backing Republican Alf Landon against Roosevelt in the election. Other backers were the American Nazi party and the German-American Bund.

The attempt to launch Landon failed, which made the Du Ponts hate Roosevelt even more. In outright defiance of Roosevelt's desire to improve working conditions for the average man, Knudsen of General Motors along with the Du Ponts instituted the speedup systems created by another prominent figure of The Fraternity, Charles Bedaux. These forced men to work at terrifying speeds on the assembly lines. Many died of the heat and the pressure, increased by fear of losing their jobs at a time when there were very few available. Irénée personally paid almost $1 million from his own pocket for armed and gas-equipped storm troops modeled on the Gestapo to sweep through the plants and beat up anyone who proved rebellious. He hired the Pinkerton Agency to send its swarms of detectives through the whole chemicals, munitions, and automobile empire to spy on left-wingers or other malcontents.

By the mid-1930s, General Motors was committed to full-scale production of trucks, armored cars, and tanks in Nazi Germany. The GM board could be guaranteed to preserve political, personal, and commercial links to Hitler. Alfred P. Sloan, who rose from president of GM to chairman in 1937, paid for the National Council of Clergymen and Laymen at Asheville, North Carolina, on August 12, 1936, at which John Henry Kirby, millionaire fascist lumberman of Texas, was prominent in the delivery of speeches in favor of Hitler. Others present, delivering equally Hitlerian addresses, were Governor Eugene D. Talmadge of Georgia and the Nazi Reverend Gerald L. K. Smith. Sloan frequently visited Berlin, where he hobnobbed with Göring and Hitler.

Graeme K. Howard was a vice-president of General Motors. Under FBI surveillance throughout his whole career with the company, he was an outright fascist who wrote a poisonous book, *America and a New World Order,* that peddled the line of appeasement, and a virtually identical doctrine to that of Hitler in terms of free trade and the restoration of the gold standard for the United States of Fascism in which General Motors would no doubt play a prominent part.

Another frequent visitor to Germany was the rugged, cheerful, hearty James D. Mooney, head of the European end of the business, directly in charge of the Adam-Opel production. On December 22, 1936, in Vienna, Mooney told U.S. diplomat George Messersmith, who despite his German family origin hated Hitler, "We ought to make some arrangement with Germany for the future. There is no reason why we should let our moral indignation over what happens in that country stand in the way." In other words, although the mass of Americans despised the Nazis, business must continue as usual. Messersmith was furious. He snapped back, "We can hardly be expected to trade with a country only so that it can get those articles which it intends to use against the peace of the world.''

In a report of December 23 to the Acting Secretary of State in Washington, Messersmith wrote, ''It is curious that Mooney and Col. Sosthenes Behn . . . both give this opinion. The factories owned by ITT in Germany are running full time and in double shifts and increasing their capacity for the simple reason that they are working almost entirely on government orders and for military equipment. The Opel works, owned by General Motors, are [also] working very well [in the same way].''

That Christmas, Mooney was in Berlin for talks with Hjalmar Horace Greeley Schacht to discuss Germany's and America's joint future in the world of commerce. He attracted the hatred of the liberal U.S. Ambassador to Germany William E. Dodd, who returned from Berlin to New York in 1937 and referred to The Fraternity in a shipboard press conference in New York harbor. Dodd was quoted in *The New York Times* as saying:

> A clique of U.S. industrialists is hell-bent to bring a fascist state to supplant our democratic government and is working closely with the fascist regime in Germany and Italy. I have had plenty of opportunity in my post in Berlin to witness how close some of our American ruling families are to the Nazi regime. On [the ship] a fellow passenger, who is a prominent executive of one of the largest financial corporations, told me point blank that he would be ready to take definite action to bring fascism into America if President Roosevelt continued his progressive policies.

Dodd's words were ignored.

On November 23, 1937, representatives of General Motors held a secret meeting in Boston with Baron Manfred von Killinger, who was Fritz Wiedemann's predecessor in charge of West Coast espionage, and Baron von Tippleskirsch, Nazi consul general and Gestapo leader in Boston. This group signed a joint agreement showing total commitment to the Nazi cause for the indefinite future. The agreement stated that in view of Roosevelt's attitude toward Germany, every effort must be made to remove him by defeat at the next election. Jewish influence in the political, cultural, and public life of America must be stamped out. Press and radio must be subsidized to smear the administration, and there must be a führer, preferably Senator Burton K. Wheeler of Montana, in the White House. This agreement was carefully hidden. But a secretary who was loyal to the American cause managed to obtain a copy and give it to George Seldes, liberal journalist, who published it in his newsletter, *In Fact*. The patriotic liberal Representative John M. Coffee of Washington State entered the full agreement, running to several pages, in the Congressional Record on August 20, 1942, demanding that the Du Ponts and the heads of General Motors be appropriately treated. Needless to say, the resolution was tabled permanently.

In 1938, Mooney, like Henry Ford, received the Order of the Golden Eagle from Hitler. On March 27, 1939, he arrived in England to confer with the heads of his British company. He learned that three of the Adam-Opel staff had been seized by the Gestapo and charged with leaking secrets of the new Volkswagen to the United States. Mooney rushed to Berlin and arranged meetings with one Dr. Meissner, who was in charge of foreign VIPs. Meissner said that even the Führer could not interfere with Himmler and the SS. Mooney reminded Meissner of his commitment to the Führer.

Meissner agreed that this trivial matter must not be allowed to interfere with German-American relations but that the men would be punished if found guilty. Mooney offered to testify on their behalf; on April 6 he went to see one of Himmler's lieutenants and on the same day he visited Ribbentrop. But he was powerless to affect the fate of his employees.

On April 19, Mooney met with the invaluable Emil Puhl of the BIS and the Reichsbank, and Helmuth Wohlthat, Göring's American-educated right-hand man in the Four-Year Plan. Mooney conferred with these men on Hitler's basic plan of the massive American gold loan that would provide the basis for the New Order. Mooney enthusiastically endorsed the scheme and promised to bring it about.

In a state of excitement he traveled to London on April 25 to see Ambassador Joseph Kennedy. Kennedy agreed to meet with Puhl and Wohlthat in Paris. Mooney talked with Francis Rodd of Morgan, Grenfell, the British representatives of the Morgan Bank. They agreed that the loan should be made to Germany through the Bank for International Settlements. Rodd said significantly that the BIS provided a flexible medium for avoiding conflict with some of the internal legal limitations on international loans—a complicated way of saying that the BIS could dodge the law whenever it felt like it.

Mooney went to Berlin on April 29. On May 1 he urged Puhl to meet with Kennedy in Paris. He promised to arrange the meeting secretly at Mooney's apartment in the Ritz Hotel. Puhl was interested. But on the following day he said he dared not make the trip because it would attract too much attention in Germany and that Wohlthat should go instead. Wohlthat agreed to go.

On May 3, Mooney called Kennedy in London. Kennedy replied that he would be willing to come on the weekend of May 5–6. But he hesitated and asked if Mooney didn't think it was advisable that he put the matter up to the White House first. Mooney said he would only do that in Kennedy's place if he thought he was a good enough salesman to get approval. Otherwise it would be taking a long chance. He added that the arrangements had been accepted in Berlin and it would not be wise to withdraw at this late hour.

After this conversation, Kennedy panicked. He called Roosevelt, who told him immediately not to make the trip. Roosevelt knew the nature of the arrangements in which Mooney was involved. There was no way he would sanction Kennedy's involvement.

Kennedy tried to reach Mooney several times. When he finally got through, Mooney chartered a plane in Brussels and flew to London. The idea of peace was clearly such an obsession he couldn't wait. On the plane, he scribbled out his notes on what was needed: a half to one billion gold loan through the BIS, a restoration of Germany's colonies, a removal of embargo on German goods, participation in Chinese markets. On Germany's side there would be armaments limitations, nonaggression pacts, and free exchange. Whatever Mooney's motives, these were pure Nazi objectives, nothing else.

Mooney went straight to the embassy from his plane and laid out the points of the peace agreement on Kennedy's desk. He begged him to see Wohlthat. Kennedy promised to put pressure on Roosevelt once more. Next morning, Mooney found Kennedy deeply depressed. Kennedy had tried to reach Roosevelt for hours, and when he had done so, Roosevelt had once again refused him.

Mooney now suggested Wohlthat should come to London. Kennedy agreed at once. Mooney called Wohlthat in Berlin and asked

him to come to London. Wohlthat obtained permission from Hitler
and Göring and arrived at the Berkeley Hotel on May 8. The meeting
was held on May 9, apparently without Roosevelt's knowledge or
approval. The Nazi economist got along well with Kennedy. Mooney
noted that the two men saw eye-to-eye on everything. Wohlthat returned to Berlin, promising his help. The press discovered Wohlthat
was in London and played the visit up tremendously with headlines
like "Goering's mystery man is here." This greatly annoyed Mooney, who had assumed the visit was secret.

Roosevelt stepped in as soon as the news was announced and forbade Kennedy to have anything further to do with the arrangement.
Mooney was greatly disappointed by this lack of rapport between the
President and Nazi Germany. It was this series of meetings with Kennedy and Wohlthat that helped to spawn ITT's Gerhardt Westrick's
visit to New York the following year, and it is significant that Mooney was high on the list of people who received and encouraged
Westrick. Roosevelt was greatly aggravated by Mooney but played
along with him in order to see what he was up to.

In the Mooney diaries at Georgetown University in Washington,
there is an eighteen-page document signed by Wohlthat that lays out
Germany's economic plans. It is quite clear that Mooney was in total
accord with these.

On September 22, 1939, Mooney had a meeting with Roosevelt.
His notes after the meeting, quoting as nearly as possible the President's actual words, suggest that Roosevelt was using Mooney to see
what Hitler was up to. Roosevelt pretended he was not interested in
telling the Germans what they should do about Hitler. That Mooney
should remind the Germans that Roosevelt had gone to school in
Germany and had a great many personal friends there. He said he
wished Germany would pipe down about domination of the world.
He discussed the question of broader distribution of goods in time of
peace and that it ought to be reasonably simple to get around a table
with the proper will and settle problems like Silesia, Poland, Czechoslovakia, and the general attitude toward Russia. Roosevelt said he
would be glad to offer himself as moderator, that the Pope could
serve a useful purpose in negotiations, and that practical suggestions
must be made satisfactory to Berlin, London, and Paris. He encour-

aged Mooney to see Hitler but to be careful in communicating the results to the White House by telephone.

Armed with this artificial, carefully calculated authorization, Mooney traveled to Europe at the same time as Roosevelt's official emissary, Sumner Welles, in March 1940. He was only one day later than Welles in audience with Hitler on March 4.

Because of the importance of Adam-Opel and the Du Ponts to the Nazi war machine, Hitler was extremely cordial. Mooney said that Roosevelt's early days in Germany had remained a nostalgic recollection; that the President's attitude to Germany was more sanguine and warm than was generally believed in Berlin; that Roosevelt would help toward a negotiated peace; that the German reporters ought to emphasize what Germany and America shared together.

Hitler smiled broadly at these sentiments. He did not want war with America: he had his hands full enough already. He wanted America to remain inactive until it either entered the Axis or was conquered. Hitler said he was delighted to hear Roosevelt's viewpoint and that Roosevelt had constructively undertaken the tasks of the Presidency. He suggested that Roosevelt would be well placed to negotiate peace. These statements were as calculated to deceive Mooney as Roosevelt's.

From the Chancellery, Mooney proceeded to the Air Ministry to see Göring, who later had him to dinner at Karin Hall. Göring played out a similar line of lies, denying among other things that Germany had any desire to affect the British colonial empire when in fact one of Hitler's burning obsessions was to retrieve his lost colonies. Wohlthat also attended the meeting at Göring's house, and everyone concurred that the gold loan must once again be pushed by Mooney with the President.

From a warship off the Italian coast in March, Mooney beseeched Roosevelt with a stream of messages calling for peace and unison with Hitler. On April 2, Roosevelt wrote to Mooney that public opinion in America was all for peace and disarmament.

Back in New York, Mooney met with Gerhardt Westrick, and joined that party at the Waldorf-Astoria in which some American leaders of The Fraternity, including Sosthenes Behn and Torkild Rieber, celebrated the Nazi conquest of France. On June 27 the Nazi

consul general in New York and local Gestapo chief, Heinrich Borchers, sent a report prepared by Westrick to Ribbentrop. It read:

> A group of prominent businessmen and politicians whom I personally
> regard as reliable in every way, and whose influence I consider to be
> very great, but who, in the interest of our operation, do not want to be
> mentioned in any circumstances at this time, suggested that I convey to
> the Foreign Ministry the following: the aforesaid group, which has the
> approval and support of a substantial number of leading personalities,
> will shortly urge upon President Roosevelt the following recommenda-
> tions: 1. Immediate sending of an American Ambassador to Berlin. 2.
> A change of Ambassadors in London. 3. Suspension of armament ship-
> ments to Great Britain until the new Ambassador to Berlin has had an
> opportunity to discuss matters with the German government.

On July 18, Hans Thomsen, chargé d'affaires in Washington, wrote
to Berlin that this group was headed by James D. Mooney. Thomsen
went on to report that Henry Ford had conveyed the same idea to him
two days earlier.

In December 1940, Mooney set off on a journey to South America
to contact some of the General Motors managers. Secretary of the
Interior Harold Ickes, in an urgent meeting with Roosevelt and Cordell Hull on December 20, asked, "Wouldn't it be a good thing if we
refuse Mooney a passport and told him why?" Roosevelt said, "That
is a good idea. Cordell, how about it?" Hull said, "Passports to
South America have never been refused." Ickes commented, "South
America is a critical zone. We shouldn't let Mooney in." But Hull
did.

The FBI apparently traced Mooney to further meetings with representatives of the German government. In a letter dated February 5,
1941, marked Strictly Confidential, James B. Stewart, U.S. consul
in Zurich, wrote to Fletcher Warren of the State Department that he
had heard from a French journalist connected to Charles de Gaulle
that Eduard Winter, GM distributor in Berlin now in Paris, acted as
a courier for Mooney, carrying secret messages to the Nazi high officials in Paris. Stewart said that Winter had a special passport that
allowed him to travel between occupied and unoccupied France. The
letter continued, "Mr. Mooney is known to be in sympathy with the
German government."

However, Stewart wondered if there was anything in the story, since he believed Mooney to be a fine person. Would Warren comment? Warren forwarded the letter to Messersmith, who was ambassador to Cuba. In his letter to Messersmith, dated March 1, 1941, Warren said: "I may say that I, personally, am rather unhappy about Mr. Mooney, and I am not sure that there is not truth in Mr. Stewart's information. There are too many rumors."

Messersmith replied to Warren on March 5, saying that in his mind there was no doubt that Mooney was transmitting messages of a confidential character to the Nazi government. He added, "Mooney is fundamentally fascist in his sympathies. Of course he is quite unbalanced . . . he is obsessed by this strange notion that a few businessmen, including himself, can take care of the war and the peace. I am absolutely sure that Mooney is keeping up this contact with the Germans because he believes, or at least still hopes, that they will win the war, and he thinks if they do that he will be our Quisling."

Messersmith sent a further letter to Warren on March 7, adding, "The attitude of Jim Mooney has a great deal to do with the attitude of some of the people of the GM Overseas Corp. who are making this difficulty about getting rid of Barletta and other anti-American representatives of GM." Barletta was GM's Cuban representative.

Questioned about these activities by Hoover's men, Mooney insisted he was a patriotic American, a lieutenant commander in the Reserves in the United States Navy, with a son on active duty with the Navy. Asked by the FBI's L. L. Tyler in mid-October 1940 if he would return the Hitler medal he said he would, "but it might jeopardize General Motors getting part of the $100,000,000 of stockholders' money invested in Nazi Germany." Clearly, along with other Fraternity members, Mooney was working for a quick negotiated peace to release those funds; but even in this time of European war, they were gathering interest toward the time when the war would be over and America would stand next to Hitler in the scheme of things. He added, "Besides, Hitler is in the right and I'm not going to do anything to make him mad. I know Hitler has all the cards." He said he was sure Hitler would win the war; that there was justice in Hitler's general position; that Germany needed more room; and that if we tried to prevent the expansion of the German people under Hitler, it would be "just too bad for us."

Soon after making these remarks, Mooney was promoted to assistant to Sloan in charge of defense liaison work in Detroit! In a special report to J. Edgar Hoover, FBI agent Tyler stated (July 23, 1941): "Men of Mr. Mooney's prominence, holding the views he holds, are potentially dangerous to national security."

Tyler was convinced, he went on, that Mooney "was threatening to the National Defense Program" that Mooney purportedly was aiding. Tyler also felt that Graeme K. Howard was a danger. He had been given a secret report from the State Department, which made clear that Sumner Welles, the Under Secretary of State, had had to threaten Howard with public exposure before Howard would agree to fire nine hundred Nazi spies working for the General Motors Export Corporation in South America.

On May 1, J. Edgar Hoover reported to Adolf Berle that he had evidence that Eduard Winter was a Nazi agent, who moved freely around Europe and had been given his position by Mooney in Antwerp just after Hitler occupied the Low Countries. Adding that Winter "hopes to be on the winning side whichever is victorious in the present conflict," Hoover stated that Winter was the son-in-law of a German Foreign Office official. He had good party connections in Germany. In a comment on this note, John Riddleberger of the State Department said, "I can easily understand how Mr. Mooney's and Mr. Winter's minds would run along the same channel with respect to the war."

Further reports on Mooney state that he had aided the Germans as director and financial contributor to the German-American Board of Trade for Commerce, which greatly aided certain Nazis. *The German-American Commerce Association Bulletin* contained pictures of Mooney standing in front of a swastika; it named him as a GACA financial contributor.

On March 21, 1942, representatives of Du Pont were reported by the U.S. Consulate in Basle to be meeting with representatives of Hermann Göring's industries at Montreux and St. Moritz. The subject of the discussions was not disclosed, but the meeting caused grave concern in Switzerland. It was alleged in reports after the war that substantial Du Pont funds were retained from 1942 on in Occupied France, gathering interest for Du Pont/General Motors.

On April 15, 1942, a curious item appeared in Gestapo reports in

Berlin. Eduard Winter, it seemed, had been arrested on suspicion of American espionage. He was now running the General Motors Adam-Opel unit in Nazi Germany and had fallen foul of Wilhelm Ohnesorge, the postminister who had similarly denounced Westrick. As in the ITT matter, Himmler stepped in and Winter was released. It was clear that, like Ford, General Motors was protected from seizure in time of war. Winter continued as usual.

On July 3, 1942, the U.S. Embassy in Panama sent a lengthy report to the Secretary of State, giving particulars of Nazi activities in the area. A paragraph read: "General Motors gives orders for molds to the Nazi firm, Erca, or via, the firm Alpa, San Martin. Both firms should be on the blacklist because they employ Nazis and work together with Nazi firms." The companies were not blacklisted.

On November 25, the Nazi alien property custodian appointed Carl Luer, an official of the government and the Dresdnerbank as manager of the General Motors Adam-Opel establishment at Rüsselsheim. This establishment manufactured military aircraft for the German government throughout World War II. It manufactured 50 percent of all Junkers Ju 88 propulsion systems; the Junkers was the deadliest bomber of the Nazi air force. It was decided by a special court at Darmstadt shortly after November 25 that the directorial board under Eduard Winter would remain unaltered.

Charles Levinson, formerly deputy director of the European office of the CIO, alleged in his book *Vodka-Cola*,

Alfred Sloan, James D. Mooney, John T. Smith and Graeme K. Howard remained on the General Motors-Opel board . . . in flagrant violation of existing legislation, information, contacts, transfers and trade continued [throughout the war] to flow between the firm's Detroit headquarters and its subsidiaries both in Allied countries and in territories controlled by the Axis powers. The financial records of Opel Rüsselsheim revealed that between 1942 and 1945 production and sales strategy were planned in close coordination with General Motors factories throughout the world. . . . In 1943, while its American manufacturers were equipping the United States Air Force, the German group were developing, manufacturing and assembling motors for the Messerschmitt 262, the first jet fighter in the world. This innovation gave the Nazis a basic technological advantage. With speeds up to 540 miles per hour, this aircraft could fly 100 miles per hour faster than its American rival, the piston-powered Mustang P150.

As late as April 1943, General Motors in Stockholm was reported as trading with the enemy. Henry Morgenthau, in an instruction given in special code, instructed W. B. Wachtler, regional manager of GM in New York, to order his Stockholm chief to discontinue trading.

Further documents show that, as with Ford, repairs on German army trucks and conversion from gasoline to wood-gasoline production were being handled by GM in Switzerland.

In April 1944 various letters between the U.S. Embassy in Stockholm and the State Department indicate that GM in Sweden was importing products of Nazi origin, including Freon, with permission from State. One letter, dated April 11, 1944, from John G. Winant said, "We are . . . of the opinion that local manufacture of a suitable refrigerant in Sweden should be encouraged, but if it proves impossible for Svenska Nordiska to obtain a suitable local product, we agree that there would be no objection to the supply of [German] refrigerant [similar to that from] I.G. Farben." The refrigerant was imported.

On April 3, 1943, State Department officials reported to Leland Harrison of the American Legation in Berne that censorship had intercepted cabled reports from Swiss General Motors to the parent company in New York showing that Balkan sales were made from stock held by General Motors dealers in Axis areas. The report continued, "It is understood that the parent company recently instructed the Swiss company to cease reporting on sales in enemy territory."

A GM overseas operations man in New York cabled Swiss GM that "We have been placed in an extremely embarrassing position by your action." However, there was no indication that the action ceased. Only that it must be authorized by the American Legation! "It is our desire," the cable continued, "that you keep the Legation completely informed of your operations and engage in no transaction to which trading with the enemy regulations of the U.S. government apply *without clearing with the Legation.*"* A copy of this telegram was forwarded by State officials to Cordell Hull with the understandable

* Author's italics.

proviso: "This cable has been sent in confidential code. It should be carefully paraphrased before being communicated to anyone."

In June 1943, when he was in the Navy, James D. Mooney's activities were still under surveillance by the FBI. He became a prime reason for a contretemps between the Duke and Duchess of Windsor and the State Department that month. Lord Halifax, the British ambassador in Washington, had written to Cordell Hull requesting that the Duchess of Windsor, who was now in Nassau with her husband, the governor of the Bahamas, should be freed from the censorship of her correspondence. This request immediately heightened grave suspicions in Adolf A. Berle. He sent a memorandum to Cordell Hull urging him to deny the request. Dated June 18, 1943, it read:

> I believe that the Duchess of Windsor should emphatically be denied exemption from censorship.
>
> Quite aside from the more shadowy reports about the activities of this family, it is to be recalled that both the Duke and Duchess of Windsor were in contact with Mr. James Mooney, of General Motors, who attempted to act as mediator of a negotiated peace in the early winter of 1940; that they have maintained correspondence with Charles Bedaux, now in prison in North Africa and under charges of trading with the enemy, and possibly of treasonable correspondence with the enemy; that they have been in constant contact with Axel Wenner-Gren, presently on our Blacklist for suspicious activity; etc. The Duke of Windsor has been finding many excuses to attend to "private business" in the United States, which he is doing at present.
>
> There are positive reasons, therefore, why this immunity should not be granted—as well as the negative reason that we are not according this privilege to the wife of an American official.

Hull called Halifax and told him the Duchess's request was denied.

General Motors went unpunished after the war. According to Charles Levinson, in 1967, after a prolonged series of detailed requests, the United States awarded the corporation a total of $33 million tax exemption on profits for the "troubles and destruction occasioned to its airplane and motorized vehicle factories in Germany and Austria in World War II."

10

The Systems Tycoon

In 1938, Nazi diplomat Fritz Wiedemann appointed the American millionaire industrial systems inventor, Charles Bedaux, as head of I.G. commercial operations on behalf of The Fraternity in Europe. Bedaux had supplied industrial systems of time and motion study to I.G., ITT, Standard Oil, General Motors, Ford, Sterling Products, and the other Fraternity members. He had introduced brutal methods of production that brought about frequent strikes in the 1930s. He was working in Paris with Torkild Rieber's Texas Corporation Nazi contact Nikolaus Bensmann.

It was Bedaux who delegated himself to inveigle the Duke and Duchess of Windsor into the Fraternity's plans for a negotiated peace. Since Hitler's rise, the Windsors had been fascinated by the Führer and his New Order in Europe.

In February 1941 the right-wing journalist Fulton Oursler interviewed Windsor at Government House in the Bahamas, publishing the results in *Liberty* magazine. The Duke declared his approval of negotiated peace to Oursler. He said, "It [the peace] cannot be another Versailles." He went on to express views that were hardcore expressions of Fraternity thinking, with their emphasis on gold as currency, Himmler's police, and the German system: "Whatever happens, whatever the outcome, a New Order is going to come into the world. . . . It will be buttressed with police power. . . . When peace comes this time, there is going to be a New Order of Social Justice*—don't make any mistake about that—and when that time comes, what is your country going to do with its gold?''

During his brief period as monarch, Windsor made every effort to overcome British prejudice against the Nazis. He became an inspiration for The Link, the British organization of highly placed Nazi sympathizers, which included in its membership some of the most prominent aristocrats in England.

The Fraternity wanted the Duke tied in more completely with them. Charles Bedaux was selected by Himmler to insure the Duke's political and economic commitment.

Sprightly, stocky and squat, with slicked-back black hair, jug ears, and the bow legs of a jockey, Bedaux first came to the United States in 1907 from his native France and became a citizen in 1916. He had served a stretch in the Foreign Legion before he arrived. He obtained a job digging his way as a sandhog through the construction of the East River subway tunnel. He scraped together what money he could and began developing a system of speeding up labor, cutting out wasted motion, and improving efficiency. In his scheme an expert would time the workers with a stopwatch. Each hour was divided into sixty Bedaux units instead of minutes. Workers who exceeded the average would be paid more and those who fell below it would be demoted or fired. By circulating booklets containing his philosophy of labor, he succeeded in becoming very rich very fast.

Bedaux's office on the fifty-third floor of the Chrysler Building in New York was designed like the refectory of a medieval monastery. He often met with his friends Lammot du Pont, and Walter Teagle, and Hermann Schmitz there—in the Chrysler's Cloud Room for lunch. He had an apartment in Greenwich Village in which he entertained his mistresses, redecorating the rooms according to the lady's background or nationality.

He married a Daughter of the American Revolution, Fern Lombard, and thereby obtained a place in the New York Social Register. He bought a château in Touraine, France, for three quarters of a million dollars. It was a former abbey, with catacombs under the golf course. He snapped up an estate in North Carolina, a hunting lodge

*Social Justice was the title of an inflammatory fascist magazine then in circulation in the United States.

in Scotland next to Walter Teagle's, and property in North Africa. An automobile buff, he crossed the Rockies by car in July 1934, and took a caravan of six cars over 9,500 miles of the Algerian and Tunisian deserts the following year.

He insinuated himself with the Windsors, offering his château to them for their wedding. Bedaux's wedding present was a statue entitled "Love," the work of Anny Hoefken-Hempel, the lover of Hjalmar Schacht. Schacht had introduced Bedaux to Fritz Wiedemann, who appointed Bedaux industrial espionage agent for the Nazi government.

As the German government's chief overseas contact for The Fraternity next to Wiedemann, Bedaux was ideally placed to snare the Windsors. He was helped by the Windsors' friend Ambassador William Bullitt, who moved the U.S. Embassy into the Bedaux château just before the fall of France.

Bedaux wanted to involve the Windsors in his international schemes. First, arrangements must be made for them to meet with Hitler and be given a tour of Nazi Germany. In the summer of 1937, according to MI-6 files in the Ministry of Defence, London, Bedaux met with the Duke of Windsor, Bedaux's close friend Errol Flynn, Rudolf Hess, and Martin Bormann in a secret encounter at the Hotel Meurice in Paris. At the meeting the Duke promised to help Hess contact the Duke of Hamilton, who had a direct link with Himmler and Kurt von Schröder to the Schröder Bank and the Worms Bank through their common membership in Frank Buchman's Moral Rearmament Movement. Hess was determined to insure an alliance with Great Britain that would continue despite Hitler's conquest. Bedaux was the instrument and Errol Flynn the glamorous accomplice. The plan was postponed; efforts were made by Hess to meet with Hamilton on several further occasions, which finally led to Hess's dramatic landing on the Hamilton estate in 1941.

The Windsors were enchanted with their visit with Hitler and their tour of Germany, and the Duchess was seen handing a bagful of money to a Nazi officer on the border of Austria.

In November 1937, Bedaux tried to arrange a state visit for the Windsors to the United States. He bombarded Washington high-ranking officials with telegrams. He wanted the Duke of Windsor to be received at the White House along with the Duchess; State Department officials planned that the Duke and the President should enjoy a Gridiron Club dinner while the Duchess appeared separately at the Women's National Press Club. Thousands of letters poured into the White House and the government departments, criticizing Roosevelt for snubbing the couple.

Bedaux and his wife arrived on the *Europa* in November to see what they could do. He had already talked with British Ambassador Sir Ronald Lindsay about the matter. The biggest blow was that Mrs. Roosevelt was "away on a lecture tour" and would be unable to receive the Windsors. Finally, it was decided by the government not to go ahead with the visit; the reasons were not officially disclosed, but Bedaux's fascist connections may have had a great deal to do with it. Appeal after appeal proved useless. Unions made clear they would picket the Duke's ship. Francis J. Gorman of the CIO Textile Workers condemned Bedaux outright for his inhuman systems. Bedaux and the Windsors were very upset.

By 1940, while Bedaux was busy undermining France in preparation for Vichy and the establishment of full-scale collaboration with Hitler, Windsor had become a member of the British Military Mission with the French Army Command. Neville Chamberlain and Winston Churchill were aware that Windsor's Nazi connections were far more serious than a mere confused sympathy would indicate.

On May 3, 1941, J. Edgar Hoover sent a memorandum to Roosevelt's secretary, Major General Watson, which read as follows:

Information has been received at this Bureau from a source that is socially prominent and known to be in touch with some of the people involved, but for whom we cannot vouch, to the effect that Joseph P. Kennedy, the former Ambassador to England, and Ben Smith, the Wall Street operator, some time in the past had a meeting with Göring in Vichy, France, and that thereafter Kennedy and Smith had donated a considerable amount of money to the German cause. They are both described as being very anti-British and pro-German.

This same source of information advised that it was reported that the Duke of Windsor entered into an agreement which in substance was to the effect that if Germany was victorious in the war, Hermann Göring through his control of the army would overthrow Hitler and would thereafter install the Duke of Windsor as the King of England. This information concerning the Windsors is said to have originated with

Allen McIntosh, a personal friend of the Duke of Windsor, who made the arrangements for the entertainment of the Windsors when they were in Miami recently. It is further reported that it is the intention of the Windsors to visit in Newport, Rhode Island, and also in Canada during the coming summer.

When Windsor asked Chamberlain for a more important job, the Duke was frozen out. Mortified, he committed himself to the appeasement group in England which remained part of The Link and still included Montagu Norman, of the Bank of England and the BIS, and Sir Harry McGowan of ICI.* In January 1940, Count Julius von Zech-Burkersroda, Nazi minister to The Hague, sent a special emissary to London to ask Windsor to tell the British government that it was useless to change Germany politically and that Windsor should help bring about a negotiated peace. Windsor was fascinated.

On February 18, according to German foreign office records, Windsor actually disclosed to Zech's emissary the details of a secret meeting of the Allied War Council. Windsor revealed that the Council had discussed in detail the situation that would arise if Germany invaded Belgium. The Council members had discussed the discovery of a German invasion plan found in an airplane that had made a forced landing in Belgium. The Council had decided that the best scheme was to set up a resistance effort behind the Belgian-French border. Some members of the Council were unwilling to surrender Belgium and the Netherlands after the humiliation of the defeat of Poland. They did not feel that a resistance plan was sufficient, and they urged the other members to defend Belgium to the last. The entire message was of such importance to the German government that it was shown to Hitler in person. Baron Ernst von Weizsäcker of the Foreign Office in Berlin wrote to Count Julius on March 2, 1940, that the report supplied by the Duke had been of interest to the Führer. He added, "If you can without inconvenience obtain further information of this nature, I should be grateful if you would pass it on to me; please do so preferably in the form of a report . . . directing it to me personally."

Had these letters slipped into the hands of British Intelligence, there is no question that the Duke of Windsor would have been arrested

*Later, Lord McGowan.

and subjected to a court-martial by Churchill. As it was, he proceeded to France at the time of the German take-over, with British Intelligence agents following him. By now it was much too dangerous for him to be seen with Charles Bedaux, who was busy setting up the Vichy take-over and having daily meetings at the Worms Bank. The Windsors proceeded into Spain via Port Bou, that favorite crossing place of people under suspicion.

After a desperate effort by Walter Schellenberg to have them returned to Germany prior to their taking over the British throne, the couple yielded to pressure from Churchill via their old friend Sir Walter Monckton and sailed to the Bahamas, where Windsor was made governor.

In their absence Winston Churchill personally made the curious move on April 7, 1941, of having U.S. Ambassador William Bullitt pay the Nazi government 55 thousand francs' annual rental on their property in Occupied Paris and 10 thousand francs' insurance plus payment to their servants and 15 thousand francs for the rent of the strong room at the Bank of France, despite the fact that the bank was directly under Hitler's control. Bedaux acted as a go-between in the arrangements since he was close to Bullitt and Nazi Ambassador Otto Abetz.

The Windsors stayed in touch with Bedaux until 1943, a fact that infuriated Morgenthau, Ickes, and Adolf Berle as well as the liberals in Congress headed by John M. Coffee and Jerry Voorhis. Bedaux schemed with Admiral Jean Darlan in North Africa in planning to destroy the British Empire; he helped to pledge Syria as a Nazi supply base for a prospective battle of Suez; and he collaborated with the Nazis in Spain, working with the Vichy leader Marshal Pétain in securing 300,000 tons of steel for Germany. Ambassador Bullitt rewarded him by making him a special attaché at a time when Bullitt was already publicly criticizing the Nazi government. Bedaux was put in charge of American property in Occupied France as a special economic advisor to Abetz and German Administrator H-J Caesar. Thus, he enabled The Fraternity to function more easily and was instrumental in approving the establishment of the Chase and Morgan banks and the Ford Motor Company in Occupied France even after Pearl Harbor.

In October 1940 he went to Africa at Pétain's request to undertake developments including railroads, power plants, water and coal production, in alliance with the Vichy General Maxime Weygand, then governor general of Africa. Bedaux presented to the German government his plans for camouflaging refineries at Abadan against Allied bombing; in return for his services he arranged for the transference of his confiscated Dutch corporation to Paris just before Pearl Harbor.

After Pearl Harbor, Bedaux was automatically arrested as an American citizen, but he was released after a month through the intercession of Abetz and the Gestapo. Because of pressure from those Germans who, like Postminister Ohnesorge, objected to dealings with the enemy, Bedaux was arrested again, on September 27, 1942. The elegant American traitor was surprised to find himself, along with his attractive wife, in the Paris Zoo, where he languished for one night in a cage normally used by monkeys.

Bedaux and his wife were released from imprisonment on the basis that he persuaded General Otto von Stülpnagel, who was in command of the German forces in Occupied France, of the necessity for France to build a strong French Africa. He was given full governmental powers to execute his plan for the construction of a pipeline from Colomb-Béchar in southern Algeria to Bourem on the Niger River in the French Sudan in French West Africa. The purpose was two-fold: The pipeline would carry 200,000 tons of water annually to different points in the Sahara for use by Rommel's army, and it would convey 200,000 tons of peanut oil from French West Africa to Colomb-Béchar for shipping by rail for reshipment by boat to Vichy. Fifty-five thousand tons of steel had been assigned by the German authorities for the construction of the pipeline, and the financing was undertaken by the Banque de Paris et des Pays-Bas.

Bedaux was authorized to hire 240 people initially, many of them from the crews engaged in the construction of the ill-fated Trans-Saharan Railway. The whole culture of peanuts in French West Africa was to be reorganized and the center of industry transferred from Dakar to Ouagadougou; and the vast and fertile area in the bend of the Niger River including parts of the Ivory Coast, French Sudan, and the Niger Colony, were to be exploited on a vast scale. Rafts constructed in French Guinea would carry hundreds of thousands of tons of peanuts a year from western Sudan via the Niger to Bourem, where presses would be erected for the extraction of the oil.

On July 22, 1942, Bedaux went to see S. Pinkney Tuck, chargé d'affaires for the United States government in Vichy. He had just had lunch with Pierre Laval. He left with the embassy a photostatic copy of the release order of the German authorities in Paris, designating him the leading expert in economic matters in France. He said he had just returned from a survey of the coal mines in the Sahara Desert, which he expected to yield 1,200 tons of coal a day; he said that the present output was 800 tons a day and that he was responsible for all the cities in North Africa having electric power. He said he was concerned with building a New Europe that would end the misery of the world; when Tuck asked him about the German attitude toward the war's future, he supplied intelligence on German problems. He said he had assisted as a technical advisor at a number of gatherings in which French and German technicians gathered. He talked of the strides the Gestapo was making in France, Major General Karl Oberg's treatment of the Jews, and execution of hostages. He suggested that the United States should trade more with Laval, pretending that Laval was unhappy with the German government. He said to Tuck, "If the American press and public opinion could be persuaded to modify their present critical attitude towards Laval, it might be possible for our Government to make good use of him."

Tuck concluded,

> I believe that this astonishing person can be classified as mentally unmoral. He apparently lacks the tradition and background which should make him realize that there is anything wrong, as an American citizen, in his open association with our declared enemies. . . . By such opportunistic tactics—which are not unmindful of Laval's—he may be attempting to find for himself a safe place in the New Order. Should this New Order fail to materialize, he evidently imagines that he will be able to justify his association with the Germans by his refusal to accept their pay.

This curious document indicates a very peculiar attitude on the part of Pinkney Tuck. Knowing full well that Bedaux was American and that he was collaborating with the enemy, Tuck nevertheless made no attempt whatsoever as chargé d'affaires to have him arrested.

On October 29, 1942, Charles Bedaux arrived at the American

Consulate General in Algiers and told Minister Robert Murphy that he was bent on his mission to aid the German government. This was almost a year after the United States was at war with Germany. It might well be asked whether a traitor would volunteer such information to an American representative if he were not assured of immunity from arrest.

In a memorandum to Cordell Hull dated October 30, 1942, Murphy gave a remarkable account of the visit. Bedaux said that he had been granted freedom to perform his mission in French Africa and "it was in that connection that he called upon me in Algiers." Unhesitatingly, Bedaux handed Murphy his German authorizations and a special set of instructions signed by Pierre Laval.

On April 12, 1943, Hoover wrote to Harry Hopkins telling him of Bedaux's arrest. Hoover revealed that Eisenhower had specifically asked the two FBI men to go to North Africa to conduct the investigation into Bedaux's activities. Although the Federal Bureau of Investigation had no authorization to handle North Africa, since its provenance was restricted to the American continent, Biddle conferred with Hoover, and as a result two prominent FBI agents were sent to Algiers by plane to interrogate Bedaux. The plane carrying them crashed. Two other agents were flown over in their place.

Acting on instructions from Hoover and Biddle, the agents, again acting entirely outside their legal and authorized provenance, showed themselves anxious to protect Bedaux from Army Intelligence. It was painfully obvious that strings had been pulled with Biddle once again. The agents went to see the officers of the French police, who produced the critical evidence of the Bedaux-Schröder Nazi conspiracy. Instead of accepting this material as evidence of treason, the FBI men accused the French detectives of planting the evidence, and they tried to have the charges against Bedaux officially withdrawn. Yet that same evidence can today be seen in U.S. Military Intelligence files.

The U.S. Army under Eisenhower was keen on having action taken, but an Executive Order of the Army Intelligence dated January 4, 1943, shows that pressure from high places was such on the Army that all plans for a tribunal were suspended. The excuse given was that the case against Bedaux "had to be watertight," while in fact it was already conclusive.

Bedaux was held for a full year in prison while nothing whatsoever was done about him. He continually protested that he had aided and abetted American businesses in Occupied Europe, a mistake since this was the last fact that anybody in high command wanted to have made public. At long last, on December 16, 1943, Bedaux was turned over to Lieutenant Colonel Herndon for military escort to the United States, arriving on December 23 at Miami, Florida. The same day, Lieutenant Colonel Crabtree of the Army Air Force suddenly released Bedaux from Herndon's custody, gave Bedaux twenty-seven hundred confiscated dollars and took all of the Bedaux papers to Washington. Army officials ordered the Customs officials (who were not normally under their provenance) to pass papers without examination by censors or Customs, then took Bedaux to the Colonial Hotel in Miami. From there, instead of going to a state prison, he was placed in a comfortable detention home in charge of Immigration, with special consideration from the authorities.

On December 28, one of Biddle's agents suddenly turned up at the Immigration station and asked the authorities to lighten what minimal restrictions Bedaux was experiencing. On December 29, Biddle ordered the War Department to withdraw completely from the case.

The cover-up continued. Bedaux gave FBI men a list of very prominent figures of commerce who could be expected to testify in his behalf in the event that he should ever come to trial. Biddle immediately suppressed the list. However, it fell into the hands of the liberal weekly, *The Nation*, which revealed the names on the list as those of "industrialists who had recently been involved in anti-Trust cases"! That meant, of course, the American figures of The Fraternity.

On February 14, 1944, Bedaux was advised by an Immigration agent that a board of special inquiry of the Immigration and Naturalization Service had "concluded that he was a citizen of the United States" and had never surrendered that citizenship. Further, the INS would order his admission into the United States as soon as certain minor formalities had been complied with. The INS man also told Bedaux that "a grand jury would be convened to inquire into his relations with high officials of the German government and the Vichy French government, and that the grand jury would consider whether he should be indicted for treason and for communicating with the enemy."

Major Lemuel Schofield had only recently stepped down as head of Immigration and members of his immediate staff were still in office, so it was unlikely that anything would have come of the grand jury hearing. However, Bedaux had become distinctly inconvenient to The Fraternity. There was a strict rule in the Immigration station that sleeping pills must not be given to prisoners, but Bedaux was allowed the special privilege of using them. On February 14, 1944, Bedaux retired to bed and swallowed all of the pills he had hoarded since his arrival on December 23. Max Lerner and I. F. Stone disclosed in *PM* and in *The Nation* that they were convinced that Bedaux was encouraged to take the easy way out. It is impossible to differ with that opinion.

11

The Diplomat, the Major, the Princess, and the Knight

Throughout World War II, Max Ilgner of I.G. Farben ran the organization known as the AO. Financed by I.G. Farben, the organization of Germans Abroad was not officially but in fact actually under Walter Schellenberg's direct control.* The leading agents for the AO in the hemisphere were Hitler's former commanding officer Fritz Wiedemann and Hitler's beloved treacherous Princess Stefanie Hohenlohe. With I.G. money and direct approval from Himmler, Wiedemann and Stefanie were the most peripatetic members of the American-Nazi international fellowship. They schemed along with Schellenberg for the downfall of Hitler and the advent of Himmler and the Schmitz Council of Twelve. They, like Himmler, dreamed of the restoration of the German monarchy. They visited the Kaiser in Doorn, Holland, until 1941, the year of his death.

Wiedemann and Stefanie entered the United States telling the FBI privately that they had fallen out of favor with Hitler. This was true, since Hitler in fact was gravely suspicious of both of them because of their connections to both the official plot to dislodge him and to the ambiguous Admiral Wilhelm Canaris, head of the Abwehr, German Military Intelligence, who himself was suspected of being a double agent. As consul general in San Francisco, Wiedemann was head

*Its nominal chief was Ernst-Wilhelm Bohle.

of the Orient Gruppe, the SD network that encompassed the whole Pacific basin including the North and South American coastal states, Thailand, Malaya, Hong Kong, mainland China, Formosa, and Japan while at the same time collaborating with the British and Americans. The Princess Hohenlohe, a widow, was his mistress, with unlimited connections in society.

The princess was half Jewish. She had been given the title of Honorary Aryan by Dr. Goebbels along with General Erhard Milch of the air force in return for her services to the Third Reich. She and Wiedemann had become romantically involved at the time of Hitler's rise to power.

Wiedemann was handsome, with black wavy hair, chiseled features, a powerful jaw, and a boxer's physique. Fluent in many languages, shrewdly intelligent, he was the toast of society on both sides of the Atlantic. The princess had been quite pretty as a young woman but had not aged well. The addition of years had filled out her figure and rendered her features far less attractive. Nevertheless, she had immense charm and vivacity; she was witty, sparkling, high-strung, and wonderful company. She was also one of the most dangerous women in Europe.

In the early 1930s, Wiedemann and Stefanie were entirely devoted to Hitler and I.G. Farben's AO. They were friendly with Lord Rothermere, British millionaire-owner of the London *Daily Mail,* who gave the princess a total of $5 million in cash to assist in Hitler's rise to power. She was less successful in France, which deported her in 1934 for scheming against an alliance between France and Poland that might have helped protect Europe from Nazi encroachment. She formed a close friendship with Otto Abetz, the smooth Nazi representative in Paris who later became ambassador and was so helpful in the fall of France. In 1938 the princess arranged a meeting between Wiedemann and Lord Halifax, the British Foreign Minister, in London, the purpose of which was to determine Halifax's and Chamberlain's attitude to Hitler. The mission was successful. As the princess had promised, Halifax told Wiedemann that the British government was in sympathy with Hitler and that he had a vision that "Hitler would ride in triumph through the streets of London in the royal carriage along with King George VI."

Wiedemann and the princess were credited by Hitler with helping to pave the way to his annexation of European territories. The Führer rewarded her with the gift of Leopoldskron Castle near Salzburg, former property of the great Jewish theatrical producer Max Reinhardt. Beginning in 1933, Wiedemann made several visits to the United States, chiefly to direct the rabid Nazi organization known as the Friends of New Germany. He aided Ribbentrop in negotiating an anti-Comintern pact with Japan, and in the spring of 1938 traveled to the Balkans to bring them closer into the realm of the Axis.

Stefanie also spent much time in Switzerland, where she linked up with German Intelligence nets, many of them connected to her former husband, Prince Hohenlohe, who had been head of Austro-Hungarian intelligence in that country in World War I.

During the British abdication crisis of Edward VIII, Lord Rothermere sent the princess from London to Berlin with a Gobelin tapestry as a Christmas present for Hitler. After Edward abdicated, Hitler cabled Ribbentrop in London, "Now that the king has been dethroned, there is certainly no other person in England who is ready to play with us. Report to me on what you've been able to do. I shan't blame you if it amounts to nothing." The princess arrived at Berchtesgaden for a tête-à-tête just after this telegram. Hitler flirted with her and touched her hair; she had always wondered if he was a homosexual and was delighted to discover that he was attracted to her. She reminded him cheerfully that there were many in Britain who would indeed "play" with the Führer even if Edward would no longer be able to do so in his new position as Duke of Windsor. She was soon to learn that the Duke of Windsor was still able to "play."

In the late 1930s, Princess Stefanie traveled continuously to London, Paris, Berlin, Salzburg, Madrid, and Rome. She was usually on Rothermere's payroll, and accepted a swastika-shaped diamond clip from Hitler and a photograph on which Hitler wrote "To my esteemed Princess." She and Wiedemann visited the United States in 1937, where they linked up to Fraternity friends such as Sosthenes Behn, Walter Teagle, and Edsel Ford. Their social position gave them great influence over prominent figures who could affect others in the Nazi cause. Hermann Schmitz rewarded the princess with a parcel of I.G. shares. At the Ritz Hotel in London a week after war broke out in September 1939, several lady aristocrats denounced her as a spy and insisted that she leave the restaurant at once. She proceeded calmly with her meal.

Later that year she was busy fighting an unsuccessful lawsuit in the London courts against Lord Rothermere for nonpayment of the amounts due to her in her travels on behalf of the Nazi cause. The case tied her up in London. Wiedemann went ahead to New York with the understanding that she would follow soon afterward. Now that Europe was plunged into conflict, their purpose was to help keep America out of the war and to unite German-Americans in business to the Fatherland. Wiedemann set up the German-American Business League, which had as its rules purchase from Germans only, a boycott of Jewish firms, and the insistence that all employees be Aryans. Financed by Max Ilgner through General Aniline and Film, Wiedemann developed the Business League while pretending to denounce the Associated Bunds organization. Among the members were the owners of 1,036 small firms, including numerous import-export companies, fuel services, dry goods stores, meat markets, and adult and children's dress shops. The League stirred up anti-Jewish feeling, financed secret Nazi military training camps, paid for radio time for Nazi plays, and publicized German goods. It ran lotteries without licenses and sold blue candles to aid its brethren in Poland and Czechoslovakia before those countries were annexed.

On September 10, just after war broke out in Europe, Wiedemann told the German-American Business League in San Francisco: "You are citizens of the United States, which has allied itself with an enemy of the German nation. The time will come when you may have to decide which side to take. I would caution that I cannot advise you what to do but you should be governed by your conscience. One duty lies with the Mother country, the other with the adopted country. Blood is thicker than ink . . . Germany is the land of the fathers and regardless of consequences, you should not disregard the traditional heritage which is yours."

The Princess Stefanie's arrival in California in 1940 was not as trivial or absurd in purpose as it seemed, accompanied as it was by a great deal of publicity including seemingly endless column mentions. Given her glamour and notorious reputation, she was asked to many social events in San Francisco and Los Angeles. The idea of a Nazi princess electrified society, even those members of it who delighted in stating their fondness for England. She was quizzed, gushed over, and interviewed incessantly. Meanwhile, she talked with the wives of business leaders, to try to influence their husbands toward the Nazi cause. She warned of the dangers of communism, and the possibility that Hitler might attack America if America were not friendly. She mentioned the wealth and prosperity of Germany.

She was a perfect agent for Nazi philosophy. She helped bring about many deals between businessmen and the I.G. Farben cartels. She continued her romantic liaison with Wiedemann. FBI agent Frank Angell and a special team tracked the two down to the Sequoia National Forest where Wiedemann and the princess spent the night together in a log cabin while the G-men lurked among the trees.

J. Edgar Hoover became so obsessed with the princess and her doings that he had squads of men following the wrong woman: the Princess Mabel Hohenlohe, an innocent American who had married into the family. Mabel and her friend, the socialite Gurnee Munn, were dogged futilely for months when they had in fact done nothing more serious than acquire a Palm Beach parking ticket.

At the beginning of 1940 the Princess Stefanie met Sir William Wiseman, baronet and Cambridge boxing Blue. Plump, with a bristling mustache and dignified air, he had been head of British Intelligence in World War I. He had become a partner in the Jewish banking company Kuhn, Loeb. Treasury documents assert that the company was aligned with the dominant group of companies in Latin America that had entered into agreement with Nazi trusts to divide up the Latin American communications business.

According to *A Man Called Intrepid,* the well-known biography of Sir William Stevenson, head of British Security Coordination in the United States, Wiseman was a member of Stevenson's staff in World War II and was delegated to spy on Wiedemann and Hohenlohe with the authorization of J. Edgar Hoover and the British government.

The FBI files contradict this assertion. Indeed, they show that Wiseman was under suspicion and investigation. Army Intelligence chiefs' memoranda show that Wiseman was unauthorized by the British or American governments to act in any negotiations whatsoever. Indeed, his activities were neither condoned nor supported by any government.

In a note dated December 14, 1940, Brigadier General Sherman Miles, Chief of G-2, wrote to J. Edgar Hoover: "I suppose it is possible [Wiseman] is another of the same group of Englishmen that has negotiated with the Nazis in the past through men like Axel Wenner-Gren, Torkild Rieber and James D. Mooney."

According to *A Man Called Intrepid,* a most inaccurate work, Wiseman was authorized by the FBI to hold a private meeting on November 26, 1940, at the Mark Hopkins Hotel in San Francisco with Wiedemann and Hohenlohe to discuss a negotiated peace with Hitler. The FBI records and Hoover's notes to Roosevelt on the matter show that the FBI's San Francisco representative N.J.L. Pieper simply got wind of the meeting and, highly suspicious of Wiseman, decided independently to monitor it.

The meeting represented the essence of Fraternity thinking. Wiseman, as the FBI reported later, made it clear that he was acting as the mediator, not for the government of Great Britain, as he later claimed, but for the appeasement group in London headed by Lord Halifax, who was soon to become ambassador to Washington. Winston Churchill had clearly defined in speech after speech, memorandum after memorandum, his position on the war: total surrender of Germany without compromise. Wiseman made clear at the meeting that Halifax and he thought differently.

The princess said she would, as a Hungarian subject, bring Hitler the peace offer from Halifax, obtaining a fake visa in Switzerland in order to enter Germany. She would intercede directly with the Führer, using his affection for her, and if that failed, she would assist in the ill-conceived Royalist/Schellenberg/I. G. Farben coup d'état in which Himmler would take over and permanently restore the monarchy. A representative of Himmler's Gestapo would then meet with Halifax in London to confirm the arrangements for an alliance with Great Britain. Wiseman irresponsibly said that now that France was out of the way, the British could offer more favorable peace terms to Germany: "The French are always the difficult ones to satisfy, and we've had to consider France in the past. France will not have to be considered now except from the standpoint that she will be reestablished like Poland."

Wiseman supplied Wiedemann at this meeting with intelligence about the way in which the Royal Navy had intercepted Hitler's plans for the invasion of England. Simultaneously, Wiedemann gave Wiseman intelligence on the workings of the German High Command. Wiseman said, "If I were advising Hitler as a friend, I would say the amount of damage you could do to America is nothing compared to the damage that can be done if you make the Americans mad. They get mad slowly but it takes them a long time to get unmad. They get hysterical and look for a spy under every sofa, and from that point of view it just takes America more into the war. From my point of view, I do not want them to do it, because I do not want to see more killing. . . . I would say that I do not want a lot of sabotage in America because it just makes the feeling so much more bitter and things so much more difficult." These words are almost identical to those found in Wiedemann's and Chargé d'Affaires Hans Thomsen's memoranda to Berlin.

Hoover kept a tight scrutiny on the three communicants from that moment on. On December 18, 1940, the FBI tapped the princess's telephone. She was calling Wiseman in New York City from California to beg him to assist her in extending her visa and avoiding deportation. Wiseman, clearly embarrassed, told her, "Please don't talk any more about it over the phone. . . . Don't say any more." The princess told him, "You know I will be eternally indebted to you. You know you will never have to regret this." Wiseman went on, "I will send you a telegram telling you when to call me and will do all I can for you."

She kept on calling Wiseman, begging him to do everything in his power to stop the newspapers from printing anything concerning her deportation. He contacted Ingram Fraser of the British Purchasing Commission, trying to pull strings in Whitehall.

On January 3, 1941, Wiseman had a meeting with Herbert Bayard Swope, a wealthy politician, who conveyed a message from Lord Beaverbrook that Wiseman was to meet Lord Halifax soon thereafter "to negotiate peace." Wiseman had a series of discussions with high-level diplomats including figures of the Australian Embassy. A useful contact in the State Department was none other than Cordell Hull's cousin, Lytle Hull. Indeed, when World War II ended, Wiedemann asserted that Lytle Hull supplied him with inside intelligence on the State Department.

Another conspirator was the United States director of the Immigration and Naturalization Service, Major Lemuel Schofield, an enormously fat man with a head like a football and large, ugly features. When there was a public outcry for the princess to leave the United States in 1940, Schofield announced that no nation would take her, thereby preventing her deportation. He became more and more deeply involved in a romance with her when Wiedemann jilted her in favor of a general's divorced wife, Alice Crockett.

Wiedemann sent Mrs. Crockett to Berlin to meet with Hitler and Himmler and determine if the German government was satisfied with his efforts. This ordinary San Francisco housewife found herself in a whirlwind of high-level meetings. She was astonished to discover that Himmler gave her a special reception. But when she returned, she turned on Wiedemann and reported him and his secret activities to the FBI. She also sued him for several thousand dollars for unpaid fees in connection with her journey to Germany. She charged that Wiedemann was in concert with I.G. Farben, General Aniline and Film, Henry Ford, and Charles Lindbergh to bring about "subversion and sabotage in the interests of the Nazi government." She said that many American government officials, as well as plant superintendents, workers, and foremen in industries, particularly the steel and munitions industries, were in Wiedemann's pay. She claimed he "employed ruffians to stir racial hate . . . and paid such ruffians from funds of the German government."

Despite the fact that Mrs. Crockett was telling the truth, and that her husband had been a prominent figure in the U.S. Army, her case was thrown out of court and she was not even granted public recognition for her efforts.

Meanwhile, Sir William Wiseman was still working hard to prevent the Princess Stefanie from being shunted off to Nazi Germany, where she might reveal too much. His guilty collusion with her is as clear as Major Schofield's in the numerous documents that have recently been declassified.

Wiseman, in a conversation one midnight with a British person whom the FBI could not identify, said that he had "done everything possible to keep the threatened deportation quiet" but he was "drastically concerned with Steffi's habit of blowing her cover."

He said in a conversation with Ingram Fraser of the British Purchasing Commission that he was concerned "to keep that hysterical creature from going off the deep end . . . from losing her head and spilling all the beans on the table." Fraser said, "This may spoil a very beautiful friendship." Wiseman said, "If the friendship spoils, we'll just have to go out and pick up another one." He added, "This gives an opportunity for a scandal on a really big scale. That's what I'm afraid of."

FBI men followed Wiseman everywhere by car, train, and plane. There was a flurry of meetings between Wiseman and Ingram Fraser. Wiseman and the Hohenlohes strongly welcomed the appointment of Lord Halifax as ambassador for Great Britain in the United States.

Lord Beaverbrook in London cabled that he wanted Wiseman to contact Lord Halifax "as soon as Halifax arrived." There were a series of mysterious meetings between Wiseman, former President Herbert Hoover, Herbert Bayard Swope, and others, apparently on the matter of the negotiated peace.

On May 20, 1941, Schofield came through. He dropped the deportation proceedings and gave an interview to newspapermen at San Francisco Immigration headquarters explaining why: "While in custody the Princess Stefanie has cooperated with the Department of Justice and has furnished information of interest. The Department believes her release from custody will not be adverse to the interests and welfare of this country. Arrangements have been made for her continued cooperation, and her whereabouts and activities will be known at all times."

The major personally conducted the princess to her luxurious apartment in Palo Alto. Dressed in a chic black crepe dress with frothy white collar, white gloves, and a black and white hat, the Nazi princess was in a good mood on May 25, 1941, as she drove around San Francisco with the Director of Immigration at the wheel. Asked by reporters wherever he went if he would explain the "interesting information" Hohenlohe had given him, the major said with a smile, "Obviously not."

Although Walter Winchell, President Roosevelt, and seemingly everybody in Washington knew that the head of Immigration and the Nazi's favorite agent were involved in an affair, her release passed without significant public protest of any kind. The strongest statement appeared in the New York *Sun*. It was: "If 130 million people cannot exclude one person with no legal right to remain here, something seems wrong."

Hoover tried very hard to obtain from the Attorney General the "important information" to which Schofield referred, but there was no reply to his or his assistant's many phone calls. In fact, FBI memoranda show the FBI couldn't even interview the princess. When Percy Foxworth of the New York FBI headquarters sent a memorandum on June 1 to Hoover saying, "It appears desirable to have Princess Hohenlohe interviewed in order that complete information which she can furnish may be available for consideration in connection with our national defense investigations . . . regarding German espionage activities," Hoover scribbled a note at the foot of the memo, "Not until we get from McGuire [Matthew F. McGuire, assistant to Attorney General Jackson] a copy of what she told Schofield, then we should ask McGuire for *clearance* * to talk to her."

Next day at a congressional committee hearing in Washington, author Jan Valtin testified that Wiedemann's consulate was a clearinghouse for the Gestapo.

By early June, McGuire had still not yet yielded up Hohenlohe's statement to Schofield. The applications went on and on. Wiedemann was still out of town by early June, filming bridges and roads and dams from Colorado to Florida.

On June 15, 1941, McGuire sent a memo to Hoover saying that the princess's statement was "in the personal possession of Lemmy Schofield and was being typed." The same day, Drew Pearson in his Washington *Times-Herald* column said that Hohenlohe had paid for her freedom with "some amazing revelations about subversive operations in this country and Britain." Hoover wrote on the article photocopy sent to his office, "Have we gotten this statement yet? Maybe if the Dept. won't give it to us we might get Pearson to supply us with a copy!"

Pearson's article went on to say that the princess had told Schofield that Wiedemann was in bad odor with Hitler because of his friendship with Himmler's friend Hess, who had just flown to England on his

* Author's italics.

famous peace mission; that she had given Immigration officials a list of Nazi sympathizers in Britain who had been trying to effect a negotiated peace with Hitler; that she had specifically named Rothermere; that she had named other German Nazi agents.

By June 20, Hoover had become exasperated by the Department of Justice's seemingly endless delays in supplying Steffi's revelations. McGuire was stalling and refused to disclose why Drew Pearson had information the FBI did not. "This is the worst pushing around we have gotten yet," Hoover wrote at the foot of a memorandum from Edward A. Tamm of his staff on the latest delaying tactic.

Meanwhile, Hoover was tireless in ordering reports on Steffi's Nazi connections.

Agent N.J.L. Pieper in San Francisco tapped several telephones to learn that Wiedemann had had a falling-out with Steffi. An informant called Pieper to say that he was a German friend of Wiedemann's who felt he owed something to the American government. He leaked the contents of a conversation he had had with Wiedemann, who said, "There is nothing the Princess could have said that would harm me. She wouldn't. Indeed, she gave *nothing* to Immigration. It was a blind so that Schofield could let her out. And there's another element. Cordell Hull's cousin, Lytle Hull, was together with Schofield in this matter. He wanted her released."

This disclosure could not be acted on by Hoover, because of his limited powers.

In mid-June 1941, under enormous pressure from Roosevelt, the government dropped a bombshell. All Nazi consulates in America were ordered closed.

Wiedemann was under orders to leave the country by July 10. He had only been in the consulate for a few weeks. Several people walked by the building and were heard by reporters to say "Good riddance." Two American sailors climbed to the roof of the consulate and pulled down the swastika flag.

The night after orders came from Washington, Wiedemann's neighbors reported smoke pouring from the chimney of the consulate with flakes of ash. Papers were being stuffed into the consulate fires while others were loaded into the official Mercedes-Benzes to be put aboard German ships bound for their homeland. There were rumors that Wiedemann had offered to tell the Hearst organization everything he knew about Nazis in America in return for being allowed to remain in the United States. But this turned out to be false.

By June 26, Hoover still did not have Steffi's report. When Wiedemann and three friends went to the Stairway to the Stars nightclub in San Francisco, patrons at surrounding tables asked to be moved away. On July 3, Edward Tamm of the FBI reminded Hoover in a memo that after two months McGuire had still failed to come up with the promised report.

On July 8, Wiedemann traveled to Los Angeles to give all of his espionage reports in person to local Consul George Gyssling. Gyssling was leaving for Germany of the S.S. *West Point*; Wiedemann was to travel to China to continue with his work linking up the German and Japanese intelligence nets. He would also meet there Ludwig Ehrhardt, Steffi's second cousin by marriage, who was to become espionage chief for the Abwehr in the Orient two years later.

On July 9 it was announced that Wiedemann and Dr. Hans Borchers, new consul general in New York, would be leaving on the Japanese liner *Yawata Maru*. The British government had failed to give assurance of the safety of agents on the Japanese shipping lines, and this made Wiedemann extremely nervous.

Suddenly the British announced that Wiedemann would be exempt from seizure under his diplomatic immunity. For some reason Wiedemann didn't believe this. Possibly he thought it was a trick, because at the last minute he chartered three planes for himself and his staff and flew via Omaha and Chicago to New York.

Hoover had them followed. Meanwhile, Steffi was in Washington at the Wardman Park Hotel. It became the talk of the town that she was continuing her affair with Schofield. On July 31, Steffi's reports still not yielded up, Schofield sent to Attorney General Biddle (who had replaced Jackson) that in order to help America, she would supply a series of articles criticizing Hitler: domestic broadcasts; short-wave broadcasts to the Axis; replies to pro-German speeches by Lindbergh, Senator Wheeler, and so on; lectures. And all these would include the following: She would attack Hitler violently, describing his "treachery, deceit and cunning," adding that he was a "sly and cunning trickster" and "doesn't shrink from murder to achieve his purposes." In August 1941 the FBI apparently gave up hope of ever receiving Hohenlohe's report. With incredible boldness, the major moved from the Raleigh Hotel to the Wardman Park on the same floor as the princess.

Princess Stefanie was in bad form, screaming constantly at the staff. Schofield had to pay enormous tips to pacify the maids. On August 9 it was announced in the Washington *Times-Herald* that the princess would publish a book in six weeks containing the "secret information" she had allegedly handed to Schofield. The FBI's Harry M. Kimball sent a memo to agent Foxworth next day saying rather plaintively, "It might be as well to yet again request this information from Mr. McGuire, pointing out the indication mentioned in the article that the press intends to fully publicize this matter within the next six weeks and that it would be most advantageous for the Bureau to have available this information prior to the time it becomes public."

At long last, on August 18, 1941, the Princess Hohenlohe was asked to leave Washington. The scandal of her affair with Schofield was such that acting Attorney General Biddle asked him to have her returned to California immediately. When Edward Tamm of the FBI got wind of this, he called Biddle. Where was the princess's statement? Biddle stated he knew nothing whatsoever about it.

At the end of August, Wiedemann was in Berlin, reporting to Himmler on his many findings. In September he was on his way by L.A.T.I. airlines to Argentina, where Nazi activities were extensive. He arrived in Rio in September, to confer with the Gestapo leader Gottfried Sandstede, who had just escaped from Buenos Aires. The Brazilian newspaper *O Globo* had a photograph of Wiedemann on the front page with the headline "Number One Nazi of the Americas." The article stated bluntly that Wiedemann was responsible only to Hitler and had left $5 million in America to finance Nazi espionage rings.

Throughout August the Princess Hohenlohe moved to the homes of various friends of Schofield's in his native state of Pennsylvania. Meanwhile, in Rio, local police searched Wiedemann's belongings and found a list of Nazi agents in California. They also determined that he was headed for the Orient, a fact he himself confirmed the following day.

Wiedemann sailed for Kobe on the *Manila Maru* via Chile on September 8. Violent demonstrations outside the embassy caused him to leave on the first available vessel. Two small bombs exploded as he drove in an armed car to the Buenos Aires wharves.*

Meanwhile, the princess was staying in a house (described as a "lovenest" by Walter Winchell) in Alexandria, Virginia. FBI men saw Schofield arriving at the house in the evenings and leaving in the mornings. She was still using the name "Nancy White."

In the days just before Pearl Harbor the princess was in Philadelphia with Schofield. Her address book was examined by the FBI during her absence from the hotel and was found to include the name of Francis Biddle's wife. Hoover made a special note of the fact.

The moment the Japanese bombed Hawaii on December 7, Hoover wasted no time. As the Princess Hohenlohe left a Philadelphia theater with her mother at 10:20 P.M. on the night of December 8, FBI agents seized her. They bundled her into a car, leaving her eighty-nine-year-old mother screaming imprecations at them on the sidewalk. Hohenlohe was fingerprinted and photographed. She tried in vain to call Schofield by telephone. She was taken to the Gloucester Immigration station in New Jersey and put into solitary confinement, later changed to dormitory accommodations where she joined four Japanese girls and a woman from New Jersey who had trampled on the American flag and who spent much of her time doing double somersaults while the princess read the reminiscences of Madame de Pompadour.

It was now confirmed by Hoover that the supposed confession the princess had made out in order to be released from deportation had never existed. McGuire's and Jackson's statements that the important document was being typed amounted to little more than a lie. Precisely why the Attorney General chose to become involved in this deception remains undisclosed.

The plot thickened in mid-January. In a report of January 15, 1942, to Hoover by Special Agent D. M. Ladd, it was made clear that the princess had "a very influential friend in the State Department whose mistress she had been; the Princess had stated that this friend had the authority to permit Axis aliens to enter the country and to keep anti-Axis aliens out of the country." The name to this day is blacked out in the report. Since Schofield's name appears in all the other reports,

---

*Wiedemann's movements are erroneously reported in *A Man Called Intrepid*.

the reference presumably is to Breckinridge Long. To this day, the FBI refuses to declassify it.

During February 1942, Hohenlohe was writing letters to her mother at the Philadelphia YWCA, full of instructions on what Schofield was to do. He was to tell reporters not to molest her, check everything before it was published, and find some way out of prison for her on the pretense she was Hungarian, not Austrian. Hoover kept careful note of all these correspondences.

The princess gave the performance of a lifetime at the camp, faking a stroke and invoking her friendship with Sir William Wiseman. Biddle proved to be most helpful, insisting that the princess should be transferred from Gloucester to a place of "the alien's choice" where she could get proper treatment.

The local inspector and the head of the Immigration station conferred with the Philadelphia U.S. Assistant Attorney who fortunately for national security evaded the order that, he pointed out, could result in the princess choosing any hospital she liked, "even though the hospital or members of its staff were suspected of German activities."

The "stroke" changed to a fit of temperament and the princess stayed where she was.

Schofield dared to make a couple of visits. He saw to it the princess was given considerate treatment. Her mother spent many hours with Schofield in offices in downtown Philadelphia, followed constantly by FBI agents. But it proved impossible to bug Schofield's office.

Roosevelt wrote to Hoover on November 28, 1941, "I spoke to the Attorney General about the Hohenlohe case and he assures me that he has broken up the romance. Also, he thinks it best not to change the present domicile as the person in question is much easier to watch at that place. Please do a confidential recheck for me."

On June 17, 1942, Roosevelt wrote again to Hoover: "Once more I have to bother you about that Hohenlohe woman. I really think that this whole affair verges not merely on the ridiculous but on the disgraceful. Is the woman really at Ellis Island?"

On July 11, it was clear nothing had been done. The President wrote to Biddle, "Unless the Immigration Service cleans up once and for all the favoritism shown to that Hohenlohe woman, I will have to have an investigation made and the facts will not be very palatable, going all the way back to her first arrest and continuing through her intimacy with Schofield. . . . Honestly, this is getting to be the kind of scandal that calls for very drastic and immediate action.''

The princess had her problems. She was being threatened with a legal action for the recovery of funds paid out and legal services supplied by her London lawyers, Theodore Goddard and Company. She tried to finance the repayment by pressing several publishers to take her memoirs; the ever-reliable Schofield managed to get her a special pass to travel to New York to discuss the matter with her agents in March. The President was getting more and more restless.

An interesting episode took place on July 16, 1942. An FBI special agent went to the visiting room of the prison on the pretext of interviewing one of the inmates. He noticed the lax conditions: a Nazi spy who had recently been arrested was speaking on the pay telephone in German without being monitored. The princess was perched on a desk; she seemed to be in good spirits and taking a letter cheerfully from a prison staff member. Apparently her skills included a mastery of shorthand. Or she may have been making a translation.

The prison staff man said boldly in conversation to the agent, ''The princess has to have personal attention, and I like to keep her company. Sometimes she helps me censor the mail!''

What this did to national security can only be guessed at. Not surprisingly, Hoover ordered an ''all-out effort to discreetly obtain information concerning the activities of the princess.''

It was reported by several plants at Gloucester that employees received raises via Schofield because of their kindness to the princess. Every effort was made to survey the princess's activities from adjoining windows; Hoover had ordered the use of ''a rooming house'' for the purpose. Unfortunately, there was no such building and ''the main street in front of the station is patrolled by Coast Guards who are suspicious of any individuals who may pass by. It would not be feasible to park a car in the proper position to observe activities without being detected by the Coast Guard.''

Hoover was drastically concerned and sent a message to his New York office reading (August 3, 1942), ''In view of the interest which has been shown in this matter by the President of the United States and the Attorney General, you are directed to obtain all developments concerning it immediately and submit the same to the bureau for the attention of the espionage section.''

The princess's luck was remarkable: it proved difficult for the law firm in London to pursue their case against her because her attorney, David Brooks, was missing in action in Singapore. This caused a delay in the case.

She began turning to the church when Schofield proved understandably cool. She asked the priest to contact Cardinal Doherty, but he declined, perhaps in part because she wasn't a Catholic as she pretended.

In order to allay or smother the President's suspicions, Attorney General Biddle decided to transfer the princess to Seagoville, Texas, a convenient distance from Washington. Schofield made sure that a contact man was planted in the camp as his stooge. At last one of the FBI men took a chance and advised the Coast Guard of his purpose in watching Gloucester station. The Coast Guard was under special instruction to watch every move the princess's mother made in case she tried to spring Stefanie loose.

Stefanie became violent at the thought of being transferred to Texas and, in the words of a report, "acted like a tigress." She said that if her captors wanted to take her out of Gloucester, "they would have to carry her." As a result, an American Legion ambulance arrived at the center with two men carrying a restraining sheet and a straitjacket. When she saw these, she announced she felt better and proceeded to the railway station in an Immigration car. As she sailed out of the camp's gate, someone was heard to say, "Is Schofield in Texas?''

The answer was in the affirmative. In fact, Schofield had preceded her there by two days. Suddenly the reason for her going to Texas became clear: She could try to escape across the Mexican border.

The princess left the train station in style. She demanded the Coast Guard carry her suitcases, and when they declined, she castigated them, accusing them of being physically weak. Stung to the quick, they obliged. When she arrived on the train, she expressed astonishment that she had not been given a drawing room but was compelled to sit in the day coach with an officer on either side of her. But she soon flirted with the two men so outrageously that they brought her a glass of white wine and some peanuts.

The baroness, her mother, was already installed at the Hotel Adolphus in Dallas. The princess arrived at Seagoville only to dash off a telegram to an Immigration official that read: IMPOSSIBLE FOR MOTHER. PLEASE DISCARD ALL CONSIDERATION OR ETIQUETTE, PURSUE AND INSIST THAT B [her code for Schofield] DOES WHAT YOU WISH. UNBEARABLE HURRY. STEFANIE.

The telegram was no problem to understand; it meant that the official, firmly in Hohenlohe's pocket, was to abandon his own caution and make sure that Schofield got her back to Gloucester with no further ado. Apparently, the heat had already proved more than a counterbalance to the chances of escape to Mexico.

The princess began threatening everybody at Seagoville, saying that she would be out of Texas in a very short time. Whether that meant she intended to go to Mexico or New Jersey was far from clear.

To confuse matters further, the same day she arrived in Seagoville, Wiedemann was reported to have arrived by submarine near Seattle.

It is scarcely surprising that Schofield was in fact in Seagoville when Princess Hohenlohe came off the train on a stretcher and was carried to the hospital for ten days despite the fact there was nothing wrong with her. She demanded use of the telephone, extended hours for visits from her mother, and sleeping powders. However, the major's influence was limited at Seagoville. The inspector in charge of Immigration, Joseph O'Rourke, ignored Schofield's pleas and made sure she had no privileges at all. He also added a couple of guards to the cyclone fence. The princess announced that no fence would hold her and she would escape and go to Mexico at the slightest opportunity. Stefanie's mother announced that she wished to be interned with her daughter as she had nowhere else to stay. Biddle conveniently placed an order for her arrest.

Desperation set in by the end of November. The princess had given Schofield some jewelry to sell for additional favors and he had failed to return it. On an impulse she called the local FBI man in Dallas and said she would personally give Hoover a full account of her activities with Lord Rothermere, her association with Fritz Wiedemann, and particularly her contact with Major Schofield. She asked to be assured that this information would not be furnished to INS. She was warned that Biddle and Schofield were very close personal friends and Biddle would ignore her. She then said that her mother had told Schofield that Stefanie was being framed and that Stefanie was about ready to go to Hoover about the case when Schofield became alarmed and paid the baroness's way back to Texas. As a last ditch stand Stefanie offered to throw in personal information about Hitler and Goebbels to insure her release. Edward Tamm of the Washington FBI, in his memo to Hoover, said that the "Princess is a very clever and, consequently, a very dangerous woman, and that she is maneuvering now to play the Bureau against the Immigration Service so she will get something out of it."

In January 1943 the princess wrote a heavily reworked version of her life and sent it off to the FBI. She told the Dallas agent John Little as she handed over this scrambled document, "What I have to tell will be as sensational as [any] saboteur's trial. What I have to tell is a 50–50 proposition. You will never regret it as long as you live. If you help my story to receive the proper attention, you will be reimbursed many, many times. I also have means in Washington where a person giving the right word will see that your career is furthered!"

She claimed she was railroaded into internment to protect Schofield's name. She said, "Anyone who comes in contact with me—it is his lucky day. This interview will make your career. My story will make headlines." She demanded to be sent to Hoover and Roosevelt "about matters which I can only relate to the President."

She became hysterical several times and then admitted, "I am a spoiled brat." She insisted that Agent Little promise to release her. She said that she knew of "secret misunderstandings" between Hoover and Schofield. She said Schofield was dreadfully afraid of Walter Winchell. She said Schofield had her jewels and she would report him to Hoover. She said, "I always tell the whole truth and nothing but the truth. And only lie when I have to."

She asked for a special board to sit on her case comprised of Hoover, Schofield, Biddle, "and anybody else who should be present."

"That is beyond imagination," Little replied.

She continued. "Ask Mr. Hoover to come here in person. I won't always be a nobody. I have friends. You'll do what you can?" She sent a letter to Hoover, grossly flattering to John Little. She then said, mysteriously, "I have something to tell you, Mr. Hoover, of a personal nature. As a result, I will be cleared!"

With blackmail in the air, Little left.

Her last words to him were, "You will make headlines!"

In a further statement she pretended that she had not been intimate with a man since 1920. ("Where some women take pleasure in giving themselves, I take pleasure in denying myself.")

The material was the mixture as before: a blend of truth and fantasy and veiled threats. It seems to have impressed somebody in Washington, because efforts were made to arrange a new hearing of the Princess Hohenlohe's case. She sent several letters to Hoover that indicated clearly she had given up on Hitler because of the news of his failures in the war. Meanwhile, her mother posed as an insane person and asked for commitment to a mental institution. She was judged mad at a state court at Dallas. She was put in a pauper's ward.

Another agent went to see the Princess Hohenlohe in November 1943 and found her extremely distraught and in an emotional condition. He described her as "a consummate actress," "her emotion . . . artificial and designed to win my sympathy."

On March 1, 1944, the Princess Hohenlohe finally got her hearing. Those present on the board were two members of the Department of Justice and one member of the FBI. The board concluded she was innocent of everything and that she should be paroled at once. She sailed triumphantly out of Seagoville—but not at once. Hoover held up the matter for some weeks. Roosevelt personally overruled the board and saw to it that the princess was not released for the duration.

In late January 1945, Stefanie tried to kill herself with an overdose of pills. How she obtained them is a mystery. The princess sent a harsh letter to Biddle and a long rambling note to Eleanor Roosevelt.

The princess was finally released a few days after V-E Day. She appeared to have suffered little from her ordeal, and Major Schofield welcomed her back with open arms. They moved to his farm near Philadelphia and lived there as man and wife. The princess reconquered New York society. Seen dancing at the Stork Club, she provoked columnist Robert Ruark into writing that soon Ribbentrop would be observed in similar circumstances.

Wiedemann was equally fortunate. During the war years he had successfully run Nazi intelligence in Occupied China from the consulate in Tientsin, guarding his safety by claiming diplomatic immunity when the American troops moved in and by pointing out that he had protected Jews there.

Arrested in China in 1945, Wiedemann turned state's evidence at Nuremberg, providing familiar information in a mélange that secured him immunity from the Nuremberg Trials. Wiedemann breezed through denazification. He was credited with being part of the plot whereby Admiral Canaris, head of the Abwehr, had hoped to remove Hitler—not, more accurately, with the Himmler plot. The FBI never sent the huge file on him and the princess to Nuremberg. They were not asked to so do. Once again, The Fraternity had closed its ranks.

12

The Fraternity Runs for Cover

The Nuremberg Trials successfully buried the truth of The Fraternity connections. Schacht, who was more privy to the financial connections than most German leaders, gave an extraordinary performance, mocking, hectoring, and pouring contempt upon his chief prosecutor—Biddle's predecessor, Robert H. Jackson. Charged with engineering the war when he had only wanted to serve the neutralist policies of Fraternity associates, he was understandably acquitted. Had he chosen to do so, he could have stripped bare the details of the conspiracy, but only once in his entire cross-examination, when he admitted to complicity in the shipment to Berlin of the Austrian gold,* did he indicate any knowledge of such matters. Never in those days on the witness stand was he asked about the Bank for International Settlements or Thomas H. McKittrick. Not even in his memoirs was there an inkling of what he knew.

Conveniently for The Fraternity, Göring and Himmler committed suicide, carrying with them the secrets that Charles Bedaux, William Rhodes Davis, William Weiss of Sterling, and William S. Farish had carried to their graves. James V. Forrestal also ended his life by suicide. In 1949 he hanged himself from the window of the Bethesda Naval Hospital in Washington, D.C., where he was suffering from

---

*But not the Czech, Belgian, or Dutch.

advanced paranoid schizophrenia. Newspapers reported him screaming that the Jews and the communists were crawling on the floor of
his room seeking to destroy him.

The rest of the conspirators lived out full life-spans.

When Germany fell, Hermann Schmitz fled from Frankfurt to a
hiding place in a small house near Heidelberg. Shuffled around between the lines in a railroad carriage, this powerful man cowered in
terror as bombs exploded about him. But he was softly handled when
the U.S. Army moved in. He was imprisoned, but well treated, thanks
to the influence of his great and powerful friends. Despite the fact
that he and his colleagues had been responsible for the deaths of four
million Jews at Auschwitz, they were not tried for mass murder as
war criminals. Instead, they were tried for preparing and planning aggressive war, and other related counts. Since they had intended to
form a world fascist state without war if possible, and since their
whole purpose was simply to render Germany equal in a United States
of Fascism, they were acquitted on the first charge. The lesser charges
resulted in insignificant sentences.

Thinner now and equipped with a distinguished Vandyke beard,
Schmitz cleverly decided not to give evidence at the trial. He claimed
illness but in fact was seldom absent. His only statement came at the
end of the hearings when he had the audacity to quote St. Augustine
and, for good measure, Abraham Lincoln, to the judges. He spent
only eight more months in prison.

Max Ilgner was equally cunning. He told the prosecutors he would
become a priest after he left prison. He did.

Espionage was not an issue in the case; no summoning of transatlantic figures was considered. Dietrich Schmitz, now on a chicken
farm in Connecticut, and Rudolph Ilgner went unpunished. In various
court hearings of the 1940s, Schmitz and Ilgner had been indicted but
the cases against them were never prosecuted.

On September 8, 1944, Roosevelt had sent a letter to Cordell Hull
that was front page in many newspapers. It included the bold statement, "The history of the use of the I.G. Farben trust by the Nazis
reads like a detective story. Defeat of the Nazi army will have to be
followed by the eradication of those weapons of economic warfare."

The powers of the Allied Military Government who favored The
Fraternity disagreed and insisted upon I.G. Farben being retained af-

ter light punishment for its leaders. Morgenthau protested to Roosevelt, who summoned him to a discussion at the Quebec Conference in September 1944.

Morgenthau laid out his idealistic and impractical Morgenthau Plan—actually the creation of Harry Dexter White. Based upon his profound knowledge of collusion, White wanted a total elimination not only of I.G. Farben but of all German armaments and chemical and metallurgical industries. He wanted Germany to become a strictly agrarian economy; Roosevelt seemed to agree. In December 1944, Roosevelt, taking his cue from Morgenthau, made a statement via John G. Winant in which he called for an abolition of the Nazi industrial war machine. But already there were some compromises in the plan. Morgenthau came under a storm of abuse from the right wing, and the ailing President was now yielding to some minor pressures and starting to back away. In February 1945, at the Yalta Conference, Roosevelt, by now grievously ill, strove to follow Morgenthau's reasoning by making the much criticized arrangements to divide Germany down the middle into eastern and western zones.

When Truman became President, Eisenhower, as commander in chief of European forces, continued to follow Morgenthau's attitude with severe edicts, calling for disruption of any Nazi source of a possible World War III. But Truman disagreed. He was convinced that to render Germany agrarian was to leave an open path for Bolshevist conquest. General George S. Patton agreed with him and began to put Nazis back in office in Germany after the war.

Those who, with ideals held high, arrived in Germany from the United States to try to disrupt the cartels were severely handicapped from the start. One of these was a promising young lawyer, Russell A. Nixon, a liberal member of the U.S. Military Government Cartel Unit. He was handicapped from the start. He came directly under Brigadier General William H. Draper, who was, along with James V. Forrestal, a vice-president of Dillon, Read, bankers who had financed Germany after World War I. Nixon quickly realized that Draper, director of the economics division, and Robert Murphy, who had moved from North Africa to become ambassador to the new Germany, were going to block his every move.

When he arrived in Germany in July 1945, Nixon found his position was virtually untenable. He had been asked to explore a tunnel that had already been bricked up.

He asked Colonel E. S. Pillsbury, Special Control Officer in charge of I.G. Farben, what had been done these several months after V-E day to carry out Eisenhower's directives on dismantling Farben. Pillsbury failed to give any information and seriously questioned whether Nixon had any jurisdiction to investigate the cartel. Nixon turned in desperation to several members of Draper's staff, only to discover that Draper had failed to give them written directives to close I.G. plants.

One man, Joseph Dodge, told Nixon he had instructed his team to dismantle an I.G. poison gas plant but that Draper had canceled the order. Again, Dodge tried to wreck the I.G. underground plant at Mannheim and again Draper intervened. Soon afterward, Dodge told Nixon, Draper arranged for both plants to obtain added business.

Frustrated, Nixon went over Draper's head. He reported to General Lucius D. Clay on December 17, 1945, that Eisenhower's orders had been deliberately violated. He charged that, contrary to Draper's statements in the press that every I.G. plant had been bombed or dismantled, none had been. He said that General Henry H. Arnold of the Army Air Force had protected I.G. and he added that despite the pleas of the Jewish councils the installations and communications systems of Auschwitz had not been destroyed.

Clay listened to Nixon's charges but did nothing about them. Nixon found that scientific and mechanical equipment in I.G. plants had been saved from removal on specific orders from Washington. Searching through files on January 15, 1946, Nixon found a letter written by Max Ilgner that gave the game away. Dated May 15, 1944, and addressed to the I.G. Central Finance Department, the letter instructed the staff to keep "in constant touch" in defeated Germany since the American authorities "would surely permit resumption of I.G. operations." Thus, the head of the N.W.7. I.G. espionage unit looked forward confidently to the future. He of all people knew the Americans he was dealing with.

Nixon was handicapped not only by the American military government, but by the British. The Labour government in England was in severe financial difficulties and wanted to make sure it had good industrial connections in Germany. Like the American government, it was busy reconstituting I.G. When Russell A. Nixon pleaded with Sir Percy Mills at meetings of the Joint Chiefs of Staff to use his influence with Clay and Draper, Mills simply held matters up further. As a result, scarcely any Nazi industrial leader was in custody by 1946.

Nixon did manage to have a few people brought in. These included Paul Denker, I.G.'s chief accountant in the poison gas division; Carl von Heider, sales director of inorganic chemicals; Hans Kugler, director of dyestuff sales; Gunther Frank-Fahle and Kurt Kreuger of Ilgner's espionage group; and Gustave Kupper, head of the dyestuffs' legal division. None of these spent any time in custody. Nixon also wanted to bring in directors of the banks that had been deeply involved with I.G., including the Deutsche Bank, the Deutsche Landersbank, the Reichsbank, and the Dresdnerbank. He wanted to ask them about the whereabouts of German looted gold and cash including the Austrian and Czech gold transferred through the BIS. Again he was blocked: Draper told Counter-Intelligence not to make the arrests. Nixon pleaded directly to Washington, and after a considerable delay Draper was overruled. But no sooner had the bank officials been taken to Army headquarters than a Major General Adcock, representing Draper, brought orders for their release. Nixon was told he had been insubordinate in going over Draper's head and should be court-martialed as a radical.

Nixon later reported to the Senator Owen Brewster War Committee in Washington that by the spring of 1946 only 85,000 of 200,000 industrial and Gestapo leaders had been arrested. He was particularly annoyed by the exemption accorded to the major Nazi industrialist Richard Freudenberg, who had worked with Göring and Carl Krauch on the Four-Year Plan and had been on the board of the Schröder Bank. When Nixon took the bold step of ordering Freudenberg arrested under mandatory arrest provision JCF 1067, the denazification board in Frankfurt voted four to one to exempt him from the provision, and Ambassador to Germany Robert Murphy ordered his release. Murphy made a statement that proved to be significant: "It is not in conformity with American standards to cut away the basis of private property." Apparently it was in conformity with American standards to restore high-ranking Nazis to their previous positions. With unconscious humor a member of the Industry Division of the

Occupying Forces confirmed Murphy's position by saying, "This man Freudenberg is an extremely capable industrialist: a kind of Henry Ford." No one could quarrel with that.

Draper sent an official to take charge of Nixon's operation in the winter of 1946. Carl Peters was in charge of Foreign Economic Administration under Leo Crowley. He was also a director of the Advanced Solvents Corporation, a subsidiary of General Aniline and Film. He had been indicted for dealing with the enemy but had pleaded nolle prosequi and had been awarded the position of colonel in the Pentagon. No sooner was he in charge of Nixon than he began securing the release of German industrialists and set up the old Norwegian plant Noramco as an I.G. subsidiary once more.

Nixon had had enough. He returned to the United States and condemned the entire protection of Nazis to Senator Kilgore's investigative committee. He charged that elements in the United States, British, and French foreign offices had consciously maneuvered to prevent the Allies from being involved in the search for Nazi assets in neutral countries, because that search would lay bare the fascist regimes in Spain, Portugal, Switzerland, Sweden, and Argentina "and would reveal all the elements of collaboration of certain industrialists in the Allied countries with these regimes."

The young, very sharp lawyer James Stewart Martin of the Department of Justice's investigative team came to Europe from Washington. He arrived at U.S. Military Command at Bushy Park, London, only to find that Graeme K. Howard of General Motors was colonel over him. Martin protested to G-2 about the General Motors–Nazi connection, and nothing was done. But he managed to find a copy of Howard's book *America and a New World Order*. Fearful of a public outcry, the Army shipped Howard home.

Martin investigated the whereabouts of Gerhardt Westrick. In the last year of the war Westrick had played an increasingly difficult and dangerous role in Germany. After Generals Fellgiebel and Thiele were hanged for treason, Westrick managed to hang on almost to the end of the conflict. He fled when Berlin was bombed and his home was destroyed. He hid out in a castle in southwest Germany. Behn, clearly afraid of the consequences if his association with Westrick became known, refused to answer his old friend's pleading letters. Instead, he arranged for Westrick to be brought by his Army associates to

Paris to give a full report to ITT's Colonel Alexander Sanders at the Hotel Claridge on the status of the ITT companies in Germany.

Westrick was given a light prison sentence and released—deeply embittered that Behn had let him be punished at all.

Martin found out that Leo T. Crowley and Ernest K. Halbach, those custodians of General Aniline and Film, when asked to supply the truth of GAF's actual ownership through I.G. Chemie, had simply referred the matter to Allen Dulles. The head of the OSS had failed to supply the required information.

At the I.G. headquarters in Frankfurt, Martin discovered files that confirmed earlier beliefs that Schmitz had laid out plans for a conquered world in which America would join in triumph. He began to understand why Schmitz and the others of I.G. had turned against Hitler. It was clear that Hitler wanted to attack the United States with Göring's bombers when sufficiently long-distance aircraft were developed. But Schmitz was loyal to his American colleagues, preferring to maintain the alliances in perpetuity. These alliances could be sustained if Himmler and/or the German generals ran the Third Reich. They would be content with Schmitz's dream of a negotiated peace.

Further evidence came to light showing the continuing connection between Schmitz and the United States during the war. In 1943 a magazine article by R. T. Haslam of Standard Oil appeared in *The Petroleum Times*. It stated that the relationship with I.G. Farben had proved to be advantageous to the United States government. A special report of I.G. Farben emphatically denied this, pointing out the innumerable benefits that Germany had obtained from her American friends, including the use of tetraethyl, without which the war effort would have been impossible, and the supply of which had been approved by the U.S. War Department. The report said, "At the outbreak of war we were completely prepared from a technical point of view. We obtained standards not only from our own experiences but also from those of General Motors and other big manufacturers of automobiles." The report also revealed that Standard had sold $20 million worth of mineral oil products including airplane benzene to I.G. The report concluded: "The fact that we actually succeeded . . . in buying these quantities demanded by the German government from Standard Oil Co. and the Royal Dutch Shell group and importing them into Germany was only because of the support of Standard Oil

Company.'' Even more damning, Martin found that I.G. had placed a 50 million mark credit to Karl Lindemann's Standard subsidiary in Germany in the Deutsch Landersbank, wholly owned by I.G. with Hermann Schmitz as chairman, *in 1944.*

Thus, it was clear that Standard's business in Nazi Germany was open as usual and that its German subsidiary was being paid handsomely for prewar agreements.

Martin and his team were hampered at every turn. He wrote in his book *All Honorable Men:*

> We had not been stopped in Germany by German business. We had been stopped in Germany by American business. The forces that stopped us had operated from the United States but had not operated in the open. We were not stopped by a law of Congress, by an Executive Order of the President, or even by a change of policy approved by the President . . . in short, whatever it was that had stopped us was not "the government." But it clearly had command of channels through which the government normally operates. The relative powerlessness of governments in the growing economic power is of course not new . . . national governments stood on the sidelines while bigger operators arranged the world's affairs.

These operators were among the obstacles faced by James Stewart Martin and his team as they began work in the fall of 1945. A year after they began rummaging through documents, many of the Nazis in Schmitz's and Hitler's immediate circle were untouched by defeat. Schmitz's fellow director of the Deutsche Bank, Hermann Abs, was now financial advisor in the British zone. Heinrich Dinkelbach, also a partner of Schmitz, was in charge of the administration of all iron and steel industries in the British zone. Yet another director of the Steel Union, Werner Carp, the closest friend of Baron von Schröder's, was released from detention and became Dinkelbach's partner.

So much for Eisenhower's orders to denazify industry. Schmitz in his prison could afford to smile. "The Nazi chieftains," Raymond Daniell wrote in *The New York Times* on September 20, 1945, "[are] in positions where they can continue to control to a large degree the machinery whereby Germany made war." Daniell continued,

> The effect of the breakdown of the denazification program . . . preserves the power of men whose nationalistic and militaristic ideas were

the very antithesis of democracy . . . in industry, in the fields of transportation and communication, the flouting of General Eisenhower's order is particularly flagrant . . . in avoiding compliance with [that] order, Army and Military government officials have shown considerable versatility. Where they have not ignored the order completely, they have got around it by reclassifying important jobs under other names and leaving the Nazi incumbent alone.

Daniell continued:

Nor has there been any known development on the plan for the disposition of the property of active Nazis, as must have been contemplated when their accounts were blocked. At present a proposal is being circulated to provide for the payment of their old salaries to executives who have been arrested and who are giving evidence to the Occupation authorities. In other words, it is proposed that those who helped the Nazis be treated as employees whose services are worth to us approximately what the Nazis paid them.

Martin made a serious discovery in October 1945. He reported that General Patton literally had sabotaged the Potsdam Agreement calling for a destruction of I.G. and that in fact it was simply being split into components and allowed to continue with several of Schmitz's minor executives continuing in higher positions. Simultaneously, the Kilgore Committee reported in Washington on November 15, 1945, that the Swiss banks led by the BIS and its member bank, the Swiss National Bank (which shared directors and staff members), had violated agreements made at the end of the war not to permit financial transactions that would help the Nazis dispose of their loot. Senator Harley Kilgore stated, "Despite . . . the assurances of the Swiss government that German accounts would be blocked, the Germans maneuvered themselves back into a position where they could utilize their assets in Switzerland, could acquire desperately needed foreign exchange by the sale of looted gold and could conceal economic reserves for another war. These moves were made possible by the willingness of the Swiss government and banking officials, in violation of their agreement with the Allied Powers, to make a secret deal with the Nazis." Martin's team, working with a special Treasury group of T-men, unraveled much of this information for Kilgore.

They found a letter from Emil Puhl to Dr. Walther Funk dated March 30, 1945, which said: "Above all I have insisted [to the National Bank] on our receiving Swiss francs in return for Reichsmarks which the Reichsbank might release for any reason. That is important as it will enable us to use these francs to transfer funds into a third country."

It was agreed by the mission to Switzerland headed by U.S. economics advisor Lauchlin Currie in 1945 that gold might be used for embassy expenses. Puhl made the Swiss buy the German gold. A further letter, dated April 6, 1945, from Puhl to Funk read: "All in all, I believe that we can be satisfied that we have succeeded in obtaining . . . arrangements for German-Swiss payments. Whatever form events will take, such connections will always exist between our countries, and the fact that there exists a contract agreement may be of considerable importance in the future. Anyway, the contrary, the breaking off of the innumerable connections, would have been a rubble pile which would have presented immense difficulties."

The day after the Kilgore Committee made these disclosures, the Treasury team along with Martin's was drastically restricted from further activities. Raymond Daniell wrote in *The New York Times* on November 16 that the experts who came to hunt down the Reich's hidden assets were suddenly relegated to obscure roles. "As a result," Daniell wrote, "140 Treasury employees are wondering tonight whether they are going to be recalled or ordered to stay on here compiling reports and making recommendations that other departments can use or ignore as they choose. Many of them feel that their usefulness here has been ended."

All through those difficult weeks Martin, his team, and the T-men clashed with Brigadier General Draper and Charles Fahey of Draper's legal division, both of whom flagrantly ignored Eisenhower's policy and the mandatory terms of the Potsdam Agreement. Russell Nixon sympathized with their largely hopeless efforts to smash Nazi economic power in Germany and overseas. He said, "Treasury experts are in the doghouse at the office of Military government." Most devastating of all, he stated that Draper had flatly refused to denazify any financial institution in Germany.

In Washington, Colonel Bernard Bernstein of the Treasury squad was delivering a powerful series of blows to I.G. before the Kilgore

Committee. He denounced Standard's synthetic rubber agreements, its $20 million contract for aviation gasoline, its $1 million supply of tetraethyl. He named Ernest K. Halbach and Hugh Williamson of GAF as organizers of direct deliveries to I.G.'s South American subsidiaries after Pearl Harbor. He charged that Du Pont owned 6 percent of I.G.'s common stock throughout World War II and that Swiss banks had uniformly refused to yield up details of I.G. Chemie. Kilgore, commenting on these statements, said, "I am profoundly disturbed by a number of recent events pointing to an attitude on the part of some of our key officials which countenances and even bolsters Nazism in the economic and political life of Germany." He said that Draper had ignored directives of six months earlier to destroy I.G.'s plants. He added that the State Department blatantly supported Draper's policy. Kilgore made clear that State Department policy did not have President Truman's concurrence.

A U.S. Military Government spokesman, who was not named, denied Kilgore's charges in *The New York Times* on Christmas Day 1945. He said it was untrue that the I.G. organization had not been broken up: that in fact "the entire I.G. question has been placed on a four-power level." He was pointing to the fact that the United States, Britain, France, and Russia all had parts of Farben because of its diffuse character; he neglected to point out that only Russia of the four powers had tried to shatter I.G.'s structure.

In July 1946, James Stewart Martin was still struggling to expose the full truth of Nazi-American business arrangements. He was not helped by the fact that Brigadier General Draper hired the adventurous Alexander Kreuter, Charles Bedaux's partner in the Worms Bank, as his economic aide.

Gordon Kern of ITT also turned up on the scene. Kern, ostensibly there to be in an advisory capacity, spent most of his time transferring the Focke-Wulf factories from the Russian to the American zone. He also arranged for ITT's Nazi factory to be used by the Army Signal Corps, which prevented its dissolution, and had Westrick brought to Switzerland to disentangle ITT's Nazi patents held in Swiss banks.

In October 1946, Senator Kilgore arrived in Germany with the Senate War Investigating Committee to try to determine why attempts to decartelize the Nazis were being obstructed at every turn. George Meader, counsel for the committee, prepared a thousand pages of testimony from scores of U.S. Army officers. A few weeks later, when the investigations were continuing, Averell Harriman (of Brown Brothers, Harriman), Jesse Jones's successor as Secretary of Commerce, sent Philip D. Reed, head of General Electric, which had suppressed tungsten carbide in favor of Krupp and financed Hitler, on an urgent mission to Berlin to confer with Draper. Simultaneously, General Lucius Clay was questioned for two hours secretly by Kilgore in Washington. The results of the questionnaire were never disclosed.

In December, Clay was back in Germany, smarting at criticisms of his activities. He arranged a meeting between Draper and Philip D. Reed at the office of his finance chief, Jack Bennett. At the meeting Richard Spencer of Clay's legal division attacked President Truman's policy on denazification and breaking up I.G. Reed reported to Harriman that the investigation of I.G. and the Americans, which was still struggling feebly along under Martin's guidance, was a symptom of Martin's "extremism" and should be brought to an immediate end.

Meader's detailed report, damning in detail and forceful in execution, was too strong even for Kilgore. He said, inter alia, "I will put it this way: that men, some men, if the Germans had ever invaded this country and conquered us, would have been the first to collaborate with the conquerors, and have been influential in decisions being made in Germany."

Secretary of War Robert B. Patterson said that he was of the opinion that Meader's statement "gave a distorted and frequently erroneous picture of the American Zone." Lieutenant General Dan I. Sultan, Inspector General of the Army, also denounced Meader, saying his charges were "unverified." Yet Meader had based his report on thoroughly reliable sources. Military officer after officer was disclosed as corrupt, unsavory, and in collusion with the Nazis.

Among the testimonies was that of Colonel Francis P. Miller who had been executive officer of Army Intelligence under Clay and had formerly been with the OSS. He charged that "Officials selected for influential economic positions in the military government had business connections at home that might influence their outlook and acts." He called for an intensified use of Army Intelligence to expose malfeasances in high office.

That December the Kilgore Committee uncovered more and more scandals. Meader introduced documents showing how Draper had told a visiting party of newspaper editors that the program of purging Nazis was holding back economic development.

There were efforts made to obtain a reversal of Truman's policy of removing patents from German hands. The leader of this attempted reversal was an executive of the U.S. Steel Corporation, who remained unnamed because of the connections to the Schmitz and Krupp steel empire. This personage called for a reopening of the German Patent Office immediately and charged that the President had jeopardized it by his policy declarations. The steel executive also wanted an outright prohibition of inspections of German plants. Phillips Hawkins pointed out that the reestablishment of patent systems and prohibition of search would be disastrous for decartelization.

General Clay had, the committee revealed, sent a stern memorandum to Draper telling him that denazification was beneficial and that the failure to denazify industry would have created major labor-management problems. He rebuked Draper loudly and clearly for opposing the removal of Nazis.

Several letters were read from James Stewart Martin showing how he had been forced into retreat. He named—but the name was not made public—an American industrialist who was trying to obtain a penicillin monopoly in Germany by buying up one American corporation after another with Nazi links, including I.G. He also charged that lobbying in Washington was allowing ITT, National Cash Register, and Singer sewing machine company to enter Germany on special licenses in defiance of presidential orders.

Kilgore was infuriated by Meader's charges and denounced him to the press.

James Stewart Martin resigned his position in frustration. His replacement, Phillips Hawkins, married General Draper's daughter.

In February 1947, Richardson Bronson, formerly Martin's deputy control officer, fired one quarter of his staff and announced that there would no longer be any decartelization of I.G. or any other heavy industry in Germany. Only small consumer-goods firms would be affected. The decision was approved by former President Herbert Hoover, who had received Hermann Schmitz at the White House in

1931. Hoover's report at the end of an investigative trip urged that I.G. and Krupp should be enabled to rebuild Germany.

Those few who raised voices against such goings-on were dismissed by the military arm as "commies." Draper still had some critics. Alexander Sacks, formerly of James Stewart Martin's staff, charged before the Ferguson Commission on decartelization in 1948 that in every way "the policies of the Roosevelt and Truman administrations have been flagrantly disregarded by the very individuals who were charged with the highest responsibility for carrying them out." Sacks was dismissed.

As for General Aniline and Film, that indestructible organ of The Fraternity, all efforts against it by Morgenthau and his successors in the Treasury proved futile. Robert F. Kennedy as Attorney General protected the company from dissolution—in his father's tradition. On March 9, 1965, GAF was sold in the largest competitive auction in Wall Street history. The buyer, offering $340 million, was an affiliate of I.G. Farben in Germany.

Those who had opposed The Fraternity were not so fortunate. In 1948 the House Un-American Activities Committee, in one of its unbridled smear campaigns, named Morgenthau's trusted associates Harry Dexter White and Lauchlin Currie as communist agents. Based on the uncorroborated testimony of one Elizabeth Bentley, a self-confessed Soviet spy who was turning state's evidence, the Morgenthau Treasury administration was smeared in the eyes of the public. White and Currie, those deeply loyal enemies of fascism, those investigators of the Bank for International Settlements, of Standard, the Chase, the National City Bank, the Morgans, William Rhodes Davis, the Texas Company, ITT, RCA, SKF, GAF, Ford, and General Motors, were effectively destroyed by the hearings. Currie disappeared into Colombia, his U.S. citizenship canceled in 1956, and White died of a heart attack on August 16, 1948, aged fifty-six, after returning home from an investigative session. While the surviving Fraternity figures flourished again, helping to form the texture of postwar technology, those who had dared to expose them were finished. The Fraternity leaders who had died could sleep comfortably in their graves—their dark purpose accomplished.

APPENDICES

Selective Bibliography

Allen, Gary. *None Dare Call It Conspiracy*. Waukesha, Wis.: Country Beautiful Corporation, Concord Press, 1971.

Ambruster, Howard W. *Treason's Peace*. New York: The Beechhurst Press, 1947.

Angebert, Jean, and Angebert, Michel. *The Occult and the Third Reich*. New York: Macmillan, 1974.

Archer, Jules. *The Plot to Seize the White House*. New York: Hawthorn Books, 1973.

Biddle, Francis. *In Brief Authority*. New York: Doubleday, 1962.

Blum, John Morton. *From the Morgenthau Diaries. Years of Crisis, 1928–1938; Years of Urgency, 1938–1941; and Years of War, 1941–1945*. Boston: Houghton Mifflin, 1959–1967.

Borkin, Joseph. *The Crime and Punishment of I.G. Farben*. New York: The Free Press, 1978.

Dodd, William E., Jr., and Dodd, Martha, Eds. *Ambassador Dodd's Diary. 1933–1938*. New York: Harcourt Brace, 1941.

DuBois, Josiah E., Jr. *The Devil's Chemists*. Boston: Beacon Press, 1952.

Dulles, Eleanor. *The Bank for International Settlements at Work*. New York: Macmillan, 1932.

Farago, Ladislas. *The Game of the Foxes*. New York: David McKay, 1971.

Gellman, Irwin. *Good Neighbor Diplomacy*. Baltimore: Johns Hopkins, 1979.

Guerin, Daniel. *Fascisme Et Grand Capital*. Paris: François Maspero, 1965.

Hargrave, John. *Montagu Norman*. London: Greystone Press, n.d. [1942].

Hexner, Ervin. *International Cartels*. Chapel Hill: University of North Carolina Press, 1945.

Hirszowicz, Lukasz. *The Third Reich and the Arab East*. London: Routledge and Kegan Paul, 1966.

Hoke, Henry R. *It's a Secret*. New York: Reynal and Hitchcock, n.d.

Howard, Graeme K. *America and a New World Order*. New York: Scribner's, 1940.

Johnson, Arthur M. *Winthrop W. Aldrich: Lawyer, Banker, Diplomat*. Boston: Harvard University Business School, 1968.

Langer, W. L., and Gleason, S. Everett. *The Challenge to Isolation*. New York: Harper Brothers, 1952.

Lee, Albert. *Henry Ford and the Jews*. Briarcliff Manor, N.Y.: Stein and Day, 1980.

Martin, James Stewart. *All Honorable Men*. Boston: Little, Brown, 1950.

Nevins, Allan, and Hill, Frank Ernest. *Ford: Decline and Rebirth, 1933–1962*. New York: Scribner's, 1962.

Peterson, Edward Norman. *Hjalmar Schacht*. Boston: Christopher Publishing House, 1954.

Quigley, Carroll. *Tragedy and Hope*. New York: Macmillan, 1966.

Rees, David. *Harry Dexter White: A Study in Paradox*. New York: Coward, McCann, & Geoghegan, 1973.

Reiss, Curt. *The Nazis Go Underground*. New York: Doubleday, 1944.

Rogge, O. John. *The Official German Report: Nazi Penetration 1924–1942. Pan-Arabism 1939–Today*. New York: Thomas Yoseloff, 1961.

Rogow, Arnold A. *James Forrestal: A Study of Personality, Politics and Policy*. New York: Macmillan, 1963.

Root, Waverley. *The Secret History of the War*. 3 vols. New York: Scribner's, 1945.

Sampson, Anthony. *The Sovereign State of ITT*. New York: Stein and Day, 1973.

Sayers, Michael, and Kahn, Albert E. *The Plot Against the Peace: A Warning to the Nation!* New York: The Dial Press, 1945.

Schacht, Hjalmar. *Confessions of the "Old Wizard."* Boston: Houghton Mifflin, 1956.

Schloss, Henry H. *The Bank for International Settlements*. Amsterdam: North Holland Publishing Company, 1958.

Seldes, George. *Iron, Blood and Profits*. New York: Harper Brothers, 1934.
——— *Facts and Fascism*. New York: In Fact, Inc., 1943.

Stocking, George W., and Watkins, Myron W. *Cartels in Action*. New York: Twentieth Century Fund, 1946.

Sutton, Antony C. *Wall Street and the Rise of Hitler*. Seal Beach, Calif.: '76 Press, 1976.

"Trials of War Criminals Before the Nuremberg Military Tribunals Under Control Council Law No. 10," Volume VIII, I.G. Farben case, Nuremberg, October 1946–April 1949. Washington: U.S. Government Printing Office, 1953.

United States Army Air Force, Aiming point report No. 1. E. 2 of May 29, 1943.

United States Congress. House of Representatives. Special Committee on *Un-American Activities and Investigation of Certain Other Propaganda Activities*. 73rd Congress, 2nd Session, Hearings No. 73 DC-4. Washington: U.S. Government Printing Office, 1934.

United States Congress. House of Representatives. Special Committee on Un-American Activities (1934). *Investigation of Nazi and Other Propaganda Activities*. 74th Congress, 1st Session, Report No. 153. Washington: U.S. Government Printing Office, 1934.

United States Congress. Senate. Hearings before the Committee on Finance. *Sale of Foreign Bonds or Securities in the United States*. 72nd Congress, 1st Session, S. Res. 19, Part 1, December 18, 19, and 21, 1931. Washington: U.S. Government Printing Office, 1931.

United States Congress. Senate. Hearings before a Subcommittee of the Committee on Military Affairs. *Scientific and Technical Mobilization*. 78th Congress, 2nd Session, S. Res. 107, Part 16, August 29 and September 7, 8, 12, and 13, 1944. Washington: U.S. Government Printing Office, 1944.

United States Congress. Senate. Hearings before a Subcommittee of the Committee on Military Affairs. *Scientific and Technical Mobilization*. 78th Congress, 1st Session, S. 702, Part 16, Washington: U.S. Government Printing Office, 1944.

United States Congress. Senate. Hearings before a Subcommittee of the Committee on Military Affairs. *Elimination of German Resources of War*. Report pursuant to S. Res. 107 and 146, July 2, 1945, Part 7. 78th Congress and 79th Congress. Washington: U.S. Government Printing Office, 1945.

United States Group Control Council (Germany), Office of the Director of Intelligence, Field Information Agency. Technical Intelligence Report No. EF/ME/1. September 4, 1945.

United States Congress. Senate. Subcommittee to Investigate the Administration of the Internal Security Act, Committee on the Judiciary. *Morgenthau Diary (Germany)*. Volume 1, 90th Congress, 1st Session,

November 20, 1967. Washington: U.S. Government Printing Office, 1967.

United States Strategic Bombing Survey. *Aeg-Ostlandwerke GmbH*, by Whitworth Ferguson. May 31, 1945.

United States Strategic Bombing Survey, *Plant Report of A.E.G. (Allgemeine Elektrizitats Gesellschaft)*. Nuremberg, Germany: June 1945.

United States Strategic Bombing Survey. *German Electrical Equipment Industry Report*. Equipment Division, January 1947.

Wall, Bennett H., and Gibb, George S. *Teagle of Jersey Standard*. New Orleans: Tulane University, 1974.

Magazines and Newspapers Consulted

The Nation; The New Republic; The Hour; Friday; In Fact; The Protestant; The New York Times; The Washington Post; The Washington Times-Herald; PM; The (London) *Times; The New Statesman and Nation; Time and Tide; The Wall Street Journal.*

Select Documentary Sources

Bank for International Settlements*

Telegrams from Merle Cochran to Henry Morgenthau, Jr.: February 14, March 14, May 9, 1939.

Memoranda from Merle Cochran to Henry Morgenthau, Jr.: April 27, May 9, May 15, 1940.

Reports on meetings of the Bank for International Settlements. 1940–1945. U.S. Consulate, Basle, Switzerland.

Resolution. H. Res. 188. 78th Congress. March 26, 1943.

Bretton Woods Conference, New Hampshire. Minutes of meetings of the U.S. delegates. July 10, July 17, July 18, July 19, July 20, 1944.

Memorandum from Orvis A. Schmidt to Henry Morgenthau, Jr. March 23, 1945.

Reports on Currie Mission to Switzerland. Minutes of meetings, memoranda to the President. April 12, May 2, May 21, 1945.

*Files available from Roosevelt Memorial Library, Hyde Park, New York.

Bedaux, Charles*

Embassy of the United States of America. Confidential Report. Vichy, May 4, 1942.

Interview with Charles E. Bedaux. Report by American Consulate, Algiers. October 30, 1942.

War Department Message. Secret. January 4, 1943.

War Department. Military Intelligence Service. Washington. Report. January 15, 1943.

Headquarters North African Theater of Operations. U.S. Army Inquiry. September 5, 1944.

Allied Force Headquarters. U.S. Army. G2. Report. February 14, 1945.

The Chase Bank—Paris**

Morgenthau Minutes. Meeting with Dr. Benjamin Anderson. April 28, 1937.

Department of State Memoranda. June 19, 1940.

Minutes of Treasury Meetings. August 26, 27, 1940.

Correspondence between Chase Bank, Paris and Châteauneuf, France, August 5, October 15, October 24, November 17, 1940.

Memoranda from Winthrop W. Aldrich to Henry Morgenthau, Jr. May 12, May 25, 1941.

Correspondence between Chase Bank, Paris, German banks, Vichy Headquarters and New York, December 30, 1941, January 3, 10, 15, 23, and 30, 1942; February 2, March 3, March 6, March 24, March 25, March 30, 1942; April 16, May 7, May 23, June 1, June 4, June 18, June 22, July 20, August 3, September 18, October 9, October 28, and December 31, 1942.

Accounts of Chase Bank, Paris, 1941–1942.

Memorandum from Randolph Paul to Henry Morgenthau, Jr. January 13, 1943.

*Files available from Department of the Army, Fort Meade, Maryland.
**Files available from the Department of the Treasury, Washington, D.C.

Accounts, Transactions, German Military Government Orders. Nazi Embassy, Paris. 1943.

Minutes of Meetings. Treasury, January 4, 13, 1944.

Report. Treasury Investigative Team, Paris, 1944.

Memoranda from Randolph Paul to Henry Morgenthau, Jr. February 3, 4, 1944.

Correspondence, Transaction List, Accounts, Memoranda between Nazi Embassy, Paris, and Chase Bank, May 22, May 30, June 8, June 29, July 3, August 10, August 16, 1944.

Memorandum from J. J. O'Connell, Jr., and Harry Dexter White to Henry Morgenthau, Jr. September 12, 1944.

Various memoranda, J. J. O'Connell, Jr., and Harry Dexter White to Henry Morgenthau, Jr. October 20, 27, 1944.

Henry Saxon to Henry Morgenthau, Jr. Memoranda. December 20, 1944.

Treasury Investigative Reports. December 30, 1944.

Harry Dexter White to Henry Morgenthau, Jr. February 12, 1945.

William Rhodes Davis*

Chapter drawn in its entirety from Davis Main File, FBI, 1937–1941, Washington, D.C.

Ford Motor Company**

Letters from Maurice Dollfus to Edsel B. Ford, September 19, October 31, November 27, 1940. October 13, 1941. January 28, February 11, August 15, 1942.

Report by Felix Cole, American Consulate, Algiers, July 11, 1942.

*File available from Freedom of Information Office, FBI Headquarters, Washington, D.C.
**Files available from Charles Higham Collection, Doheny Library, University of Southern California, Los Angeles.

Telegram from John G. Winant, U.S. Embassy, London, to Cordell Hull, October 20, 1942.

Telegrams from Leland Harrison, U.S. Minister in Berne, Switzerland, to Cordell Hull, October 29, December 4, 1942.

Reports by John J. Lawler to Henry Morgenthau, Jr., December 9, 10, 11, 1942 (includes transcripts of Edsel Ford's letters to Maurice Dollfus in Occupied France).

Accounts reports and details of transactions, Ford Motor Company, Dearborn and Poissy, December 11–12, 1942.

Report by Randolph Paul to Henry Morgenthau, Jr., May 25, 1943.

Report by Leland Harrison to Cordell Hull, December 13, 1943.

Report by John G. Winant to Cordell Hull, April 3, 1944.

General Motors *

Report by James D. Mooney to Adolf Hitler, n.d. (presumably January 1940).

Letter from James D. Mooney to Adolf Hitler, February 16, 1940.

Summarized statement of Hitler's conversation with James D. Mooney, March 4, 1940.

Notes covering James D. Mooney's visit to Göring, March 7, 1940.

Letters from James D. Mooney to Franklin D. Roosevelt, Rome, Italy,. March 11, 15, 1940.

Letter from Franklin D. Roosevelt to James D. Mooney, April 2, 1940.

Detailed program of meetings in Berlin and London in 1939 by James D. Mooney, January 24, 1941.

Letter from James D. Mooney to Franklin D. Roosevelt, February 21, 1941.

Report by J. Edgar Hoover to Adolf A. Berle, Jr., May 1, 1941.

FBI Reports, Various, 1942.

*Files available from Georgetown University Library, Washington, D.C., FBI, and National Archives Diplomatic Records Room.

Report by Leland Harrison to Cordell Hull, March 21, 1942.

Report of U.S. Embassy, Panama, June 26, 1942.

Report by U.S. Embassy, Buenos Aires, July 20, 1942.

Reports by John G. Winant to Cordell Hull, October 20, 1942.

Report by Jacques Reinstein to General Motors, April 2, 1943.

Telegram from U.S. Embassy, London, to Cordell Hull, May 18, 1944.

Report from U.S. Embassy, La Paz, Bolivia, to Cordell Hull, February 10, 1944.

Report from John G. Winant to Cordell Hull, April 11, 1944.

Princess Stefanie Hohenlohe, Fritz Wiedemann, and Sir William Wiseman*

Chapter drawn in its entirety from FBI Main Files on these individuals, Washington, D.C., 1940–1945.

ITT and Radio Corporation of America**

Telegram from American Legation, Bucharest, Rumania, to the Treasury, January 3, 1941.

Notes and Memoranda by E. H. Foley, Jr. and Herbert Feis to Sumner Welles, March 24, 25, 26, 1941, and October 9, 1941.

Undated draft on unification of Mexican telephone systems. Treasury files. 1941.

Censored conversation intercept. Hans Sturzenegger and Hugh Williamson, Basle and New York, June 24, July 3, 1941.

Memorandum from E. H. Foley, Jr., to Henry Morgenthau, Jr., September 8, 1941.

*Files available from FBI.
**Files available from National Archives and Records Service: Social and Industrial Records Room, Washington, D.C.

Memoranda from Breckinridge Long to Harry Hopkins, January 5, January 12, 1942.

Seized records, January-March 1942. ITT, South America.

Detailed reports of TTP, South America, State Department File, 1941–1942.

Staff memorandum for members of the interdepartmental advisory committee on hemisphere communications, Allen W. Sayler, January 13, 1942.

Intercepted conversation. Cia Radio International of Brazil, February 11, 1942.

FBI report. February 14, 1942.

Memo to Thurman Arnold from Robert Wohlforth, February 20, 1942.

Memo from R. T. Yingling to Breckinridge Long, February 26, 1942.

Censorship reports, January-May 1942.

Memoranda to Sumner Welles, from Breckinridge Long, April 21, 1942.

Memoranda of Breckinridge Long on meetings on ITT and RCA/Consortium, June 26, July 13, July 14, July 20, August 10, August 11, 1942. Also August 25 and September 21, 1942.

Censorship reports May-December 1942.

Special report on Mexican telephone merger, State Department, 1942.

Special report, State Department, August 20, 1942.

Minutes of meetings of the IHCAC, September-December 1942.

Intercepted communications, 1942–1943.

Report on leakage of shipping information. Office of Censorship. July 24, 1942.

Report on evasions of communications regulations and cable communications with the Axis. December 7, 11, 14, and 15, 1942.

Report on Axis pressure on ITT. November 18, 1942 (no source given).

Questionnaire, responses, and reports. U.S. Commercial Company to Henry A. Wallace, 1942–1943.

Breckinridge Long memoranda to the State Department, 1943.

FBI reports. ITT. Main File, 1943.

Censorship intercepts. ITT. April 14, 1943.

Minutes of meeting between W. A. Winterbottom and Breckinridge Long, August 16, 1943.

ITT. Intelligence report. Bartholomew Higgens to Wendell Berge, September 20, 1943.

Memorandum to Secret Intelligence Service, Berlin, FBI. September 12, 1945.

Interrogations of Baron Kurt von Schröder, November 20–25, 1945.

Interrogatory reports: numerous. Gerhardt Westrick. 1945 (no day or month).

SKF*

Memorandum re SKF. Heinrich Kronstein. March 6, 1942.

Secret memorandum. Foreign Economic Administration. Lauchlin Currie to Oscar Cox, February 4, 1944.

Memorandum for Foreign Economic Administration. Control groups in Sweden and their German tie-ups, 1944.

Memorandum from Captain W. D. Puleston to Lauchlin Currie. Foreign Economic Administration, March 15, 1944.

SKF Industries, Inc. report, 1944.

Jean Pajus draft report. Swedish ball-bearing business, May 1944.

Foreign Economic Administration. Memorandum for the files of the Economics Intelligence Division, May 1, 1944.

Miscellaneous telegrams from Ambassador Herschel Johnson in Stockholm to the Department of State. Encoded, May 1944.

Memorandum by Franklin S. Judson. Foreign Economic Administration, May 11, 1944.

Telegram. Stockholm Legation to Foreign Economic Administration and Secretary of State, May 13, 1944.

*Records available from National Archives and Records Service, Suitland, Maryland.

238 TRADING WITH THE ENEMY

Securities and Exchange Commission. Memorandum covering interviews with E. Austin and Ernest Wooler. Foreign Economic Administration file, May 19, 1944.

Memorandum of interview with J. W. Tawresey. Franklin S. Judson. June 7, 1944.

SKF. Introduction and summary. Jean Pajus, Foreign Economic Administration, September 15, 1944.

Telegrams received. American Legation, Stockholm, to Secretary of State, Washington, D.C., October 9, 1944.

Memorandum by Jean Pajus to Lauchlin Currie and Frank Coe, Foreign Economic Administration, November 2, 1944.

Complete summary of SKF wartime activities. Jean Pajus, 1945.

Standard Oil of New Jersey*

Report to Sumner Welles by Herbert Feis, March 31, 1941.

Report by John J. Muccio, Chargé d'Affaires, U.S. Consulate, Panama, to Cordell Hull, May 5, 1941.

Report by H. E. Linam, Standard Oil, Caracas, Venezuela, to Nelson Rockefeller, July 9, 1941.

Report by Major Charles A. Burroughs, G-2, Columbus, Ohio, to Headquarters, July 15, 1941.

Report from American Legation, Bucharest, Hungary, to State Department, August 5, 1941.

Report from E. H. Foley, Jr., Acting Secretary of the Treasury, to Cordell Hull, October 30, 1941.

Report by E. H. Foley, Jr., to the Senate Special Committee on Defense, April 30, 1942.

Letter from H. E. Linam, Standard Oil, to Dr. Frank P. Corrigan, U.S. Embassy, Caracas, Venezuela, June 8, 1942.

*Records available from National Archives and Records Service, Diplomatic Records Room.

Report from Samuel F. Gilbert to Donald Hiss, State Department Foreign Funds Control, July 14, 1942.

Letter from John J. Muccio, U.S. Embassy, Panama, to Cordell Hull, August 24, 1942.

Report by Leland Harrison, U.S. Embassy, Berne, to Cordell Hull, October 3, 1942.

Report by Daniel J. Reagan, Commercial Attaché, Berne, November 6, 1942.

Telegram in code from Leland Harrison to Cordell Hull, December 8, 1942.

Report by Jacques Reinstein to John N. Bohannon, Standard Oil, December 26, 1942.

Report from U.S. Embassy, London, to Cordell Hull, December 29, 1942.

Cable in code from Jacques Reinstein to U.S. Legation, Berne, January 20, 1943.

Telegrams from Leland Harrison, U.S. Legation, Berne, to Cordell Hull, January 28, 1943.

Report from Adolf Berle to U.S. Legation, Berne, February 27, 1943.

Telegrams from Leland Harrison, U.S. Legation, Berne, April 15, 21, 1943.

Telegrams from John G. Winant to Cordell Hull, May 5, 15, 17, and 18, 1943.

Reports from C. F. Sabourin to F. P. Corrigan, U.S. Embassy, Caracas, Venezuela, June 9, 1943.

Report from Frank P. Corrigan to A. T. Proudfit, Standard Oil of Venezuela, June 24, 1943.

Licenses permitting trading with enemy nationals. Various. 1943.

Sterling Products, Inc./General Aniline and Film*

Reports. Foreign Economic Administration, 1942, 1943.

Memorandum. Charles Henry Lee to John E. Lockwood. Foreign Economic Administration. July 19, 1941.

*Records available from FBI and from National Archives Diplomatic Records Room and Records Service, Washington, D.C.

Memorandum. Dean Acheson to Jefferson Caffrey. n.d. [1942]

Memorandum. J. Edgar Hoover to Adolf Berle. Alleged German agents in Brazil. May 26, 1942.

Memorandum. E. Schellnebergger. Chief, Commercial Intelligence. Department of Commerce. June 9, 1942.

Memorandum. Dean Acheson to the American Ambassador, Paraguay. June 29, 1942.

Memorandum. George Messersmith to Cordell Hull. July 14, 1942.

Memorandum. J. Edgar Hoover to Adolf Berle. July 28, 1942.

State Department Memorandum to the Chargé d'Affaires, Buenos Aires. September 11, 1942.

Memorandum. Frederick B. Lyon for Adolf Berle to J. Edgar Hoover. September 16, 1942.

Memorandum. Robert A. Scotten to State Department. September 21, 1942.

Memorandum. J. Edgar Hoover to Adolf Berle. September 28, 1942.

Memorandum. J. Edgar Hoover to Adolf Berle. October 3, 1942.

Memorandum. Frederick B. Lyon to J. Tannenwald. January 12, 1943.

Correspondence. Philip W. Thayer to State Department. August 1943.

Memorandum. Flemming T. Liggett, FBI, to J. Edgar Hoover. December 30, 1943.

Texas Company*

Enclosure to Dispatch No. 10008 of February 12, 1940, from U.S. Embassy, Mexico City, to State Department.

Memorandum from U.S. Embassy, Montevideo, Uruguay, to Lawrence Duggan, State Department, June 5, 1940.

Report of the U.S. Legation, Costa Rica, to Cordell Hull, June 13, 1941.

Military Intelligence Division Report, October 9, 1940.

*Records available from National Archives and Records Service, Diplomatic Records Room.

Memorandum from J. Edgar Hoover to Adolf Berle. February 10, 1942.

Report by A. R. Randolph, Acting Commercial Attaché, Guatemala. December 8, 1942.

Division of the American Republics Report. December 28, 1942.

Miscellaneous authorizations. A. R. Randolph. 1943.

Memorandum from Leland Harrison, U.S. Legation, Berne, Switzerland, to State Department. January 27, 1944.

Memorandum from Leland Harrison, U.S. Legation, Berne, Switzerland, to State Department. January 30, 1944.

Selected Documents

HEADQUARTERS FIFTH CORPS AREA
OFFICE OF THE CORPS AREA COMMANDER
FORT HAYES, COLUMBUS, OHIO CAB

OFFICE CHIEF OF STAFF
MIL. INTELL. DIV.
2267 - 32
JUL 17 1941
WAR DEPARTMENT

G-2

July 15, 1941

SUBJECT: Standard Oil Company of New Jersey Ships Under Panamanian
Registry.

TO: A. C. of S., G-2,
        War Department
        Washington, D. C.

1. A report has been received from Cleveland, Ohio, in which it is
stated that the source of this information is unquestionable, to the
effect that the Standard Oil Company of New Jersey now ships under Panamanian registry, transporting oil (fuel) from Aruba, Dutch West Indies
to Teneriffe, Canary Islands, and is apparently diverting about 20% of
this fuel oil to the present German government.

2. About six of the ships operating on this route are reputed to
be manned mainly by Nazi officers. Seamen have reported to the informant
that they have seen submarines in the immediate vicinity of the Canary
Islands and have learned that these submarines are refueling there. The
informant also stated that the Standard Oil Company has not lost any
ships to date by torpedoing as have other companies whose ships operate
to other ports.

For the A. C. of S., G-2,

CHAS. A. BURROWS,
Major, Military Intelligence,
Asst. A. C. of S., G-2

1941 JUL - 16 AM 4:34

Memorandum from R.T. Yingling, State Department attorney, to Assistant Secretary of State Breckinridge
Long

February 26, 1942.

Mr. Long:

It seems that the International Telephone and Telegraph Corporation which has been handling traffic between Latin American countries and Axis controlled
points with the encouragement or concurrence of the
Department desires some assurance that it will not be
prosecuted for such activities. It has been suggested
that the matter be discussed informally with the Attorney General and if he agrees the Corporation can be
advised that no prosecution is contemplated.

This office feels that no formal opinion of the Attorney General for its future guidance is necessary in
view of Resolution XL on telecommunications adopted at
the Consultative Meeting of Ministers of Foreign Affairs of the American Republics, held at Rio de Janeiro
in January of this year. If the International Telephone and Telegraph Corporation feels that activities
of the nature indicated above which it may be carrying
on at the present time in Latin America are within the
purview of the Trading with the Enemy Act it should apply to the Treasury Department for a license to engage
in such activities.

Le:RTYingling:LEY:SS

DEPARTMENT OF STATE

Memorandum of Conversation

STRICTLY CONFIDENTIAL   DATE: September 9, 1942.

SUBJECT: Telecommunication Circuits With the Axis Maintained by
Argentina and Chile.

PARTICIPANTS: The Secretary (later); Assistant Secretary Long;
Mr. Hackworth, Legal Adviser (later); Mr. Bonsal, RA;
Mr. Daniels, RA; Mr. Halle, RA; Mr. Reinstein, A-A;
Mr. Tannenwald, FF; Mr. deWolf, IN.

COPIES TO: A-L , A-A , FF , Le , IN

Memorandum of a Meeting in Mr. Long's Office (Later Adjourned
to the Secretary's Office)

Mr. Long pointed out that after months of conversation the American interests in the Consortium Trust (Radio Corporation of America) had done nothing actually to bring about a closure of the circuits maintained with the Axis by the Consortium companies in Argentina and Chile. He said they had proved what degree of control they could exercise over these companies by what had been accomplished in the course of General Davis' visit to Buenos Aires and Santiago, and that consequently he had no doubt but what they could order the companies to suspend the operation of the undesirable circuits. He said that the RCA representatives were coming to see him at 3 p.m. today, and that he had in mind telling them to do what was necessary in order to shut down the circuits by midnight tomorrow (September 10).

Mr. Bonsal suggested the advisability of informing the Argentine and Chilean Governments in advance of the contemplated action, pointing out that the politi-

cal consequences of doing otherwise might have wide
ramifications involving the basic policy governing
our relations with the two republics. Specifically, he
said, action taken by the companies in response to an
initiative from this Government to close the circuits
might raise the whole question of control by national
governments over public utilities operating within
their own jurisdiction. He felt that one of the consequences might be that nationalistic interests would
point out that the public services in these countries
were controlled by Washington, rather than by the national governments which should properly have jurisdiction.

Mr. Long expressed the view that, should the Governments be notified of the proposed action in advance, they would immediately call in the Axis
representatives and that then we would have a fight on
our hands. Mr. Bonsal felt that, in any case, we should
be much better informed than we were of what the legal
and political consequences of such action would be before we embarked on it.

The suggestion was advanced by Messrs. Daniels and
Halle that it might be sufficient to have the RCA representatives be prepared to issue the necessary orders
immediately when the Department gives them word to go
ahead. This suggestion was based especially on the
possibility that the Chilean Government might cut the
circuits in the near future on its own initiative, and
that since such initiative would lead the country
nearer to a complete diplomatic break with the Axis, it
would be preferable to company initiative.

The meeting thereupon adjourned to the Secretary's
Office, where Mr. Long placed the problem and various
considerations that had been advanced before the Secretary. The Secretary, citing the vital economic
assistance that we were extending to Argentina, especially in the way of iron and steel shipments, said
that we had a right to expect a good deal more coopera-

tion in return than we were getting. He said that,
while he had not been in close touch with the situation
in Argentina over the past few months, he felt the time
had come when we should deal more severely with the
Argentine Government. Consequently, he favored Mr.
Long's proposal to ask RCA to have the circuits aban-
doned by midnight tomorrow. Mr. Bonsal expressed his
view that we should have more information on the provisions of the franchises under which the companies were
operating before proceeding further. The Secretary
said that he felt the question of what the franchises
provided concerned the Consortium and the Consortium
companies rather than this Government. It was agreed
that, because of indications that the Chilean Government would not oppose company initiative in this matter, the Chilean authorities should be notified in
advance. In the case of Argentina, the Secretary expressed no objection to our having the company take the
action forthwith.

RA:LHalle:MM

248

DEPARTMENT OF STATE

Memorandum of ~~TELEPHONE~~ *Conversation*

DATE: May 24, 1943.

SUBJECT: Communications.

PARTICIPANTS: Colonel Sarnoff, RCA

Mr. Long.

COPIES TO: PA, IN.

Messages fr B.A. by Axis powers to their Govts

•PO   1—1403

    I talked to Colonel Sarnoff on the telephone and explained to him that we had reason to believe that more messages than the agreed 700 code-groups a week were being sent from B. A. by the Axis powers to their Governments. I told him I could not disclose down there the source of our information. In an effort to obtain additional information our representatives down there had approached Hayes. Hayes had seemed to them noncooperative. There may have been very sound reasons why he refused to disclose the exact number of messages sent in code-groups by each of the Axis representatives to their Government. However, there didn't seem to be any reason why the managership should not request a report on all code-groups being sent over a period of time, day by day, and to include a report on all belligerents, and that if he would obtain that information through confidential channels we would be appreciative. I suggested it be not done by telegraph or telephone and suggested the mail, but offered to make the pouch available.

    Colonel Sarnoff replied that he would talk to Mr. Winterbottom but he saw no reason why we should not do it and that he would communicate with us if they wanted to use the pouch.

    After receipt of this information we will be in a better position to judge what our policy should be.

B. L.

A-L:BL:lag

May 25 1943

Secretary Morgenthau

Randolph Paul

A short time ago a brief investigation was made of the files of the Ford Motor Company of Dearborn, Michigan, in order to determine the extent of its relationship and its control over its French subsidiary. Since the investigative report is rather lengthy, I have attached hereto a summary thereof which discloses that from the fall of France to July 1942—the date of the last letter in the files from Ford of France to Ford of America: (1) the business of the Ford subsidiaries in France substantially increased; (2) their production was solely for the benefit of Germany and the countries under its occupation; (3) the Germans have "shown clearly their wish to protect the Ford interests" because of the attitude of strict neutrality maintained by Henry and Edsel Ford; and (4) the increased activity of the French Ford subsidiaries on behalf of the Germans received the commendation of the Ford family in America.

I am sure you will want to read the attached report. We propose to submit informally copies of the investigative report to Military Intelligence, Office of Naval Intelligence, Federal Bureau of Investigation and other similar investigative agencies.

If you are in agreement, please so indicate below.

(Initialed) H.E.P.

Attachment.

(Signed) H. Morgenthau, Jr.

Approved: _____

RRShwartz:rhb 5/22/43

By Jean Pajus—June 1944

Memorandum by Jean Pajus, Foreign Economic Administration

June 1944.

MEMORANDUM ON SKF

In the current investigation on SKF the following
points are important:

1.   The important foreign files, including the
correspondence between SKF in this country and SKF
Sweden, and other foreign countries have been destroyed by order of the American SKF officials. According to an interview with Mr. William Batt it is the
custom of the American SKF to destroy its files every
seven years. It is extremely significant that Mr. Batt
ordered the destruction of all foreign correspondence
for the years prior to 1941 and 1942. Orders to destroy
these files came down three days after Sweden was
blocked by the United States Treasury in 1941.

2.   Ever since the war began the Swedish company
has been giving orders to its American affiliate with
respect to volume of production, prices, and other
matters of major policy. At one time it appears that
the Swedish company deliberately withheld the shipment of necessary machinery to curtail production in
this country for about eight months. All ball bearing
machinery for SKF companies must be imported from Sweden and, consequently, the parent company can dictate
changes in ball bearing production in foreign countries.

3.   All of these orders from the Swedish parent
company came through the Swedish Legation in Washington, thus escaping the normal channels of censorship.

4. There is a very considerable investment of German capital in the Swedish company. At the time of the merger of the German companies into the VKF Combine, under control of the Swedish SKF, a very substantial block of shares in the Swedish company was given to Germany. The shares received by the Germans were so-called B shares—those without voting rights—but the evidence is clear that the Germans have a very important position in the determination of all major matters of policy. In fact, the former manager of the German ball bearing is now manager of the Swedish company.

5. The largest share of SKF's production is located in Axis-controlled Europe, 52% in Germany and 64% in Germany and France.

6. There is considerable evidence of a direct German interest in the United States Company. Just prior to the last war the Hess-Bright Company, owned by the German Munitions Trust was purportedly sold to the Swedish SKF. The Investigation made by the Alien Property Custodian at that time indicated great doubt in the validity of the sale to the Swedes. A cash transaction of $2,800,000 reported paid to the Germans by the Swedish Company for the property was never traced. In fact the whole investigation was a fraud, since the final report submitted by the United States Secret Service was written by the vice president of SKF. Other evidence indicates that the Swedish company merely acted as a front for the German company and that that situation still exists.

7. Further evidence to show how the German and Swedish interests are inextricably linked is the fact that in 1912 SKF Sweden purchased 50% of the Norma Ball Bearing Company, Cannstadt, Germany. This purchase was necessary in order to secure access to German patents and to make sales in the German market from which it was previously excluded by the German Ball Bearing Cartel. In 1912 they joined the German cartel and be-

came a licensee under the Conrad Patent. In 1929 the Norma Company was merged into VKF and a further German interest in the Swedish Company took place.

The Norma Company of America, a branch of the German Norma Company, was taken over by the Alien Property Custodian upon our entering into the war and, subsequently, was sold to American interests in 1919. At that time William Batt acted as an attorney in fact for the Norma Company. This indicates how closely knit Mr. Batt's interests with the Germans have been in the past.

8.   Until 1940 Mr. Batt was a member of the board of directors of the American Bosch Company which has since been seized by the U.S. Alien Property Custodian. This company attempted to cloak its German ownership under a purported sale of the properties to Swedish interests affiliated with SKF just prior to our entrance into the present war. The Alien Property Custodian nevertheless seized the properties on the ground that the transfer was fraudulent. It is reported that, at the time of the American Bosch investigation, a memorandum was prepared by the Treasury Department on Mr. Batt's connections with German companies, which was sent to the White House. The memorandum raised the question of the desirability of allowing Mr. Batt to hold a prominent position in the War Production Board in the light of his business affiliations.

9.   Numerous letters in the SKF files indicated that Mr. Batt was under orders from the Swedish company to supply the Latin American market, irrespective of current war orders in the United States; and that all sales in the United States should be based primarily on the long-term business interests of the company rather than the needs of the war effort.

At the present time an FEA representative is in Sweden attempting to purchase the SKF production in Sweden for $30,000,000. In the light of the above facts

it would seem that action other than that of purchase
could be effected to get the results desired.

The following steps are suggested:

a. Declare null and void the voting trust
   agreement now placed by Swedish SKF in the
   hands of Mr. Batt.

b. Seize the SKF properties in the United States,
   placing them under the Alien Property Custodian.

c. Place on the U.S. Proclaimed List all SKF companies in Sweden and Latin America.

d. Encourage American firms to export ball bearings to Latin America to compete with the SKF
   monopoly in those countries.

e. Place on the U.S. Proclaimed List all major
   Swedish companies affiliated with SKF., i.e.,
   Asea, Atlas Diesel, Separator, Etc.

f. Block all transfers of funds from Latin American subsidiaries to Sweden.

g. Eliminate the Swedish cartel in ball bearings
   in Germany after the war.

h. Eliminate the Swedish monopoly in France and
   Japan.

i. Seize all patents belonging to SKF Sweden and
   SKF Germany and other patents held by SKF subsidiaries in Europe.

TREASURY DEPARTMENT

INTER OFFICE COMMUNICATION

DATE   FEB 1 2 1945

TO   Secretary Morgenthau

FROM   Harry White   *HDW*

Information re. Chase Bk. activities in Paris:

    You will recall that on September 12, 1944, we reported to you that a study of an exchange of correspondence in New York between Chase, Paris, and Chase, New York, from the date of the fall of France to May 1942 disclosed that (1) the Paris branch collaborated with the Germans; (2) Chase was held in "very special esteem" by the Germans; (3) the Paris manager was "very vigorous" in enforcing restrictions unnecessarily against Jewish property; and (4) the home office took no direct steps to remove the Paris manager as it might "react" against their interests. We were then aware that the Paris branch of Chase acceded to the demands of the Germans to continue normal operations, even though both the Guaranty and National City had refused and substantial liquidation ensued.

    On the basis of this report, you agreed with our recommendation to investigate Chase in France. As of the present date our investigation of the Chase records in France confirms the above mentioned findings, and discloses the following additional information:

    1. S. P. Bailey, an American citizen who was in charge of the Paris office in June 1940, felt that it was desirable to, and actually commenced to, liquidate the Paris office. Some time thereafter and certainly by June 1941 his powers were revoked when the home office conferred authority on Niedermann who thereafter successfully ran the Paris office during German occupation, and Bertrand who remained at Chateauneuf in then unoccupied France.

    2. Although Chase in New York did not, so far as is presently known, send instructions for the Paris branch after February 4, 1942, there is thus far no evidence that Chase even attempted to veto any transactions of the Paris

- 2 -

office or between the office in the Free Zone and the
office in Paris even when such contemplated transactions
were the subject of requests for instructions.

3. Between May 1942 and May 1943, deposits in the
Paris office virtually doubled. Almost half of the increase
in deposits took place in two German accounts.

4. About a month after United States' entry into the
war, the Chase attorney in Paris advised that it was a
matter of "the most elementary prudence" to block American
accounts notwithstanding that no such instructions had been
issued by the occupying authorities. We are awaiting further
reports as to whether the suggested action was taken.

5. In May 1942 the Paris branch advised a Berlin bank
that certain instructions of the latter had been carried
out and that the Paris branch "are at your disposal to continue to undertake the execution of banking affairs in
France for your friends as well as for yourselves ***."

I will keep you advised of further developments in the
investigation of Chase and the other American banks in Paris.
In this connection you might be interested in reading the
attached cable received yesterday from Hoffman in Paris which
describes a meeting he held with Mr. Larkin who was apparently
sent to Paris by Aldrich to try to straighten up the Chase
offices. Larkin reported that Aldrich and the New York board of
Chase were very much concerned over the situation in the Paris
office of Chase, and that it was Larkin's job "to get to the
bottom of the situation and make the necessary adjustments in
personnel." It is significant that Larkin emphasized the fact
that Chase, New York, had been cut off from the Paris branch since
the United States entered the war. This does not agree with our
findings which disclose that between the date of the fall of
France and May 1942, Chase, New York, was kept advised about
activities in Chase, Paris.

Attachment.

Ref: 1634/21/43
No: 366

His Majesty's Ambassador presents his
compliments to the Secretary of State and has the
honour to state that His Royal Highness, the Duke
of Windsor, Governor of the Bahamas, has enquired
whether the United States Government would be so
good as to grant exemption from United States
censorship to the correspondence of the Duchess
of Windsor. Lord Halifax would be grateful for
such sympathetic consideration as can properly
be given to this enquiry.

BRITISH EMBASSY,

WASHINGTON, D.C.,

31st May, 1943.

DEPARTMENT OF STATE

ASSISTANT SECRETARY

DIV. OF FOREIGN A...
JUL 2 - 1943
DEPARTMENT OF STATE

June 18, 1943

<u>Memorandum</u>

I believe that the Duchess of Windsor should emphatically be denied exemption from censorship.

Quite aside from the more shadowy reports about the activities of this family, it is to be recalled that both the Duke and Duchess of Windsor were in contact with Mr. James Mooney, of General Motors, who attempted to act as mediator of a negotiated peace in the early winter of 1940; that they have maintained correspondence with Bedaux, now in prison in North Africa and under charges of trading with the enemy, and possibly of treasonable correspondence with the enemy; that they have been in constant contact with Axel Wenner-Gren, presently on our Blacklist for suspicious activity; etc. The Duke of Windsor has been finding many excuses to attend to "private business" in the United States, which he is doing at present.

There are positive reasons, therefore, why this immunity should not be granted -- as well as the negative reason that we are not according this privilege to the wife of any American official.

A.A.B. Jr.

A-B:AAB:ES

Index